Flying Across America

Flying Across
America

The Airline Passenger Experience

Daniel L. Rust

University of Oklahoma Press : Norman

Library of Congress Cataloging-in-Publication Data

Rust, Daniel L.
    Flying across America: the airline passenger experience /
    Daniel L. Rust. /
        p. cm.
    Includes bibliographical references and index.
    ISBN 978-0-8061-3870-1 (hardcover : alk. paper)
        1. Aeronautics, Commercial—United States—Passenger traffic—History.
        2. Air travel—United States—History. I. Title.
    HE9787.R87 2009
    387.7'420973—dc22

1 2 3 4 5 6 7 8 9 10

Contents

Acknowledgments

With my deepest gratitude I acknowledge the many people who assisted me in making this book possible. The Center for Transportation Studies at the University of Missouri–St. Louis, under the direction of Ray A. Mundy, generously covered the cost of obtaining the images found in this book and provided a great place for me to work and study. I appreciated the cheerful help of the center's administrative assistant, Betty Jo Ditmeyer. My mentor, colleague, and friend Carlos A. Schwantes provided invaluable guidance and encouragement as I researched this book. He shaped the way I view history and the world of transportation, and I can only hope to be as academically productive as he. Thanks also to Katherine G. Aiken, Richard B. Spence, and Richard C. Davis at the University of Idaho, who reviewed an early version of this book.

Several people contributed to this work in special ways. Charles C. Quarles answered my questions and provided resources from his extensive collection of airline artifacts. Additionally, John T. Corpening loaned me rare ephemera from the nonscheduled airlines. Through Nancy A. Wright of Air Mail Pioneers, I had the pleasure of contacting Robert E. Burness, Jr., who generously supplied several photographs related to aviation in San Francisco.

I received excellent assistance from a number of archivists and librarians: Charles Lamb and Erik Dix, University of Notre Dame Archives; Steven K. Gragert, Will Rogers Memorial Museums; Bette Davis Kalash, Jesse Davidson Aviation Archives; Tim Nelson, Thomas Jefferson Library at the University of Missouri–St. Louis; Ron Goldfeder, St. Louis Museum of Transportation; Rose Krause, Northwest Museum of Arts and Culture; Clark Skillman and Latanne Steel, C. R. Smith Museum; Erik Carlson and Paul Oerkrug, McDermott Library at the University of Texas at Dallas; Pat Donelson, Chase County (Kansas) Historical Society; and Ed Nolan and Elaine Miller, Washington

State Historical Society. I am especially grateful to the staff at the St. Louis Mercantile Library, including Gregory Ames, Charles Brown, Deborah Cribbs, John Hoover, and Miranda Rectenwald.

Many others aided in the creation of this work: Barbara Young Welke, University of Minnesota; Stephen A. Haller, Golden Gate National Recreation Area; Robert Chandler, Wells Fargo Historical Services; Michael Lombardi, Boeing Company; Kimble D. McCutcheon, Aircraft Engine Historical Society; H. Roger Grant, Clemson University; Don Michelson; and Joe Orr and Foe Geldersma, Airline History Museum at Kansas City. Thanks also to University of Missouri–St. Louis student Chastity Jackson for inspiring me to research the travel challenges that disabled passengers encounter.

My extended family provided encouragement and assistance throughout the research and writing of this book. I particularly appreciate the research assistance I received from my sister-in-law Dana Williams, and my father-in-law, Daniel M. Williams. My father-in-law and my mother-in-law, Elizabeth A. Williams, have been a constant source of support and encouragement. Thanks to Dana and Vivian Wriston of Shawnee, Oklahoma, for their generous hospitality during my trips to the University of Oklahoma Press.

This book is a testimony to the love and devotion of my wife, Lisa; my children, Evan, Dillon, and Liana; and my parents, Tony and Marilyn Rust. My wife and children too often endured my frequent absence as I researched and crafted this book over the course of several years. Their understanding and their emotional support were invaluable to me throughout the process. I thank my parents for sacrificing their time and resources so that I might attain the educational status I enjoy today. I also thank them for encouraging me in my pursuit of academic excellence and my affinity for aviation history. My father passed away in 2003 and, even though I know it is not possible, I wish I could hand him a copy of this book just to see his face light up as he would exclaim, "You did it, Tiger!" And, most important, I thank God for his providential leadership and innumerable blessings in my life.

FLYING ACROSS AMERICA

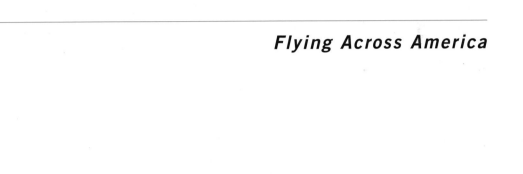

Flying Across America

Introduction

The crowd pushed forward for a closer view. They did not seem to comprehend that the flying machine resting on the racetrack at Sheepshead Bay, Long Island, needed a clear path ahead to become airborne. The aircraft's lanky pilot, wearing a brown business suit and a jaunty cap, could wait no longer. He suddenly climbed aboard, started the engine, and watched as people retreated before his noisy contraption. He taxied into position, held up a moistened finger to determine the wind direction, clenched his teeth around an ever-present cigar, and took off into the sky. Calbraith Perry Rodgers had started an amazing journey to become the first person to fly all the way across the continental United States in an airplane. The date: September 17, 1911.

Only eight years earlier, two brothers from Dayton, Ohio, had flown the first powered heavier-than-air craft a few hundred feet across the sand dunes of Kitty Hawk, North Carolina. Because of the Wright brothers' secrecy, few Americans, except some residents of Dayton and Kitty Hawk, knew of their progress until 1908, when Orville Wright publicly flew an airplane at Fort Myer, Virginia, before members of the U.S. military. During a demonstration flight, a cracked propeller caused the airplane to crash, seriously injuring Wright and killing Lieutenant Thomas Selfridge—the first casualty of an airplane accident. Even so, the War Department purchased one of the Wrights' aircraft for possible military application. That same year, Glenn Curtiss flew an aircraft called the *June Bug* an astounding distance of one mile to win the *Scientific American* trophy. And in September 1910, before a crowd of 200,000 spectators, Thomas Scott Baldwin became the first person to fly across the Mississippi River at St. Louis. At the controls of the *Red Devil*, an aircraft that he himself had built, Baldwin crossed the river twice to collect a $3,000 prize.

Aviator Thomas Scott Baldwin completes the first flight over the Mississippi River at St. Louis, September 10, 1910. Baldwin had disassembled his aircraft, the Red Devil, and sent it via rail from New York to St. Louis, where he earned $3,000 for flying across the river twice. During his record-making flight, he flew under a span of the famous Eads Bridge, seen in the background. (From the *St. Louis Globe-Democrat* Archives of the St. Louis Mercantile Library at the University of Missouri–St. Louis.)

To most people, airplanes were a novelty not worthy of serious consideration as a means of travel. In 1910, perhaps only one in a thousand Americans had even seen an airplane, usually at an air meet, where aviators vied for who could fly at the highest altitude, make the most accurate landings, or carry out the sharpest turns. The city of Los Angeles hosted the first major air meet in January 1910, where the most famous aviators, including Glen Curtiss and Lincoln Beachey, competed for cash prizes. The French flyer, Louis Paulhan, came out on top, with winnings totaling $19,000. Attending the meet was newspaper baron William Randolph Hearst. What he witnessed fired his imagination and prompted him to set up a $50,000 prize for the first person to fly an airplane across the United States within a span of 30 days, and no later than October 1911.

The state of aviation technology prevented anyone from seriously competing for the Hearst prize until practically the last minute. A race-car-driver-turned-aviator named Robert Fowler and a former jockey named Jimmy Ward began attempts early in September 1911. On September 17, Cal Rodgers became the third contestant, setting out to fly from Long Island, New York, to Los Angeles.

Rodgers had learned to fly that summer at the Wright brothers' training facility in Ohio. The Armour Meat Packing Company of Chicago sponsored his attempt and emblazoned the name of its soft drink subsidiary, *Vin Fiz*, on the wings of his brand-new Wright EX Flyer. Two propellers, connected by a chain-drive transmission to a 35-horsepower engine, drove the spruce-and-canvas aircraft at speeds approaching 60 miles per hour. Anticipating hardships, Rodgers and the *Vin Fiz* traveled aboard a three-car supply train that carried fuel and a store of spare parts and engines. Among his entourage were his mother, his wife, and reporters. Charles Taylor, the Wrights' master mechanic who had designed and built the first and subsequent engines for the brothers' models, agreed to accompany Rodgers to keep the *Vin Fiz* airworthy as he flew it across the country.

Rodgers followed railroad tracks and other landmarks as he doggedly endured a series of misfortunes during his transcontinental odyssey, making nearly 70 aerial hops and surviving 15 crashes along the way. As he neared his goal, thousands of people congregated each time the *Vin Fiz* stopped. After covering nearly 4,000 miles, the *Vin Fiz* arrived in Pasadena, California, with only a vertical rudder and a couple of wing struts original to the aircraft when it had left Long Island 49 days earlier. Even though Rodgers had exceeded the travel time required to win the Hearst prize, his successful arrival in Los Angeles made him a national celebrity. However, as was often the case with early flyers, Rodgers met an untimely demise in an airplane crash only five months after completing his transcontinental journey.[1]

With an ever-present cigar between his lips, Calbraith "Cal" Rodgers stands beside his Wright EX Flyer on September 17, 1911, ready to begin his epic journey from Long Island, New York, to California. Note the light construction of the airplane, as well as the propellers and chain drive in the right foreground. Rodgers piloted the aircraft while seated in a chair fully exposed to the weather. (Courtesy of the George Grantham Bain Collection, Library of Congress reproduction no. LC-DIG-ggbain-09719)

This promotional map traces Cal Rodgers's transcontinental route from New York to Chicago, then to San Antonio, and across the Desert Southwest before his arrival on the Pacific coast. Inset photos feature the Vin Fiz railcar as well as several images of Rodgers's aircraft after numerous mishaps. (Courtesy of Imagination Counts, LLC)

The popular press reported Cal Rodgers's transcontinental feat as a sensational story, but the flight demonstrated little practical use. Trains reigned as the premier means of long-distance travel, with plush railcars, many of them Pullman sleepers, offering unmatched luxury. Scarcely a decade old, the automobile required a network of surfaced roads before it could challenge the railroads' supremacy. Cal Rodgers's flight may have pointed to the future of airborne travel, but the idea of scheduled passenger air travel from coast to coast awaited a watershed event that was to come 16 years later.

In May 1927 a 25-year-old pilot named Charles Lindbergh dared to fly solo across the Atlantic Ocean from New York to Paris in a single-engine Ryan airplane called *The Spirit of St. Louis*. The epic flight covered 3,610 miles, mostly over trackless ocean, in 33 and a half hours and showed the reliability of aircraft and aircraft engines designed in the preceding decade. If one young person in a single-engine airplane could fly nonstop across the Atlantic, what would be possible with larger commercial aircraft? Crowds jammed New York City streets to welcome the "Lone Eagle" home with a ticker-tape parade, and *Time* magazine named Lindbergh its first "Man of the Year." Suddenly, long-distance passenger air travel captured the public's imagination.[2]

Firsthand accounts of transcontinental air travel began to appear in the popular press in 1927. For the next three and a half decades, numerous coast-to-coast air passengers recorded and published their experiences for a curious public in magazines such as *Collier's, World's Work, Good Housekeeping, Ladies' Home Journal, Sunset,* and *Atlantic Monthly.* As a body of literature, these articles provide eyewitness accounts of the birth of this last phase of transcontinental travel. The first phase of transcontinental travel had begun with the overland journey of the Corps of Discovery, led by Meriwether Lewis and William Clark from St. Louis, Missouri, to the mouth of the Columbia River and back again in 1804–1806. The expedition set out from Wood River, Illinois, at about 4 P.M. on May 14, 1804. After an odyssey to the source of the Missouri River in present-day Montana, across the Rocky Mountains, and down the Snake and Columbia rivers, they arrived within sight of the Pacific Ocean on November 7, 1805. Several members of the expedition kept journals, filled with their observations and detailed accounts of events along the way. Republished in several editions, the Lewis and Clark journals continue to fascinate historians and general readers alike.

Others who followed in Lewis and Clark's footsteps also kept journals. Narcissa Whitman recorded her observations as she traveled from Missouri to the Pacific Northwest with her husband, Marcus, and another missionary couple, Henry and Eliza Spaulding, in 1836. Whitman and Spaulding became the first European women to cross the North American continent—forerunners of the immigrants who would brave the Overland Trail in the coming decades. During this second phase of transcontinental travel, thousands of pioneers from towns such as Independence, Missouri, set out on the Overland Trail in springtime, hoping to arrive in Oregon or California within six months. Hundreds of pioneers who migrated westward during the mid-nineteenth century wrote about their adventures along the trail. Published and unpublished pioneer journals of the hardships involved, especially for the women and children, constitute an invaluable resource.

In addition to explorers and Overland Trail pioneers, some passengers on scheduled transcontinental transportation left accounts of their experiences as participants in the third phase of coast-to-coast travel. Before the creation of the transcontinental railroad, those wishing to travel from cities along the U.S. Atlantic coastline, such as New York, to the towns and gold fields of California chose between two means of public transportation—seagoing vessel or stagecoach. If traveling by sea, passengers could select a five-month, 17,000-mile trip around the southern tip of South America or a month-long, 6,000-mile journey via a shortcut across the Isthmus of Panama. Both posed great risks, such as shipwreck or lethal tropical diseases. Completion of the Panama Railroad in 1855 shortened the Panama crossing from five days to five hours, significantly reducing passengers' chances of contracting diseases. If neither of the seagoing options appealed to prospective transcontinental travelers, they were left with an arduous trip via stagecoach from Missouri across the wilderness to San Francisco.[3]

How FAR is an hour?

IS it 4 miles or 400? It depends on how you travel! When grandpa was a boy, he spent most of a Saturday getting to town and back in a buggy.

But today he can step into an airliner and cross the country before the sun goes down.

To thousands of people who travel by air, miles are merely minutes . . . oceans and continents, hours.

Today, the Airlines maintain the fastest passenger, mail and cargo schedules in the world—serving hundreds of U. S. cities and scores of foreign countries.

For the Army and Navy, the Airlines also operate an armada of transport planes that reduce *surface days* to *air hours* in getting vital goods and personnel to every fighting front.

Yet the 180-mile-an-hour speed on which the Airlines base their present schedules will probably seem slow indeed, when the giant transports of the future lift their wings to global skies.

What that speed will be—how far it will take you in 60 minutes—can only be conjectured by this fact: Our aircraft builders are now making military planes that fly more than 400 miles an hour— *7 miles a minute!*

＞   ＞   ＞

When you travel by Air *make reservations early; please cancel early if plans change.* When you use Air Express *speed delivery by dispatching shipments as soon as they're ready.* Air Transport Association, 1515 Massachusetts Ave., N. W., Washington, D. C.

IF YOU CAN'T GO OVER, COME ACROSS . . . BUY BONDS!

THE AIRLINES OF THE UNITED STATES

AIR TRANSPORT GETS THERE FIRST...PASSENGERS...MAIL...AIR EXPRESS

As evidenced in this advertisement from the 1940s, the airplane radically altered people's perception of time and distance. An hour spent in the confines of a horse-drawn buggy would transport a passenger only a small fraction of the distance a passenger could cross in a modern airliner. (From the author's collection)

Stagecoaches traversed the central transcontinental route on a regular basis for the first time in the 1850s. The federal government subsidized stage runs between San Diego, California, and San Antonio, Texas. Twice each month, a stage made the journey with passengers and mail in approximately 38 days. The Butterfield Overland Mail soon eclipsed the San Antonio and San Diego Mail Line to become the first truly transcontinental stage line. On September 16, 1858, John Butterfield's Overland Mail Company inaugurated stagecoach service between Missouri and California. Its coaches made one-way trips in three weeks.[4]

The completion of the first transcontinental railroad signaled the start of the fourth phase of transcontinental travel. Convinced that a coast-to-coast rail link was vital to the nation's development, the federal government funded the line's construction. In an epic contest, the Union Pacific laid down rails west from Omaha, Nebraska, while the Central Pacific started construction in the opposite direction from Sacramento, California. The two lines met amid great celebration at Promontory, Utah, in 1869. The nation was transformed. No longer would wagons bear pioneers and their belongings to their homesteads in the West, nor would stagecoaches carry people across the continent. The railroads carried people coast-to-coast in 8 to 10 days, rather than several weeks.[5]

Railroad passengers of the 1870s left written records of their experiences aboard the transcontinental trip. The natural wonders and arid climate of the West, as well as the food and accommodations aboard the trains, found their way into personal accounts of coast-to-coast rail travel. Such accounts noted few features east of the Mississippi River because of the familiar topography of green fields and rolling wooded hills.[6]

The early transcontinental motorists, participants in the fifth phase, likewise left a written record. Dr. Horatio Nelson Jackson's amazing 1903 road trip from San Francisco to New York City, a 6,000-mile journey taking 63 three days, earned him a place in history as the very first person to cross the continent in an automobile. He and mechanic Sewall K. Crocker overcame one hardship after another as they traveled across the roadless wilderness of the nation's interior. Jackson published his experiences in magazine articles and in book form. Many who followed in Jackson's tire tracks, including some who traveled on buses, also published their own accounts, creating a sizable body of literature.[7]

A time line connecting the personal travel accounts of transcontinental explorers, overland pioneers, coast-to-coast ship and stagecoach passengers, early transcontinental railroad passengers, and hearty coast-to-coast motorists concludes with the firsthand accounts of transcontinental airline passengers. Air travel was the last phase of transcontinental travel because of its unparalleled swiftness. From Lewis and Clark, who spent 13,000 hours just getting from St. Louis to the Pacific Ocean, to the Overland Trail pioneers who typically covered nearly the same distance in around 4,400 hours, to seaborne travelers going from New York to California in about 700 hours, to stagecoach passengers going from Missouri to California in 500 hours, to railroad travelers making the journey in less than 120 hours, the speed of each transportation mode increased significantly.

Although not evident in Cal Rodgers's nearly 1,200-hour odyssey, aircraft speeds surpassed all other modes. Starting in the late 1920s, airplanes whisked passengers from coast to coast in less than 48 hours. Transcontinental travel times quickly fell to 36 hours in 1930, then to less than 24 hours two years later. Fifteen hours coast-to-coast was common in the mid-1930s. Immediately after the Second World War, the scheduled time across the continent via airliner dropped to 10 hours. And with the introduction of jetliners on transcontinental routes in 1959, the new standard became 5 hours, lasting into the twenty-first century.

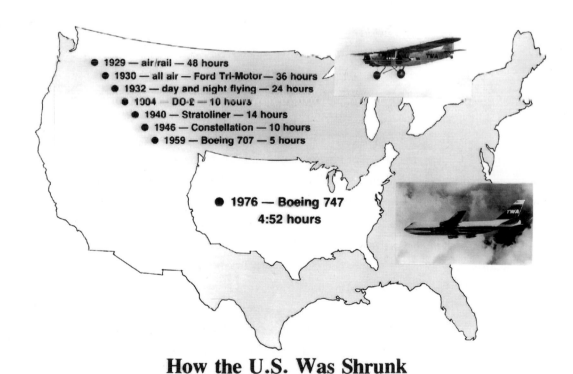

- 1929 — air/rail — 48 hours
- 1930 — all air — Ford Tri-Motor — 36 hours
- 1932 — day and night flying — 24 hours
- 1934 — DC-2 — 18 hours
- 1940 — Stratoliner — 14 hours
- 1946 — Constellation — 10 hours
- 1959 — Boeing 707 — 5 hours

- 1976 — Boeing 747
  4:52 hours

How the U.S. Was Shrunk
Transcontinental Travel Times 1926-1976

Within the brief span of 30 years, transcontinental travel times shrank from 48 to 5 hours. As graphically represented here, advances in aviation technology brought the two coasts closer together than ever before. (From the TWA Archives of the St. Louis Mercantile Library at the University of Missouri–St. Louis.)

Firsthand accounts of transcontinental air travel traced this rapid evolution in speed and the accompanying changes in the air travel experience. In the span of a half century, this form of travel across the continental United States evolved from a novel, adventurous, and physically and financially draining proposition, into a jet-speed, comfortable, comparatively inexpensive, pedestrian occurrence. Personal accounts constitute snapshots of different segments in the evolution of domestic air travel.

This book is based primarily on firsthand accounts written within months of the recorded travel experience. The impressions were still fresh in the authors' minds—not tainted with fond reminiscences of past glory only recently recognized as deserving of publication. Rather, these passengers wrote with an immediate purpose in mind. Because as late as 1960 only 10 percent of American adults had taken even one commercial flight, most people experienced the "golden age" of air travel vicariously. For the vast majority of Americans, reading about the flying experience was as close as they would come to setting foot in a commercial airplane until the coming of the jet airliner. Even then, it would be the mid-1970s before a majority of Americans had made an airplane flight. Recognizing this situation, authors who wrote about their air journeys attempted to inform the nonflying public of the advantages and sensations of taking a trip across the country in an airliner.[8]

Although ever-greater speed was a dominant theme, many other themes appeared throughout these narratives. As aviation technology advanced, passengers noticed an increasing disconnection from the actual flying experience. Air passengers, who once flew in open-cockpit biplanes a few hundred feet from the ground, found themselves decades later in pressurized metal tubes streaking across the sky at near the speed of sound, 35,000 feet

above the earth, while eating hot food, drinking cold beverages, watching an in-flight movie, and occasionally glancing out of a small porthole at the seemingly still landscape below. Between these two extremes was a rapid evolution in passenger comfort and safety.

Another aspect of the air journey that has been instrumental in transforming it from an adventure to a routine event is falling air fares. Published personal accounts of transcontinental air travel bore witness to the increasing affordability of air travel. What was once available to only the wealthiest adventure seekers has now become affordable to most Americans, who now give as much thought to riding an airplane across the continent as they once did to taking a subway or bus ride downtown.

By the 1970s, articles showcasing the air travel experience had virtually disappeared from the pages of America's popular magazines. The sights, sounds, and sensations of commercial passenger flight no longer warranted published firsthand accounts. While transcontinental air travel remained the setting for many published stories, the experience of air travel no longer took center stage.

In an age of airline deregulation and concern about terrorist attacks, the transcontinental airline passenger may find it worthwhile to pause and reflect on an amazing evolution that has culminated in swift, efficient, and affordable coast-to-coast air travel.

Flying with the Mail

1

The highly polished propeller reflected the brilliant California sun, as cars filled with curious people streamed onto Crissy Field, on the San Francisco beachfront. The ceremony this day, June 30, 1927, marked the beginning of a new era in transcontinental travel. The U.S. Post Office would hand over the western portion of the transcontinental airmail route to a private contractor, and—for the first time—passengers could fly aboard commercial aircraft along the airway. The name on the contract and on the planes designed to fly the route belonged to a businessman from Seattle—William E. Boeing.

Boeing Air Transport

Born in Detroit in 1881, Boeing was the son of a German immigrant who made a fortune in the timber and mining industries. After dropping out of Yale in 1903, Boeing followed in his father's footsteps by going into the lumber business, which took him to Seattle five years later. The young, wealthy bachelor took his first airplane flight in 1915 and, with the help of friend George Conrad Westervelt, started the Boeing Aircraft Company. It built training airplanes for the U.S. Navy during the First World War, but canceled contracts at war's end led to the company to build bedroom furniture and boats to stay in business. William Boeing and company pilot Eddie Hubbard established an airmail route from Victoria, British Columbia, to Seattle in 1919, flying a Boeing aircraft. This service met ships arriving from Asia and brought their airmail to Seattle days before the ships docked at the city.

Commercial aviation played a small role in the Boeing Aircraft Company's early history. As evidenced by its war contracts, Boeing sold most of its aircraft to the military. However, when the U.S. Post Office offered for bid the two transcontinental airmail route

segments, one from San Francisco to Chicago, and other from Chicago to New York, Eddie Hubbard and Boeing engineer Claire Egtvedt approached William Boeing about bidding on the western segment. They believed that the key to success would be a modified version of an aircraft Boeing called the Model 40. The U.S. Post Office had previously rejected the design as a replacement for its venerable de Havilland DH-4s because it was underpowered. At the Post Office's insistence, the same Liberty engine that pulled its DH-4s powered the Boeing 40. Developed during the war, the liquid-cooled, 350-horsepower Liberty engine provided reliable service but weighed 900 pounds when complete with radiator and fluids. Revisiting the rejected aircraft design, Hubbard and Egtvedt thought that Boeing 40 mail planes equipped with new Pratt & Whitney Wasp radial engines, which weighed 650 pounds and produced 425 horsepower, could carry the mail over the diverse topography between San Francisco and Chicago more profitably at a lower postal pay rate than any would-be competitor might. The men emphasized that the Boeing 40 could be modified to carry two passengers in addition to the mail, generating passenger revenue that would make possible an even lower pay rate for carrying mail.

William Boeing was initially skeptical. But when he mentioned the idea to his wife, Bertha, she responded with enthusiasm. After a sleepless night pondering the opportunity, he gave his approval. The Boeing Aircraft Company placed a bid to carry the mail halfway across the continent for $2.88 per pound.[1]

The federal government received a wave of messages protesting the Boeing airmail bid. Many critics asserted that the bid was ridiculously low. The well-established Western Air Express, already carrying mail and passengers between Los Angeles and Salt Lake City, had submitted the second-lowest bid—for $4.25 per pound—and those familiar with contract airmail could not believe anyone could operate the San Francisco–Chicago route for a lower price. Boeing's proposed charge for carrying mail nearly 2,000 miles equaled what the Post Office was currently paying to move mail between Boston and New York City. If Boeing won

At Crissy Field in San Francisco, William Boeing's wife, Bertha, christens a Boeing 40A at the inauguration of contract airmail services between San Francisco and Chicago, June 30, 1927. William Boeing stands to the far left. In a similar ceremony 26 years later, Bertha Boeing would break a bottle of champagne over the nose of the Boeing 367-80 – the prototype leading to the 707 jetliner and the military's KC-135. (From the collection of Robert E. Burness, Jr.)

The Boeing Company

William E. Boeing, of Seattle, incorporated his aircraft manufacturing business in 1916 as the Pacific Aero Products Company. Renamed Boeing Airplane Company the following year, the firm produced seaplanes for the U.S. Navy during the First World War. The firm survived the glutted postwar market by manufacturing furniture and boats, while producing limited numbers of aircraft under license for the military. Nevertheless, Boeing persevered in developing its own military and commercial designs, including the Model 40A biplane with capacity for mail and two passengers in an enclosed cabin. William Boeing joined with Pratt & Whitney president Frederick Rentschler in 1929 to create United Aircraft and Transport Corporation (UATC) as a holding company. A year later UATC included the Boeing Aircraft Company, Chance Vought Corporation, Hamilton Aero Manufacturing Company, the Pratt & Whitney Aircraft Company, Sikorsky Aviation Corporation, the Stearman Aircraft Company, and the Standard Steel Propeller Company, in addition to several airlines. Boeing produced the innovative Monomail airplane in 1930 and the revolutionary Model 247 airliner in 1933. Federal antitrust legislation resulted in the breakup of UATC in 1934. Boeing Airplane Company emerged independent from airline operations, now under United Air Lines. Disenchanted with the ordeal, William Boeing retired from the aviation business for good in 1934.

In 1935 Boeing produced the Model 299, a large four-engine bomber, for the U.S. Army. The 299 would evolve into the rugged B-17, made famous during the Second World War in the skies over Europe. Boeing also produced the four-engine Model 314 Clipper and the first commercial airliner with a pressurized cabin, the Model 307 Stratoliner, capable of cruising at altitudes of 20,000 feet. Both aircraft flew for the first time in 1938.

Boeing's aircraft production rate peaked during the Second World War, when the company produced 362 airplanes in March 1944. The company manufactured strategic bombers such as the B-17 and B-29, attack bombers, cargo and troop gliders, flying boats, torpedo airplanes, and even trainers during the war. Cancellation of military orders after the war compelled Boeing to reduce its workforce by 70,000 people as it struggled to attract orders for its commercial Stratocruiser airliner. Fortunately for the company, the newly created U.S. Air Force adopted the KC-97 aerial refueling tanker to extend the range of its aircraft. Boeing also scored successes with the B-47, an elegant swept-wing jet bomber, and the B-52 long-range bomber, which is still in frontline military service more than 50 years after it was first produced.

The company took a significant financial risk in 1952 when its leadership, headed by president William Allen, decided to develop a large, swept-wing jetliner that could also serve as the basis for a military aerial refueling tanker. The legendary Boeing 707 and KC-135 came from the prototype Model 367-80, which first took to the sky in 1954. Boeing produced the outstanding medium-range 727 in 1963, followed four years later by the short- to medium-range 737. The 737 evolved into one of the best-selling jetliners of all time, with the five thousandth copy delivered in 2006. The Boeing 747 jumbo jetliner first flew in 1969, then reigned supreme with the largest passenger capacity of any airliner for the next 37 years. Boeing followed with the 767 in 1981, and one year later the 757 took to the sky. The Boeing 777, sized between the 767 and the 747, few in 1994. Two years later Boeing merged with Rockwell International Corporation, and in 1997 it merged with McDonnell Douglas Corporation to become the largest aircraft manufacturer in the world. The more fuel-efficient 787 jetliner heralded a continuation of the Boeing legacy in the large commercial aircraft industry. Even before its first flight in 2008, Boeing had received orders for more than 600 of the mostly composite-construction jetliner. Besides commercial and military aircraft, Boeing has also produced numerous other products such as missiles, hydrofoil watercraft, light-rail vehicles, and space-related products.

William Boeing (far left) stands in front of a postal service mail plane with other officials at the start of Boeing Air Transport Corporation's airmail contract in San Francisco. The new Boeing 40A began flying the route to Chicago the next day, replacing the Post Office's de Havilland DH-4 seen here. (From the collection of Robert E. Burness, Jr.)

the contract, critics charged, it would mean financial ruin for the fledgling air transportation industry because other contractors could not earn money at such low levels of compensation. And, many suspected, Boeing Aircraft had entered into commercial aviation to keep the employees in its Seattle factory busy. Although the latter was true, Boeing's entrance into contract airmail service would prove the critics wrong. But convincing the Post Office was no easy task. Before accepting the Boeing bid, postal officials demanded that William Boeing personally guarantee the fulfillment of airmail contract operations and that U.S. senator Wesley Jones of Washington should testify to Boeing's character.[2]

The Post Office and Boeing Aircraft Company inked a contract in January 1927. The firm quickly built and flew a prototype Boeing 40A by mid-May. Weeks later, despite the absence of experimental runs to prove the correctness of the company's assumptions regarding the type's economic performance, a fleet of twenty-four 40As stood ready for service.

In the spring of 1927, Boeing Aircraft Company birthed a subsidiary named Boeing Air Transport (BAT) for the express purpose of fulfilling the airmail contract. On July 1, BAT assumed responsibility for airmail between San Francisco and Chicago. As the subsidiary's president and general manager, William Boeing, along with his wife and a gleaming Boeing 40A, participated in a June 30 hand-over ceremony at San Francisco's Crissy Field, near where the Golden Gate Bridge would soon be built. Bertha Boeing struck the aircraft's propeller hub with a bottle of tonic water mixed with orange juice, christening the craft *The City of San Francisco*. Nearly three decades later, Bertha Boeing would christen another Boeing triumph: the first American-made commercial jet airliner, the 707.

San Francisco postmaster James Power swore in William Boeing as an official mail carrier at the 1927 ceremony. As cameras clicked, Power handed the first sack of mail to Boeing, and BAT was in business. The company earned a profit from the start. As Boeing later observed, the air-cooled Pratt & Whitney Wasp engine made the difference. The 40A carried mail and passengers across the Rocky Mountains "instead of radiators and water."

As airmail pilot Art Vance looks on, Postmaster James Power hands the first sack of contract mail to William Boeing. With this symbolic gesture, the transcontinental airmail route was no longer a government enterprise. (From the collection of Robert E. Burness, Jr.)

From its first day of operations, Boeing Air Transport welcomed passengers to fly the longest passenger airline route in the world—1,950 miles—between Chicago and San Francisco. The new service owed much to the pioneering efforts of those who blazed the coast-to-coast airmail route and built an infrastructure on the ground that made safe passage in the air possible.[3]

The U.S. Air Mail Service

The U.S. government has a long history of funding communications and transportation improvements. Based on the economic and political benefits of binding the regions of the nation together, the government provided capital for canals and inland waterways and for the construction of the National Road linking Illinois with the Atlantic Coast. The first telegraph line in the United States, built in the 1840s, also owed much to federal assistance. In the nineteenth century, scores of companies received 131 million acrews of land—approximately 7 percent of the country's total area—and millions of dollars in subsidies to build a network of railroads linking the country together with rails of steel.

Aviation was no exception to this trend. Just as private enterprise could not build a canal or rail system in the nineteenth century without governmental assistance because financial returns on private investments were many years distant or unlikely to materialize, very few financiers in the early twentieth century considered aviation to be a worthwhile investment. Starting in 1910, stunt pilots carried a few pieces of mail to gain publicity and win prizes. In June 1910, Charles K. Hamilton earned a $10,000 prize for carrying a letter from New York governor Charles Evans Hughes to Pennsylvania governor Edwin Stuart in Philadelphia and back again to New York City. Two newspapers, the *Philadelphia Public Ledger* and the *New York Times,* had offered the prize money, hoping that news of the feat would increase circulation. But more than a year elapsed before the first official airmail flight took place on September 25, 1911, at the very time Cal Rodgers was making his way across the continent. Sworn in as the first U.S. airmail pilot, Earl Ovington carried pouches of mail six miles between the site of an air show near Mineola, New York, and the Mineola post office without compensation. Other aviators, including Katherine Stinson, carried letters at air shows in the following years. But not until the spring of 1918, with the war still raging in Europe, did the U.S. Congress appropriate $100,000 for the first regularly scheduled airmail service.[4]

Employing U.S. Army pilots, the service began on May 15, 1918, from the Washington, D.C., polo grounds. An array of dignitaries, including President Woodrow Wilson, attended the event. They witnessed Lieutenant George L. Boyle climb into the cockpit ready for the flight, only to discover that the plane's engine refused to start. Minutes passed before someone checked the gas tank—it was empty. The crowd laughed as mechanics scrambled to fill the tank. At last, Boyle took off, bound for Philadelphia. But he mistakenly flew around, rather than past the Chesapeake Bay, away from his destination. Upon landing 24 miles away from his starting point, Boyle's craft flipped over, and the mail was transferred to a train for transport to Philadelphia.

Despite the inauspicious start, army pilots completed 270 flights between the nation's capital and New York City before the Post Office Department took over flying the mail on August 12, 1918. From the beginning, the Post Office viewed its airmail service as an incubator for civil aviation in the United States. And its successful demonstration of putting aircraft into commercial use did spur the development of new routes. The airplane's only advantage over the train was speed, and its speed advantage was best realized over long distances. Airmail reached westward from New York to Chicago on July 1, 1919, and then to Omaha, Nebraska, on May 15, 1920. Following the tracks of the original transcontinental railroad, airmail service came to San Francisco on September 8, 1920.

As late at 1920, airmail pilots flew only during daylight hours. Trains carried airmail at night and during periods of foul weather, because no facilities on the ground or equipment on the planes existed to permit such flying. But when criticism of the airmail service as inefficient and financially unfeasible gained footing on Capitol Hill and a new president, Warren G. Harding, let it be known that he would veto any airmail spending bill that Congress might pass, the Post Office decided to demonstrate that it was capable of night operations. On February 22, 1921, airmail pilots left both coasts to make connections with relief pilots across the continent—a Pony Express in the sky. As night fell, a series of bonfires lit the way for the intrepid pilots traversing the central plains. Pilot Jack Knight became a national hero when he not only flew his assigned segment from North Platte to Omaha, Nebraska, but continued east in a blinding snowstorm over a route that he had never flown before, all the way to Chicago. Thanks in no small measure to Knight's skill and daring, the airmail arrived in New York 33 hours and 20 minutes after leaving San Francisco. The flight proved the worth of night flying and possibly saved the airmail service from extinction.[5]

Private Contractors Carry the Mail

In the summer of 1920 the Post Office retained the transcontinental route, but because of a lack of Congressional funding, it abandoned the route between Washington, D.C., and New York as well as one connecting St. Louis with Minneapolis via Chicago. Lights and flares on aircraft and placement of lighted airway beacons along sections of the route permitted regular day-and-night transcontinental airmail service to start on July 1, 1924. Now coast-to-coast airmail took, not 78 hours flying only in daylight, but less than 35 hours flying around the clock. Such speeds beat the fastest trains across the continent by at least three days. Railroad executives began complaining to their representatives on Capitol Hill that the airmail was costing them significant business, particularly from banks using airmail to shorten the float time of checks from coast to coast. In February 1924, U.S. representative M. Clyde Kelly of Pennsylvania, chair of the House Post Office Committee and well-known friend of railroad interests, introduced a bill into the House of Representatives authorizing the postmaster general to contract with private air carriers for domestic airmail service. Kelly had watched the airmail service mature under the direct auspices of the federal government and believed that it was time for the Post Office to give up running the airmail at the direct expense of the American taxpayer. The Post Office had lost money on airmail every year except 1918. According to Kelly, private contractors should carry the airmail, with mail payment acting as a subsidy. Kelly's bill easily passed Congress with little debate. President Calvin Coolidge signed it into law on February 2, 1925.

Under the authority of the Contract Air Mail Act of 1925—or the Kelly Act, as it came to be known—the Post Office awarded contacts to seven operators to carry mail over eight routes, each linked to the transcontinental airmail line. On April 3, 1926, the Ford Motor Company became the first contractor to start service, when its planes carried mail between Detroit and Chicago. Three days later, Varney Air Lines, which eventually became part of United Air Lines, started airmail service between Elko, Nevada, and Pasco, Washington, effectively linking the Pacific Northwest with the transcontinental route. Western Air Express (WAE) and its resourceful president, Harris M. "Pop" Hanshue, began to carry mail on April 17, 1926, between Los Angeles and Salt Lake City. Both Western Airlines and TWA would later claim WAE's start date as their own earliest origins. In fact, most U.S. major airlines would eventually claim lineage to one or more of the companies that operated the first 12 contract airmail routes.[6]

On July 1, 1927, the Post Office turned over the western portion of the transcontinental line to Boeing Air Transport. Exactly two months later, National Air Transport began to carry mail between Chicago and New York. The Post Office airmail operation officially ceased to exist, and a bevy of fledgling airlines now stretched their wings.

Early Commercial Air Travelers

Air passenger service in the United States was limited for quite some time. The first scheduled airline in the world, the St. Petersburg–Tampa Airboat Line, lasted for only a few months, shuttling passengers across Florida's Tampa Bay in 1914. Most contract mail carriers in the 1920s indirectly entered the passenger business. Mail took priority over passengers because mail paid the bills and was in fact the reason for the airlines' existence. People wishing to make the newspaper headlines sometimes persuaded the mail carriers to allow them to fly with the sacks of mail. On one occasion a newlywed couple convinced an airmail contractor to let them ride 500 miles among the mail sacks for a cost of $2,000. Most potential air passengers considered the flying conditions too harsh and the price too steep, and contract airmail carriers simply did not wish to carry passengers when they could earn more money with less effort by carrying mail.[7]

One exception to the rule was Western Air Express, the earliest predecessor of what would become TWA. This pioneering airline flew passengers along with the mail almost from the airline's inception. Harris "Pop" Hanshue had founded WAE to fly the contract mail route between Salt Lake City and Los Angeles in the spring of 1926. Only one month after its first scheduled flight, WAE carried its first passenger. Ben Redman paid a

Pictured here in 1927, the de Havilland DH-4 mail plane was the workhorse of the Post Office's transcontinental service. Made of wood and canvas, the modified de Havilland mail plane was about to pass into history after seven years of flying over mountains, plains, and deserts between the nation's two coasts. (From the collection of Robert E. Burness, Jr.)

$90 fare for the eight-hour trip from Los Angeles to Salt Lake City. When the volume of airmail allowed, passengers became a regular feature on WAE. More than 200 intrepid souls flew as passengers on the airline in 1926. Seated on two removable seats or on mail sacks in an open cockpit, hardy passengers braved deafening noise and whatever Mother Nature served up as Western's Douglas M-2 mail planes soared over the arid Southwest.[8]

Although the majority of airline passengers were men, women formed a strong minority. One of the first female airline passengers in the American West was Maude Campbell of Salt Lake City. In early June 1926 she gamely shelled out $180 for a round-trip flight on WAE between Salt Lake City and Los Angeles. The line's alert traffic manager made Miss Campbell's flight a public celebration. Upon arrival at the airport, she donned a special flying suit, compliments of the airline, to protect her from the elements during the flight. Pilot Alva DeGarmo told her that the onboard toilet facilities consisted of one tin can, if she cared to use it. He also outlined the proper deployment of her parachute in case of an emergency.[9]

After the plane touched down in Los Angeles, airline president Hanshue presented Campbell with a spray of gladiolas as news cameras snapped photographs. Her fair complexion glowed red from the stinging wind and, despite the cotton she placed in her ears before putting on a helmet at the start of the flight, she suffered a minor degree of deafness because of the roar of the engine. As for the tin can, Miss Campbell later confessed, "I waited until we got to Las Vegas. It was the only thing to do."[10]

Another woman made aviation history when she became the first passenger to fly on Boeing Air Transport from Chicago to San Francisco in July 1927. Jane Eads, a reporter for the *Chicago Herald and Examiner*, climbed into a Boeing 40A at night in Chicago. Boarding a Boeing 40A was an ordeal for a woman in a skirt or long dress. She first climbed a stepladder situated at the trailing edge of the wing next to the fuselage. Standing on the wing itself, several feet from the ground, she then had to bend her body in half to slip through the low opening into the cabin.

Once inside, Eads curled up on the upholstered bench and slept during most of the night except for brief stops in Iowa City and Omaha, where she changed planes. In Iowa City, she wrote: "Before landing I was too frightened to write. The plane tipped and tilted and dropped. I just threw down my pencil and hung on. . . . It was the most exhilarating feeling I've ever experienced in all my life." The airplane touched the earth again in North Platte, Cheyenne, and Rock Springs, before another airplane took over from Salt Lake City. The hot desert air prompted Eads to change into a light summer dress during the flight—no small feat in the confines of the Boeing's cabin. Stops in Elko and Reno meant that the plane was near its destination.

A Varney Air Lines (part of the United Air Lines system) pilot accepts an air mail letter from a young woman. Note the location of the cabin doors on the four-passenger Boeing 40B. Climbing aboard was no simple matter for passengers, especially for women in skirts and dresses who had to walk on the wing before bending down to fit inside the door frame. (Northwest Museum of Arts and Culture / Eastern Washington State Historical Society, Spokane, Washington. L87-1.1561-32)

San Francisco welcomed Miss Eads less than 24 hours after leaving Chicago. The same journey aboard a regular train would have delivered her to San Francisco about 40 hours later.[11]

Soon after Jane Eads's historic flight, George J. Mead, vice president and chief engineer at Pratt & Whitney Aircraft Company, took a scheduled flight on the Boeing Air Transport line to see how well the Boeing 40A's Wasp engines performed in service. Mead was the sole passenger in a Boeing 40A flying over the midwestern states and baking in the summer heat. Despite flying at night, the heat was so intense that he kept the sliding windows closed, hoping that it was cooler inside than outside the aircraft. Even over Nevada and California on the following day, Mead could not decide which was worse: the blast of hot air through the open windows, or the stifling heat inside the cabin with the windows closed. He concluded that it was a no-win situation until the pilot mercifully climbed to more than 8,000 feet, where the cooler air refreshed his passenger. Throughout the daylight portion of his trip, Mead could often look down and see the Union Pacific Railroad tracks and even sections of the Lincoln Highway, carrying what looked like miniature automobiles. Cars and trains seemed slow to Mead as his Boeing passed them all at twice their speeds.[12]

Will Rogers, Avid Flyer

Another early BAT passenger who appreciated air travel's speed was humorist Will Rogers. Hailing from Claremore, Oklahoma, Rogers was an American icon, entertaining audiences with his earthy humor and keen political and cultural commentary. He appeared in many movies and toured with the Ziegfeld Follies. His syndicated newspaper column entertained and informed more than 40 million people daily. And Will Rogers loved to fly. He flew with the likes of Charles Lindbergh, General Billy Mitchell, and Wiley Post, who went around the world in a Lockheed Vega named the *Winnie Mae*.[13]

Affectionately known as the "patron saint of aviation," Rogers routinely took to the sky aboard commercial aircraft at a time when few people of note ventured into the air. Though not a pilot himself, Rogers nevertheless exercised his considerable influence as a national commentator to promote flying to the American people. His tireless work on behalf of air travel earned him induction into the National Aviation Hall of Fame in 1977. Proclaiming the advantages of air travel, Rogers recorded the details of one of his adventures, a trip from Los Angeles all the way to New York and back, in a two-part 1928 article for the *Saturday Evening Post*, spiced with a generous dash of his trademark humor.

Will Rogers poses in front of an American Airlines airplane during one of his many trips on commercial airlines. Before his death in an airplane crash with aviator Wiley Post in Alaska in 1935, no other American had so tirelessly promoted the advantages of commercial air travel. (Courtesy of Will Rogers Memorial Museums)

Although he liked flying, Rogers complained about the first part of his trip—getting to the airfield: "It took just an hour and a half to drive through the traffic to the field. Ain't autos grand? What would we do without them? If we had a dirt road, with no expense to the taxpayers, we would have got over there with a horse and buggy in about forty minutes." From the passenger's perspective, airports should have been built close to commercial and residential areas. However, all airports needed a certain amount of open space. Airplanes required clear zones with no obstructions for safe departures and landings. Such open spaces were most often found on the outskirts of towns, where tall buildings did not pose a hazard. Additionally, inexpensive real estate beyond the city limits meant that multiple acres of open land could be purchased for much less than property closer to the central business district. The noise of airliners taking off and landing also made the airports less-than-gracious neighbors.[14]

Given the distance between passengers' businesses and homes and the nearest airport, driving to and from the airport could prove time-consuming as well as dangerous. Rogers wrote that the pilot of his airplane, Jimmy James, arrived with his wife and children in the family car at the airfield: "They have come to see that he got through the dangerous part of his journey O.K." Roger's irony was thinly veiled. While most of the American public thought air travel inherently dangerous, they gave little consideration to taking auto trips in which they were more likely to suffer injury and even death. The same holds true in the twenty-first century.[15]

Before departing Los Angeles in the small aircraft, Rogers warned his wife to take care driving home from the airfield and to wire the Salt Lake Airport to confirm that she had arrived home safely. Rogers was the one who seemed to be making the more dangerous journey, but he turned the tables by emphasizing the reservations he had concerning his wife driving to their home in Los Angeles unharmed.

Rogers put on a recently purchased flying suit and took his seat amid the overflow of mail sacks in the front cockpit of the WAE biplane. He relaxed, placing his complete confidence in the pilot.

The Pilot Mystique

DEDICATION
Will Rogers
FIELD
OKLAHOMA CITY
JUNE 28, 1941

Many early airline passengers, including Will Rogers, viewed pilots through the romantic prism of the most famous ones, such as Charles Lindbergh and Jack Knight. Aerial record setters dominated the front pages of American newspapers, making the pilots seem larger-than-life. The speed of air travel, and the romance of winging through the sky, contributed to the aura surrounding them. After all, pilots were the fastest men on earth—participating in the cutting edge of technological advancement.

Most Americans in the 1920s and 1930s still believed that only the daring or the foolish would ride in an airplane, let alone take the controls of one. Therefore, pilots were admired as virile figures who bravely rode the clouds "by the seats of their pants." By necessity and training, pilots had to withstand high-altitude conditions and amplified gravitational forces that were wholly foreign to those who remained on the ground. Pilots needed faster reflexes and exceptional depth perception. Clearly, these men were extraordinary.[16]

Besides training and skills, their manner of dress also distinguished them from practitioners of other arts. Because they were exposed to the elements in open cockpits, they donned a wide range of outfits to stay warm while aloft. Some wore heavy street clothing but added multiple layers of wool sweaters, leather vests, and overcoats, before topping off such ensembles with sheepskin jackets. Other pilots simply donned a flying suit over stylish business clothing. Still others arrived at the airport in simple work clothes and donned a leather coat and greasy overalls before braving the frigid skies. Early airline pilots exhibited a great deal of individuality in how they suited up for their daunting task.[17]

Their physical appearance could inspire reverence. In December 1928, during a stop at Bellefonte, Pennsylvania, a passenger saw two pilots deep in conversation next to an aircraft. These men regularly flew open-cockpit biplanes between Chicago and New York City. While they talked, the passenger noticed how they resembled "Eskimos in their ungainly flying suits, with helmets and goggles on their heads and great fur-lined moccasins over their shoes." The passenger stood in awe of them.[18]

Besides bulky apparel, early airline pilots wore a sidearm, in accordance with Post Office regulations. The Post Office wished to make sure those who transported the mail could fend off anyone attempting to take postal property by force. Of more utilitarian interest, however, the handguns became instruments of personal survival when pilots and their handful of passengers encountered trouble in the air and found themselves alone on the ground, in a vast wilderness.[19]

Many passengers thought the sidearms a strange sight. One passenger, who described the airmail pilots as "short stocky chaps, made broader in appearance by their many layers of clothing," likened them to "animated teddy-bears," with handguns "strapped to their thighs in approved 'bad man' fashion." Such sights only added to the pilots' mystique.[20]

In addition, the calm demeanor of pilots gave them an air of superiority and self-reliance. Even after completing long, physically and psychologically taxing flights, pilots emerged looking unruffled and relaxed. A passenger with the airmail in 1927 marveled that despite the gauntlet of forces the pilot of his flight had to overcome, this man never seemed anxious or disturbed: "He stepped down from his cockpit at the end of the run as cheerful, collected, and unworried as if he had not just done a day's nerve-racking labor." The pilot's unconcerned swagger reflected confidence in his own abilities to do a job few others would venture.[21]

As demonstrated in this 1930 advertisement featuring the Ford Tri-Motor, airlines and aircraft manufacturers alike understood that the perceived danger of air travel kept many Americans from taking to the sky.

Will Rogers worshipped airline pilots. He called them a "great bunch of men" who were "the most careful ones in the world." Admitting his own cowardice regarding many things, Rogers had so much confidence in the skill and character of the airline pilot that he crawled into the passenger compartment "like a baby crawling into its mother's arms." Just as the mother would not let harm come to her child, Rogers believed the pilot would make sure he delivered his passenger safely to the destination. (His confidence was ultimately to prove fatal, however. Rogers met an early death as a passenger of Wiley Post when their aircraft crashed soon after takeoff near Point Barrow, Alaska, on August 15, 1935.)[22]

Los Angeles to New York in 1927

The WAE pilot of Rogers's 1927 flight departing Los Angeles pointed the craft's nose toward Salt Lake City. He navigated according to the "iron compass," as early aviators called railroad tracks. Stretching between important cities and cutting through the lowest point between mountains, railroad tracks proved a reliable means of aerial navigation during daylight. Bound for Salt Lake City, WAE pilots simply followed the railroad tracks from Los Angeles across the Mohave Desert to an intermediate stop at Las Vegas.

Founded in the opening years of the twentieth century, Las Vegas remained little more than an oasis where a few thousand hearty folks lived next to the rail line. How different from the Las Vegas of the early twenty-first century—the most visited city on the planet, with over 37 million tourists every year. The Las Vegas of 1927 offered Will Rogers few amenities besides a space to stretch his legs during his airplane's refueling.[23]

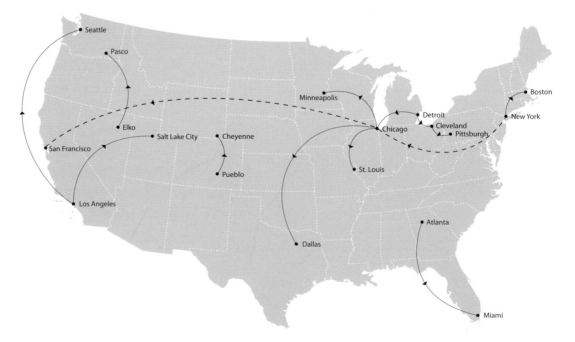

First Domestic Contract Air Mail Routes

The Air Mail Act of 1925, also called the Kelly Act in honor of its sponsor, U.S. Representative M. Clyde Kelly of Pennsylvania, authorized the Postmaster General to contract for air mail service. The first twelve contractors under the Kelly Act all started service by April 1927. They acted as feeder routes (see map on opposite page) funneling mail to the transcontinental route which the Post Office operated until awarding the Chicago-San Francisco segment to Boeing Air Transport and the New York-Chicago segment to National Air Transport in 1927. Both Boeing and National Air Transport became part of United Airlines.

Contract Air Mail (CAM) Route Number	Company (successor company)	Route	Started Operation
CAM 1	Colonial Air Lines (American Airlines)	New York-Boston	June 18, 1926
CAM 2	Robertson Aircraft Corporation (American Airlines)	Chicago-St. Louis	April 15, 1926
CAM 3	National Air Transport (United Airlines)	Chicago-Dallas	May 12, 1926
CAM 4	Western Air Express (TWA and Delta Airlines)	Los Angeles-Salt Lake City	April 17, 1926
CAM 5	Varney Air Lines (United Airlines)	Elko, Nevada-Pasco, Washington	April 6, 1926
CAM 6	Ford Air Transport (United Airlines)	Detroit-Cleveland	April 3, 1925
CAM 7	Ford Air Transport (United Airlines)	Detroit-Chicago	July 31, 1925
CAM 8	Pacific Air Transport (United Airlines)	Los Angeles-Seattle	September 15, 1926
CAM 9	Charles Dickenson (Northwest Airlines)	Chicago-Minneapolis	June 7, 1926
CAM 10	Florida Airways Corp.	Atlanta-Miami	June 1, 1926
CAM 11	Clifford Ball (United Airlines)	Cleveland-Pittsburgh	April 21, 1927
CAM 12	Western Air Express (Delta Airlines)	Pueblo, Colorado-Cheyenne, Wyoming	May 31, 1926

Back in the sky, the pilot passed notes to Rogers, pointing out landmarks and interesting facts. One note explained that the pilot was following the Union Pacific tracks all the way to Salt Lake City and that Zion National Park was in view. Rogers appreciated the information, especially the assurance that the pilot knew their location. Then came another message: "Wild horses!" The plane flew low over the herd, but, to Rogers's disappointment, they seemed indifferent to the aircraft's presence. Excitement was in store for Rogers, however, when his pilot spotted the WAE plane heading for Los Angeles and approaching from the opposite direction. Rogers held onto his seat as the pilot cut the engine and swooped down to greet his WAE colleague.

On the ground in Salt Lake, Rogers bought his ticket for Chicago while waiting 20 minutes for the connecting BAT plane's departure. He paid $60 to fly to Salt Lake, then $142 more to reach Chicago. For his second fare he had a seat in a Boeing 40A's enclosed cabin. Stepping inside, he sized up the airplane's passenger accommodations, noting that the side-by-side seating arrangement was similar to day coach seats on a railroad, but narrower. Rogers found the space "nice and comfortable," with an electric dome light in the metal ceiling. He marveled at the small windows on either side of the compartment. The windows slid back to open, allowing air into the cabin as desired.[24]

The comfort of Rogers's cabin changed when an executive from New York's Labor Bank climbed into the seat next to him. The two seats were comfortable for one person, but two adults fitted like sardines in a can. Rogers explained to his readers: "Now when I told you this seat was narrow, I didn't just put that in there to make more words. It is either terrible narrow or this old Labor boy keeps spreading out. He is a big husky thing. . . . I would turn my shoulders crosswise and still he would spread over onto my side. . . . The specifications in these planes might call for two people, but not one prosperous Labor leader and a well-fed actor at the same time." He concluded that the cabin was designed for "one frail woman accompanied by a male contortionist."

Another passenger recorded a similar experience in a Boeing 40. In a virtual replay of Will Rogers and the banker, a passenger named Myron M. Stearns shoehorned himself in Chicago next to a gasoline salesman headed for Reno. Stearns wrote: "The seat in the little cabin was hardly wide enough for the two of us. But we squeezed in, and a mechanic shut the door. It was like the inside of a small coupe, with a window in the upper part of the door at each side. The roof was close above our heads." That same roof met Stearns's head with a wallop when the plane encountered some rough air over Nevada. After the salesman got out at Reno, Stearns had no one to wedge himself against when the airplane began to buck. He was happy, however, for the extra space, as both he and the salesman were by no means skinny men.[25]

In Will Rogers's case, he may have enjoyed more space if he had not brought along a generous quantity of food from home. Knowing that the airlines served only complimentary box lunches, his wife, Betty, had packed some food for his trip. So when Rogers became hungry during the flight, he opened the travel bag he had carried aboard with him. After getting past the clothing inside it, he discovered a treasure trove of food, including sandwiches, baked chicken, and ham, as well as some pie and chocolate cake. Rogers claimed that his wife had read that Charles Lindbergh carried only a ham sandwich to eat during his nonstop flight from New York to Paris, so she determined to make "a sucker out of his commissary department."[26]

At Salt Lake City, airline personnel handed Rogers a box lunch and a bottle of coffee. Western Air Express and Boeing Air Transport pioneered aerial meal service in the skies over America. These lines set the precedent of including en route food service in the price of a ticket. Meals aboard steamships were also complimentary to any passenger, unlike meals on railroad lines. Railroads charged an additional fee for each meal served. Given the three or more days required for a train to travel coast-to-coast, the cost of the luxurious meals could prove substantial for a passenger with a healthy appetite. However, the transcontinental airline passenger needed fewer meals when covering the same distance because air travel required less time. As airlines understood that passengers digested lighter foods more easily, they served complimentary meals, typically a chicken sandwich or two with an apple and a small dessert. And pilots such as Jack Knight were known to share their personal homemade lunches with passengers on occasion.[27]

Rogers accepted the box lunch and carried it with him aboard the Boeing 40. The New York banker, armed with his own box lunch and coffee, joined Rogers. The two men ate their food, and then Rogers brought out more from his bag and shared some with his fellow passenger. Will Rogers did not mind sharing his food. But with such limited space in the cabin, eating made the men feel more crowded in an already tight environment.

More box lunches awaited Rogers in the airplane from Omaha to Chicago. Tongue firmly in cheek, Rogers greeted coffee and breakfast in Chicago with glee after a "day and night of fasting." At Chicago he transferred to an open-cockpit plane again. National Air Transport (NAT), soon to join Boeing Air Transport and other lines as one entity called United Air Lines, held the mail contract from Chicago to New York. After paying NAT's $200 air fare to New York, Rogers found himself crammed into his seat, surrounded by mail sacks.[28]

National Air Transport, operating the eastern section of the transcontinental airmail route, flew over the most feared portion of airway in the United States. Called the "hell stretch," the airway over the Allegheny Mountains in Pennsylvania was subject to terrible storms and fog and provided few places for safe landings because of the series of ridges and valleys running directly across it. NAT used Douglas M-3 mail planes on the route, with primitive passenger accommodations among the mail sacks in the front cockpit. During NAT's first year operating the route, only 168 passengers rode with the airline. Most, like Rogers, transferred from BAT Boeing 40As in Chicago. NAT had doubled its passenger fare to $200, effectively discouraging all but the most determined air traveler from attempting to fly the airline.[29]

After an intermediate stop at Cleveland, Rogers's NAT plane encountered turbulence over the Alleghenies on the way to New York, due to a severe rainstorm that had paralyzed most transcontinental air traffic for several days. The mail plane started "rocking and bucking like a bronc," and Rogers became airsick, vomiting on the sacks of mail as well as on his flying suit. Although he was an avid promoter of air travel, he made no excuses for airsickness. He explained to his audience, most of whom had never set foot in an airplane, that there were many similarities between the motion of an airplane and an ocean liner. Just as a rough sea will induce sea sickness in ocean liner passengers, rough air could cause air passengers to feel their stomachs going up and down with the plane's motion, inducing airsickness. Understandably, Rogers lacked his original enthusiasm when greeted by the sight of box lunches on the return flights a few days later.[30]

Rogers's airplane made a forced landing in a Pennsylvania farmer's rain-soaked pasture—apparently a long way from New York City. But Rogers soon discovered that the airports were a significant distance from New York City too. He explained the irony: "I want to tell you now it don't do you any good to fly to New York. After I finally got out to [Hadley Field], I found I dident [sic] lose any time by landing at Beaver Falls, Pennsylvania; in fact I was nearer New York than Hadley, or even Mitchell or Roosevelt Field. You lose more time getting into the city than you save by flying there."[31]

The U.S. Post Office had established Hadley Field near New Brunswick, New Jersey, as its eastern terminus for the transcontinental airmail line. The fast mail train could reach the field from New York General Post Office in an hour. The primary reason for an airfield so far from New York City was it lacked the fog and smoke that were found closer to the city. The field was later abandoned for a new one that the city of Newark prepared closer to New York City.[32]

Rogers returned westbound from New York during the dark of night. Looking out of their aircraft, early air passengers understood that, in the words of Second Assistant Postmaster General Paul Henderson, "an airway exists on the ground, not in the air." This was especially true at night. Airmail and passenger airline pilots relied upon lighted airways to tell where they were and if they were on course. Without such navigational aids, they were sailors adrift in the midst of a dangerous ocean of seemingly endless plains, mountains, and valleys.[33]

The Lighted Airway

Under the able leadership of Paul Henderson, the Post Office built the first sections of lighted airway with high-intensity rotating beacons across the center of the nation from Chicago to Cheyenne. By January 1929 the transcontinental lighted airway from San Francisco to New York was complete. Four years later, two more transcontinental airways were lit. By early 1932 the Department of Commerce had installed more than 2,000 beacons throughout the United States. These beacons came in three varieties: airway beacons to guide pilots along an airway from one city to another, airport beacons to ensure safety in the skies at and around airports, and landmark beacons, warning pilots to avoid navigational hazards.[34]

The airway beacons were the most numerous and held the greatest fascination for passengers. The Commerce Department had detailed regulations regarding their construction. Federal plans required an airway beacon every 10 to 25 miles apart along a commercial airway. Additionally, such beacons adorned emergency landing fields, approximately 30 to 50 miles apart in areas lacking established landing fields.[35]

Each airway beacon rotated on top of a 51-foot open steel tower. A tower of that height put the rotating beacon above most surrounding vegetation and obstructions and permitted it to illuminate the horizon rather than shining upon the ground. Where conditions warranted, crews installed towers ranging from 20 feet to nearly 90 feet in height.[36]

At night, pilots and passengers first saw the most visible part—the rotating lamp. Those installed in the 1920s were usually standardized at 24 inches in diameter. By the early 1930s, larger, 36-inch-diameter lamps at each side of the beacon came into common use. One side of the lamp had a clear lens; the other side showed either red or green. A red light meant the beacon was not at an emergency landing field. However, a green beacon light indicated that an emergency landing field was nearby. Airway lamps rotated at 6 rpm—six clear flashes and six flashes of either red or green every minute. The beacons each projected a million-candle-power shaft of light at an angle of 1.5 degrees above the horizon. A pilot could see the flash of the rotating beacon up to 40 miles away.[37]

The beacon tower straddled the middle of a 70-foot-long concrete arrow pointing in the direction of the next beacon in sequence along the airway. At the arrow's fletching end stood a 10-by-14-foot building—the powerhouse. Inside the yellow structure were generators to power the rotating beacon. If adequate electrical power was available locally, the powerhouse reverted to a storage shed. On one-half of the roof, large black letters, contrasting with the overall yellow color, displayed the beacon's number, based on its location along the airway. The other side of the roof declared the air route, based on the first letters of the airway's terminal cities.[38]

Located between Laramie and Cheyenne, Wyoming, at 8,500 feet above sea level, the Sherman Hill light beacon was the highest airway beacon in the world. Light beacons such as this one provided pilots with an unerring navigational aid across the darkened night landscape of the nation's interior. (Courtesy of Jesse Davidson Aviation Archives)

Installing the beacons was only the beginning. Someone had to maintain them in good working order. The Commerce Department delegated that task to the Lighthouse Bureau, which assigned various airways to lighthouse districts on both coasts. For instance, as of the fall of 1929, the Eighteenth Lighthouse District, San Francisco, was responsible for four airways, including the section from San Francisco to Reno along the transcontinental airway. Airways across the heartland became the responsibility of two "maintenance organizations," based in Salt Lake City and Dallas. The Salt Lake City airway engineers ensured the operation of the transcontinental airway from Reno to Omaha.[39]

The mechanics caring for airway beacons throughout the nation needed the "combined talents of a high-wire artist, gasoline engine mechanic, electrician, bookkeeper, and mountain climber." Whenever a pilot or even a local citizen reported a beacon outage, a mechanic traveled to the beacon and made the necessary adjustments or repairs. Mechanics also periodically refueled the gasoline tanks of self-powered beacons.[40]

To the trained eye, airway beacons flashed a coded message, identifying their location along the airway. Each of the 10 beacons stationed along every 100 to 250 miles of airway had a number between 1 and 10. The numbering simply repeated for the next 100 to 250 miles and so forth. Every rotating beacon flashed a pattern based on its location within its particular stretch of airway. The Morse code mnemonic for the beacon order was *When Undertaking Very Difficult Routes, Keep Heading By Good Methods*. Therefore, a pilot could determine his location along an airway by the Morse code letter a beacon flashed.[41]

Night Flights

Passenger Myron Stearns, flying across the Midwest at night in 1928, could not help but notice the flashing beacons: "Ahead a level finger of light swung about in a circle, flashing bright each time it passed us: a Department of Commerce air beacon marking the route." As he continued his journey, Stearns enjoyed a night flight between Cheyenne and Salt Lake City. Darkness closed in around Stearns's plane, yet the way ahead was never in doubt as the pilot "followed a trail of flashing beacons, the revolving mail-route lights." For the passenger, flashing light beacons served as a visual reminder that the plane was on course—a reassuring thought as the aircraft winged its way through the inky black of night.[42]

Will Rogers noted, on his way back across the country in 1927, that airway beacons between Chicago and New York were at 10-mile intervals, instead of the 25-mile intervals between beacons farther west. Weather conditions, such as haze and storms, reduced visibility more often over the Alleghenies than across the Rockies. The beams from eastern beacons crossed so that pilots could always keep a beacon in sight unless dense fog enveloped the land.[43]

Some transcontinental air passengers in the 1920s, such as Will Rogers, expressed pure joy at night flying. Rather than fear, the onset of darkness and the revelation of lights upon the ground delighted the eyes of those winging above the landscape. Rogers had previously flown over Germany at night, but this trip was his first over the United States in darkness. Peering from his window at the blackness outside, Rogers watched the flashing beacons with interest. He noticed how some of the beacons were near "a row of little lights what kinder looks like the size of a baseball park." These were emergency landing fields.[44]

Rogers also marveled at Chicago's lights as his airplane approached from the east. Myriad streetlights illuminated the city's transportation grid. He could even "see the dark outline of the lake and thousands of automobile headlights moving like bugs." Enraptured, Will Rogers commanded the reader: "Ah, say, fly over a Big City at night. Daytime is like slumming compared to seeing a big, lighted City from the air at night."[45]

Speed

Such views mattered little to executives who valued air travel purely for its speed. C. R. Borkland was the business manager for *Popular Aviation* magazine in Chicago. He needed to get to San Francisco quickly late in 1927 and preferred to travel at the weekend and during the night so that he would not waste precious time. His BAT flight was scheduled to leave Chicago on a Saturday evening, but subzero temperatures and snow kept the Boeing 40A on the ground until about 3:30 A.M. Sunday morning. An hour and a half later, Borkland's plane landed in Iowa City, just long enough to refuel before continuing to Omaha. Passengers stepped from the airplane to stretch their stiff legs briefly, while airline personnel exchanged mail between the connecting aircraft. Then it was across the plains to North Platte and Cheyenne.

Borkland's airplane climbed into a blue sky from Cheyenne at noon. Blizzard conditions soon developed, forcing the pilot to make an emergency landing near Elk Mountain. A local property owner invited the two passengers and the pilot inside for food and warmth until the storm subsided. A couple hours later the skies cleared and a small crowd witnessed the Boeing climb westward over the snowy landscape. Wishing to save time, the pilot put down at an emergency landing field to refuel. The frigid wind chilled Borkland and the others to the bone during the brief stop, and the elderly man in charge of the field and his wife appreciated the passengers' assistance in refueling the airplane. The caretaker reluctantly waved good-bye as the Boeing 40A climbed skyward. Borkland sympathized with the loneliness in the Wyoming wilderness experienced by the emergency field caretaker, who longed for company because several weeks could pass without any human contact.

Four hours after leaving Cheyenne, Borkland's plane touched down at Salt Lake City. Darkness prevented air travel across Nevada at night because the lighted airway beacons were not yet installed over that section of the transcontinental airway. The pilot brought his two passengers to a hotel, and another airline employee returned them to the airport for a 7:00 A.M. departure. After stops in Elko and Reno, Borkland marveled at the stunning beauty of the Sierra Nevada and relished the warm sunshine flooding through the window into the Boeing's cramped cabin. After a few minutes in Sacramento, just long enough to hand over mail, the flight continued to Oakland, bringing Borkland to his destination almost 2,000 miles from snow-shrouded Chicago. Despite weather delays, Borkland lost only half-a-day's work.

While air travel cost more than rail travel, business professionals such as Borkland believed that the price was acceptable because of the superior speed and therefore the time savings of aircraft. Contrasting rail and air travel, Borkland challenged his readers to ponder more than the obvious price: "Figure the expense of berths, meals, tips and all the other little extras you never can remember and have to lump on the swindle sheet as 'misc.' Then put a conservative value on your wasted time, the time you spend reading magazines on the train, looking out the window, trying to sleep nights, trying to stay awake daytimes so you can sleep nights." Air travel on weekends and during nights kept business travelers from wasting precious time in transit on weekdays. The business traveler actually saved money using the airlines. After totaling all the expenses associated with rail travel, Borkland believed that the features of air travel, including superior speed and scheduling, coupled with fewer hidden costs, would lure business travelers to the airlines.[46]

Yet before well-heeled executives would consider abandoning their Pullman cars for airplane cabins, a distinct revolution in the very concept of commercial aviation was necessary. Accomplishing this feat would take a large amount of capital, a great deal of careful planning, a rugged aircraft with a trusted brand name, and the personal attention of the most famous aviator—Charles Lindbergh.

The Tri-Motor Era

2

In the euphoria following Charles Lindbergh's nonstop flight from New York to Paris in the summer of 1927, many business leaders saw great opportunities in commercial aviation. Stock values of aviation-related companies rose to heady heights. Along with radio, aviation became the darling of Wall Street in much the same way as investments in information technology led the way in the 1990s. Investors purchased $400 million in aviation securities between 1927 and 1929. One of the best-financed of such enterprises inaugurated service in July 1929. Transcontinental Air Transport—TAT—boasted a combination air-rail service that sped passengers from coast to coast in 48 hours—half the time required aboard the fastest scheduled train.

Creation of TAT

Few airmail contractors routinely transported passengers in 1929. Boeing Air Transport carried passengers along the central transcontinental route in Boeing 40As, but BAT was first and foremost a contract airmail carrier. Passengers took a figurative and sometimes literal backseat to the mail. Charles Lindbergh sought to remedy the situation. The famous aviator dreamed of establishing an aerial transcontinental link catering specifically to passengers. Along with some wealthy backers from St. Louis who had financed his 1927 flight to Paris, Lindbergh approached Henry Ford, suggesting that he should join them in creating a transcontinental airline. After Ford refused, Clement M. Keys, a Wall Street financier and leader in aviation business, joined forces with Lindbergh and the St. Louis investors. Together they sought financial ties with railroad companies. A joint air-rail operation made sense. Airliners would naturally follow railroad tracks for navigation between the two coasts, stopping at cities along the way where railroads already had stations. Additionally, if darkness or weather prohibited flying, air passengers could take a train along the route. Two rail lines, the Pennsylvania Railroad and the Atchison, Topeka, and Santa Fe Railroad, combined with the other parties to form Transcontinental Air Transport for the express purpose of creating a luxurious, safe, and swift air-rail passenger service from coast to coast.[1]

Railroad executives in the late 1920s never envisioned that, less than three decades later, airlines would surpass railroads in volume of domestic intercity passengers. The president of the Pennsylvania Railroad, W. W. Atterbury, wrote at the commencement of TAT service that "the railroads will remain, of course, the backbone of the nation's transportation system." An official from the Santa Fe Railroad was also unconcerned about competition from air transportation because, in his opinion, only those people in the greatest hurry would need the speed of air travel. From the railroaders' point of view, Transcontinental Air Transport was foremost a train ride with portions of the trip accelerated by aircraft.[2]

Because of the railroad's extensive involvement, the general public perceived the creation of TAT as the railroad's taking to the sky. Contemporary writers and promotional literature emphasized that TAT passengers could sleep well while aboard the finest rail accommodations at night and soar on the wings of flying Pullmans during the day. As one author put it, here was a clear case of "railroads sprouting wings."[3]

Railroads were important for another reason. Until navigational beacons lit the way, TAT's planes would not fly at night. Rather, aircraft shuttled passengers during daylight hours between key points where they transferred to trains for an overnight trip to meet another aircraft to take them via air for the next portion of the journey.

Readying TAT for Passenger Service

In 1928, Transcontinental Air Transport began preparations for service between New York City and Los Angeles. With Clement Keys as president and Charles Lindbergh as chairman of the TAT technical committee, the line was ready for its first transcontinental passengers by the next summer.[4]

Less than two years after his flight from New York to Paris propelled him onto the world stage, Charles Lindbergh wearied of the public adoration showered upon him. He threw his energies into building TAT, playing a key role in designing TAT's route across the continent. He oversaw the selection of intermediate airports across the nation, most lacking airport facilities capable of handling the large aircraft that Lindbergh believed the line should use. Some of the sites that he selected lacked airfields, including Winslow and Kingman,

Charles A. Lindbergh's nonstop flight
from New York to Paris in 1927 caused
business leaders to recognize the potential
of commercial aviation and provided an
invaluable boost to the industry. While
Americans were investing hundreds of
millions of dollars in aviation, Lindbergh,
as chairman of Transcontinental Air
Transport's technical committee, had
a major role in designing the airline's
passenger route across the country and
establishing safety measures. (Courtesy
of the George Grantham Bain Collection,
Library of Congress reproduction no. LC-
DIG-ggbain-35317)

C.A. LINDBERGH   No.1

Arizona; Clovis, New Mexico; and Waynoka, Oklahoma. TAT purchased land and made its own landing facilities at each of these locations.[5]

Lindbergh established a significant precedent for safety when he demanded the creation of 72 weather reporting stations along TAT's transcontinental route. Before departure, TAT pilots would know the current weather conditions from coast to coast, thanks to a private teletype service linking every TAT station. Accurate weather reports and predictions contributed greatly to the airline's safe operation.

Charles Lindbergh selected the all-metal Ford 5-AT-B Tri-Motor aircraft to form TAT's airliner fleet. The line needed to convince passengers that they were in a safe, luxurious, and efficient environment. This started with the use of the proven, all-metal Ford, a name that Americans already knew and trusted. The public understood that Ford automobiles were dependable and rugged, attributes applicable to the trimotor craft. The airplane sported three radial piston engines: even with one engine stopped, it could still keep flying, thus assuaging passenger fears of forced landings due to engine failure.

Costing $57,000 each, TAT's Ford airliners carried only 10 passengers rather than the usual 15. Radio communication equipment and provision for a uniformed cabin attendant took up some of the weight and space made available with the removal of five seats. The extra space also allowed more legroom between the 10 wicker seats, soon to be replaced by aluminum chairs, bolted to the floor on either side of a center aisle. Seatbelts were attached to the plane and not the chairs, providing an added measure of safety. Even the hulking appearance of the Ford Tri-Motor conveyed a message of ruggedness, dependability, and safety.[6]

Lindbergh provided another important element to the new service—his name. TAT became known as the Lindbergh Line, invaluable brand recognition that other fledgling operators could not claim. The famous phrase "the Lindbergh Line" remained even after TAT became part of Transcontinental and Western Airlines, or TWA.

After the investment of millions of dollars in facilities and equipment and many months of careful preparation, the entire TAT system between New York and Los Angeles operated for two weeks before the official start of the service. Approximately 260 passengers traveled on TAT before the inaugural commercial flight in July 1929. The line followed a strict schedule. Westbound from New York City, TAT passengers left Pennsylvania Station at 6:05 P.M. aboard a luxury Pullman train called the *Pennsylvania Railroad Airway Limited* bound for Columbus, Ohio. The *Airway Limited* took passengers over the Allegheny Mountains, which were notorious for hazardous flying conditions. Arriving at 7:55 the next morning, passengers climbed aboard a Ford Tri-Motor at Port Columbus—TAT's own airport about

by plane
and train

TAT
TRANSCONTINENTAL AIR TRANSPORT INC

MADDUX
AIR · LINES

Coast to coast

eight miles from downtown—and departed for Waynoka, Oklahoma, 120 miles northwest of Oklahoma City. The aircraft stopped in Indianapolis, St. Louis, Kansas City, and Wichita along the way. Passengers dined at the Santa Fe Railroad's Harvey House in Waynoka before continuing their overnight journey aboard a Santa Fe Railroad Pullman train to Clovis, New Mexico. Another Ford awaited passengers there for the continuation of their trip to Los Angeles, with intermediate stops in Albuquerque and in Winslow and Kingman, Arizona, arriving in Los Angeles at 5:52 P.M. local time. The eastbound system worked the same, only in reverse, with a scheduled Los Angeles departure at 8:45 A.M.

One of those earliest passengers was S. L. Gabel, president of the Summerill Tubing Company, in Bridgeport, Pennsylvania. Gabel noted how low the Fords traveled over much of the route. Between Indianapolis and St. Louis his plane flew so low that people on the ground waved at the passing airplane and dogs tried to chase it. On the eastbound return, a thunderstorm between Albuquerque and Clovis forced the pilot to fly particularly close to the earth. Herds of cattle and innumerable jackrabbits scattered as the plane lumbered overhead. Another passenger recorded flying so low over portions of Missouri that she witnessed flocks of sheep scatter and chickens scramble. The Ford typically cruised at between 1,000 and 4,000 feet elevation. Over mountains in Arizona and California the pilot took the airplane to more than 7,000 feet.[7]

Five months after the start of coast-to-coast service, TAT merged with Maddux Air Lines to form the short-lived TAT-Maddux, adding passenger connections between Los Angeles and San Diego. The logo for the new enterprise clearly shows the importance of both railroads and airplanes to TAT's transcontinental service. (From the collection of Dr. Charles C. Quarles)

TAT's Inaugural Flight

The official start of TAT's public service on July 7, 1929, was a gala event in New York. A band played "California, Here We Come," and passengers posed with Amelia Earhart and other VIPs for pictures. Large crowds, with Henry and Edsel Ford among them, were on hand at Port Columbus to watch passengers, including five women, board TAT's *City of Wichita* and *City of Columbus*. TAT had named each of its 10 Fords after a city that the line served—in the same way that railroads named locomotives.

The two Fords landed at intermediate stops. After leaving St. Louis, passengers gazed down at the passing farmland and dined on a lunch of cold chicken and potato salad. The meal came complete with iced tea and fresh strawberry shortcake. West of Kansas City, many passengers developed airsickness as the planes bucked in turbulent air at low altitude.[8]

On the ground in Waynoka, special vehicles called Aero-Cars sped passengers the five miles from the airport to the rail depot. Aviation pioneer Glenn Curtiss had designed the vehicles for TAT to carry up to 14 passengers in style between airports and rail stations. A Studebaker roadster pulled each Aero-Car, whose plus interior design mimicked that of the Ford Tri-Motors.

During this inaugural westbound flight across the continent, the only significant mishap took place in Clovis. The first of two Tri-Motors took off without incident, but a combination of "unfavorable circumstances," in the words of a news reporter, befell the second Ford as it attempted to take off. Because of a strong wind gust, combined with engine trouble, the pilot applied the brakes as the craft careered through plowed earth before its left wing struck the side of a hangar, breaking several windows. Fortunately, the airplane hit the building at a relatively slow speed, and all aboard emerged unhurt. Company officials persuaded passengers to board a spare aircraft, which departed only 30 minutes later than scheduled.[9]

The next morning, a host of celebrities and dignitaries came to see the two TAT planes leave the Los Angeles airfield in Glendale for New York City. Hollywood actors Douglas Fairbanks and Mary Pickford arrived in a yellow luxury car. They waved to the spectators filling grandstands erected for the momentous occasion. Standing on a stepladder, Pickford broke a bottle over the nose of one plane, christening it *The City of Los Angeles*. This aircraft and its companion soon filled with 10 passengers each.[10]

TAT's inaugural eastbound flight from Los Angeles had none other than Charles Lindbergh at the controls. His new bride, Anne Morrow Lindbergh, rode as a passenger. In a letter written to her sister Constance Cutter Morrow during the flight, Mrs. Lindbergh observed that the TAT Ford Tri-Motor was a decided step up for passenger comfort: "It is beautifully comfortable and businesslike; I feel as though I were in a private

The inaugural trip of the Airway Limited, in July 1929, officially commenced TAT's coast-to-coast service. This group of distinguished people, including Amelia Earhart (the woman in front of the word "New"), posed for pictures and a band played, "California, Here We Come," before the train left New York for an overnight trip to Columbus. (From the TWA Archives of the St. Louis Mercantile Library at the University of Missouri–St. Louis)

TAT passengers transfer from an Aero-Car to a Ford Tri-Motor.
Aviator Glenn Curtiss designed the Aero-Car especially for
transporting TAT customers between rail depots and airports.
(From the TWA Archives of the St. Louis Mercantile Library at the
University of Missouri–St. Louis)

car." Marveling at the adjustable leather-clad seats, the dainty curtains, and the shaded electric lights, she wrote to her sister: "I am crazy to have you take this trip. You simply must. Even Mother would enjoy it."[11]

Flying mostly for pleasure, women constituted approximately one-quarter of TAT's passengers during the line's brief existence. TAT catered to its passengers, particularly the female ones, as no other domestic line had previously. Women in the 1920s wore primarily skirts and dresses, their legs exposed to the numbingly cold air so closely associated with early air travel, so they particularly appreciated the Ford Tri-Motor's floor heating ducts. Forced air, warmed by the engine exhaust manifold, flowed through the cabin. In reality, the heating system seldom kept passengers warm in cold weather, as openings in the rear of the plane sucked air from the heating vents and windows out of the cabin during flight. The Ford Tri-Motor earned the nickname "flying icebox" because of this deficiency.[12]

During warm weather, passengers could open small vents near the floor of each seat to provide a draft of outside air. Open vents allowed in more than air during takeoff and touchdown on the typical earthen landing fields of the era. If passengers neglected to close their vents, mud splattered on their feet.

On the inaugural eastbound TAT transcontinental trip, the airliner following the one Charles Lindbergh piloted carried a passenger named Velva G. Darling, whose outstanding account of her experiences on the trip from Los Angeles to New York was published in *World's Work* magazine. Stepping into the Ford's cabin in California, Darling could hardly contain her admiration of the aircraft's interior. She deemed it a work of art. A new product called Aero-board lined the walls. One-eighth inch thick, it consisted of a thin layer of balsa wood sandwiched between sheets of aluminum and acted as a sound and temperature insulator while providing the interior decorator with a ready, smooth canvas. TAT wished for an interior unlike that of a railcar or automobile cabin. It was to look modern and cheerful and provide a sense of comfort to passengers, many of whom had probably never flown before. To accomplish this, TAT hired a relatively obscure artist from Greenwich Village, New York, to decorate the interior with colors he considered best for air travel. The designer painted the ceiling cream and the walls lavender, with chrome paneling accents to convey a sense of strength and safety. As *Airway Age* put it, TAT had designed all aspects of the cabin interior "to impress the traveler with the fact that flying is safe, stable, and conducted on an orderly basis."[13]

Examining the cabin, Darling marveled that everything, from "the polish of the panels on the walls to the electric cigar lighters, individual lamps with parchment shades, rugs, and sliding glass windows," exuded "a subtle feeling of confidence." The window beside each seat could be opened or closed at the passenger's whim, and silk window shades dropped down if the passenger wished to block the light from outside. Fluffy curtains

The interior of a TAT Ford Tri-Motor featured wicker seats, a hand strap and a light beside each seat, curtained windows, and a paneled interior. To the right of the cockpit door is an altimeter so that passengers could know the plane's altitude. (From the TWA Archives of the St. Louis Mercantile Library at the University of Missouri–St. Louis)

surrounded three sides of each window, giving them a decidedly feminine touch. Seat covers, headrests, and even seat belts matched the cabin's color scheme. Alongside each seat, passengers discovered an ashtray.

In the event that food or drink spilled on the floor, the entire cabin could be washed after removal of the seats, window coverings, and lampshades. TAT had purposefully sought out washable materials for cabin construction that would not readily absorb odors. When a cabin needed a thorough cleaning, an airline employee simply took a pressurized water hose and washed it from the front down the sloping floor to the rear. Designers realized that keeping a spotlessly clean cabin environment promoted confidence in the air service.[14]

Another feature new to air travel in the United States was the onboard attendant. While European airlines boasted young men serving passengers in flight as early as 1919, airlines in the United States were slow to adopt the practice. Stout Air Services, flying between Detroit and Grand Rapids, Michigan, became the first American carrier to employ aerial stewards in 1926. Two years later, Western Air Express placed stewards on its

A courier serves liquid refreshment to passenger aboard a Ford Tri-Motor. Note the courier's uniform, patterned after the dress of naval officers, and the Spartan overhead storage suitable only for hats and other small articles. (From the TWA Archives of the St. Louis Mercantile Library at the University of Missouri–St. Louis)

flights along the Model Airway between San Francisco and Los Angeles on an experimental basis. Pan American Airways also hired young men to attend air passengers' needs.[15]

The male attendants on TAT flights (called couriers, because young men with a similar title escorted tourists on side trips for the Santa Fe Railroad) filled a role that women would eventually assume on commercial airliners. One TAT passenger wrote that the courier on her flight was "a college boy, tall, clean-cut, intelligent, obviously thrilled with the idea of being on this first flight, and very eager to make each passenger as comfortable and happy as possible." The sons of wealthy TAT investors, these young men brought the passengers to the airfield from a downtown collection point, delivered catered meals to the waiting airplanes, and handled baggage. A courier weighed each bag to ensure that passengers did not exceed the 30-pound limit, storing the bags in a retractable bin inside the wing. Inside the cabin, another courier hung passengers' coats in a rear compartment that also featured receptacles specifically designed for golf bags. Hats, reading materials, and other small, lightweight articles could ride in racks constructed of netting and aluminum tubing along the walls above the rear seats.[16]

At the start of the flight, a courier pointed out the lavatory located at the rear of the plane, complete with sink, toilet, towel rack, and trash can—all made of aluminum. Distributing small packets containing cotton and chewing gum, the courier instructed passengers to put the cotton in their ears to help muffle some of the deafening noise pervading the cabin, and to chew the gum to help clear their ears during changes in altitude. TAT offered magazines especially for women, such as *Vogue* and *House Beautiful*, and the courier handed maps of TAT's route to each passenger for precise identification of landmarks, rivers, cities, and mountain ranges seen along the way. Flying across the continent engendered a new appreciation in passengers for their nation's size and geographic diversity. Many if not most of TAT's first passengers had never flown over the continent's interior, so maps were an important resource to satisfy their natural curiosity and gave them a connection with the landscape slowly rolling by beneath them.[17]

Writing legibly during flight was possible despite the vibrations of the motors as well as motion induced by frequent air turbulence. Throughout the flight, the courier provided reading and writing material to any passenger who requested it. If passengers wished to write letters or play card games, the courier attached a table to the passenger's seat. To communicate to someone on the ground, passengers could write a message and give it to for the courier; the message would then be sent via radio to a nearby city and relayed by wire to the intended recipient.[18]

The cabin attendant served lunches and beverages from a kitchenette in the rear of the airplane and offered passengers selections of cold sliced meats, prime roast beef, bread and olives, served on trays. Meal service aboard the Ford Tri-Motor contained dangers for stewards and passengers alike. Velva Darling described the scene when a courier served lunch as the plane neared Kingman: "The courier was standing beside me serving coffee. The cups, the small milk bottles, sugar, the coffee container, and spoons were in a basket on his arm. Suddenly the plane jumped, leaped forward and up like a frightened horse! A milk bottle popped out of the basket and landed in my lap. Everyone made a grab for the small aluminum table in front of him and held on for dear life." After that episode, the passengers continued eating and drinking even though the plane encountered more rough air, albeit less severe than the first episode. TAT passengers ate from custom-made porcelain plates, metal cups, and gold-plated utensils, and a sudden pitching of the aircraft could turn these implements into projectiles capable of doing harm. Dangerous or not, the valuable food service items, including lavender-colored napkins, proved an irresistible temptation for passengers to take as souvenirs.[19]

Besides the great care taken to create a comforting atmosphere in the aircraft cabin, TAT attempted to soothe passengers' safety concerns by carefully canvassing the nation to select the most careful and experienced pilots available to fly its airliners. Each of the original 16 TAT pilots possessed an average of 3,000 hours flying time, including about 500 hours in trimotor aircraft. Because people in the late 1920s thought of pilots more as barnstormers taking great risks than as professional, competent airmen, the airline crafted a professional image for its flight crews. It discouraged conversation between pilots and passengers during flight to prevent unwanted distractions in the cockpit. TAT pilots wore finely tailored blue uniforms and received the labels of "captain" and "first mate," hoping that passengers would associate the men in the cockpit with their dependable nautical namesakes. (Women were excluded from this fraternity in the sky until the 1970s.) Typically in their mid-thirties, TAT pilots downplayed their youthfulness to passengers and emphasized their experience.[20]

Passenger comfort on the ground also mattered to TAT. It was common practice in the late 1920s for pilots to park airliners on the landing field, forcing passengers to trek across the grass to a hangar or terminal building. Airline planners realized that women wearing high-heeled shoes had difficulty walking across the often rain-soaked sod of landing zones. Thus, TAT took measures to ensure that its passengers walked on firm surfaces between terminals and aircraft at each of its landing fields. Additionally, TAT personnel rolled black-and-orange-striped awnings on wheels from the terminal to the aircraft door to keep passengers out of the weather. Rather than forcing passengers to wait in some hangar side office during intermediate stops, TAT provided attractively decorated and inviting terminal facilities. A few minutes on the ground allowed passengers a brief respite from the deafening noise in the plane's cabin and provided an opportunity to stretch, walk around, send telegrams, and use the restroom before reboarding the aircraft.[21]

The inaugural eastbound passengers arrived in New York City within the 48 hours that TAT had advertised. They had traveled more than 2,000 miles, 900 of which was aboard trains. Subsequently, some passengers often covered a higher percentage of the miles on rails, as bad weather frequently kept the Tri-Motors grounded. When that occurred, an employee met arriving passengers at the train station, informing them that they would continue their journey on a train rather than a plane. This happened so frequently that some said TAT stood for "take a train."[22]

The Evolution of Air-Rail Combinations

Transcontinental Air Transport never turned a profit. Even before the stock market crash of October 1929, the airline struggled to meet its expenses. TAT provided a top-class service designed for those who could afford to pay $350 one way, coast-to-coast—a price tag equal to about $4,000 (or supersonic Concorde fare) at the turn of the twenty-first century. Only a small number of business executives found the cost worth the extra time savings. Moreover, a tragic accident only two months after the start of service led to a steep decline in passenger numbers. On September 4, 1929, a TAT plane carrying eight passengers struck a mountainside in California during a thunderstorm, killing all aboard. The next month the New York stock market crashed, followed by the greatest economic decline the nation had ever known. TAT never recovered. In its 18 months of operation, the company lost $2.7 million.

TAT was not the only transcontinental air-rail combination, however. The Universal Aviation Corporation established service between New York and Los Angeles in June 1929. Passengers took the New York Central Railroad from New York City to Cleveland and, aboard one of Universal's Fokker trimotors, continued to Garden City, western Kansas. The Atchison, Topeka, and Santa Fe Railroad delivered passengers the rest of the way to Southern California, 67 hours after leaving the East Coast.

Western Air Express also claimed a rail connection to New York from its easternmost terminal in Kansas City. But a scheduled travel time of nearly 80 hours because of awkward rail connections east of Kansas City made this coast-to-coast link less than popular. A third, and more complicated, air-rail transcontinental connection opened on August 4, 1929. Passengers traveled west from New York on the New York Central Railroad to St. Louis for transfer to a Southwest Air Fast Express (SAFE) trimotor airplane, which carried them to the west Texas town of Sweetwater, where they boarded the Texas and Pacific Railway for overnight passage to El Paso. From there, they completed the trip to Los Angeles aboard Standard Air Lines, less than 70 hours after their journey's start.[23]

Postmaster General Walter Folger Brown, a Republican who assumed his position after the 1928 election of President Herbert Hoover in 1928, witnessed this jumble of transcontinental connections among dozens of local airlines and resolved to create a coordinated national system of mail and passenger air service. He saw that the fledgling contract airmail carriers, utterly dependent on income from mail pay, had little incentive to purchase new and larger aircraft. If given the proper incentives,

Brown reasoned, the airlines could eventually increase passenger traffic to the point that mail subsidy could be reduced or even eliminated. Intent upon creating combined mail-passenger service within a nationwide air system of several large competitive transcontinental airlines and a complementary network of feeder airlines, Brown sought to control the competitive bidding process for airmail contracts so that he could shape the airline industry according to his vision.

The McNary-Watres Act of 1930 gave Brown the tools that he needed. Under the act, the airlines received airmail compensation according to space available in their aircraft rather than according to the actual weight of mail carried. The change encouraged the airlines to purchase larger aircraft to earn more money by filling the surplus mail space with passengers whose fare was pure profit for the airlines. The act also gave the postmaster general the authority to award airmail contracts to the "lowest responsible bidder," empowering Brown to pass over low bids from all but the most experienced airlines.[24]

Brown invited airline executives from the airmail contractors to a series of meetings in May 1930. There he single-handedly cajoled and threatened various contactors to merge operations and ensured through rigged bidding that the largest companies were left with the prized long-term contracts. Later derided as "spoils conferences," the meetings set the course of aviation development in America. Boeing Air Transport and National Air Transport, under the corporate umbrella of United Aircraft, retained the airmail contract between New York and San Francisco. The postmaster general forced a merger between Western Air Express and Transcontinental Air Transport, creating Transcontinental and Western Air. TWA would become one of the first airlines to fly passengers coast-to-coast in its own aircraft when the line inaugurated Ford Tri-Motor service between New York and Los Angeles on October 25, 1930. A southern coast-to-coast route went to American Airways, a line newly created out of many smaller entities, based on Universal Air Transport, Colonial Air Transport, Robertson Aircraft Corporation, and Southern Air Transport. American would link Los Angeles with the Atlantic Coast via Dallas and Atlanta. Brown ensured that only three of the 27 airmail contracts nationwide did not go to large holding companies such as United or American. Brown thus reshaped the nation's airway map, limited competition between airlines, and set the pattern for the growth of the trunk lines.[25]

Hoping to attract more female and young passengers, American Airlines placed on this system map cover an image of a smiling woman and two happy children climbing the stairs to a departing flight. (From the author's collection)

Women as Passengers

Operating under the McNary-Watres Act, the large transcontinental lines quickly purchased bigger three-engine planes that could carry more than 10 passengers as well as hundreds of pounds of mail. TWA led the way with its fleet of Fokker and Ford Tri-Motors, each carrying at least 10 passengers. With more seats available than ever before, airlines and aircraft manufacturers placed advertisements in many printed periodicals with nationwide readership aimed at potential passengers—particularly females. An advertisement for the Ford Motor Company in the July 1929 issue of *World's Work*, for example, depicted an airport scene viewed from the waiting area out toward the runway. In the foreground, a multitude of passengers, luggage at their sides, milled about and engaged each other in conversation. Half of the people in the waiting area were women—youthful women of means, dressed smartly in the styles of the era. The title under the illustration read: "When Women Fly." Although the text was concerned mostly with praising female pilots, it also made clear that women were important passengers. Ford Tri-Motors carried a variety of women—"tourists, business women, sightseers even"—showing the world that air transportation was a reliable and pleasant means of travel. The advertisement proudly proclaimed: "Man no longer flies alone!"

Not only did the Ford Motor Company take out advertisements declaring women to be enthusiastic passengers on the trimotor airliners that the company manufactured, but it also sponsored ladies' luncheons in trimotors flying over metropolitan areas. Convincing women to come aboard for a short flight and a meal, while giving them an aerial view of the city, seemed to be a good way to introduce air travel to upper-class women who might have not been tempted to take longer and seemingly more dangerous flights.

Katherine A. Fisher of Detroit took at least three of these luncheon flights, recounting her experiences for the readers of *Good Housekeeping* in 1930. Her first luncheon aloft was over Detroit during an air show. Because the flight was only the second time she had been in an airplane, Fisher approached the experience as a novice. She attempted "to sit lightly" when the airplane took off, but soon settled back and enjoyed the rest of the flight. Looking around, she noticed that Ford had outfitted the interior of the airplane with a kitchenette for meal preparation, "comfortable chairs attractively upholstered, curtained windows, and a colorful interior," reminding the author of conditions aboard an ocean liner.[26]

A hostess prepared and served the food. Mary Barber, director of home economics for the Kellogg Company, emerged from the kitchenette, bearing a delightful bowl of chicken consommé served with cheese wafers, followed by a pineapple salad with marinated tomato slices. Fisher especially enjoyed fresh radishes, olives, and celery served with bran muffins, and dessert featured coffee and scrumptious macaroons. Despite a few bumps of rough air, the women ate well and enjoyed the scenery, along with the opportunity to do something novel yet elegant. Fisher took pleasure in gazing from her window at the seemingly miniature buildings, golf courses, and patterns in the earth around the Motor City. From her point of view, the primary drawback was the obligatory sign language while in flight. The roaring engines and the sound of the air rushing past the plane produced noise levels approaching 115 decibels—near the threshold of pain. Audible conversation was not an option. The ladies resorted to pantomime until they safely returned to earth. Fisher's account expressed great enthusiasm for air travel, and in all likelihood she took a regular commercial flight whenever possible thereafter.[27]

Yet aircraft manufacturers, airlines, and airports could do more to attract female patronage than conducting aerial luncheons. Curtis Publishing Company issued a report in 1930 that included suggestions for drawing more women to air travel. Among the report's recommendations was that airports install pleasant outdoor landscaping and create tidy waiting rooms and attractive restaurants. One airport feature particularly vexing to women at that time was an absence of covering between the ramp where the airliners parked and the terminal building. Although air travel boasted an absence of coal smoke and cinders—the bane of rail travel in the age of steam locomotives—the walk across the ramp exposed passengers to all the elements found in an open field. Some type of covering, perhaps similar to the canvas awnings that TAT used, could keep sun and rain and even the ever-present dust off of female passengers, as well as men.[28]

The Curtis report advised airlines to keep their aircraft clean—especially the onboard restrooms. Passenger comfort should rank high on the list of priorities for airlines and airframe designers. By bringing an artistic touch to the cabin environment, pleasant surroundings and comfortable seating could put women at ease while flying. Besides this, all airline and airport employees, from the janitor to the reservation counter attendant to the flight crew, should treat customers—particularly women—with great courtesy. Airlines took recommendations such as these to heart and strove to create an agreeable air travel experience for women as well as men.[29]

Air travel did appeal to women, as evidenced by the fact that women wrote and published more firsthand accounts in the early 1930s than at any other time in the history of transcontinental air travel. Taking a trip on an airliner across the country was a novelty, but what was especially significant was that women emerged from the 1920s more independent-minded and willing, in growing numbers, to travel great distances. Several women—some well known, others more obscure—recorded their observations for the reading public, beckoning other women to take to the sky aboard the transcontinental airlines.

The interior of the terminal at Lambert–St. Louis International Airport, built in the 1930s, took many cues, such as wooden benches and architectural design, from railroad stations. (From the *St. Louis Globe-Democrat* Archives of the St. Louis Mercantile Library at the University of Missouri–St. Louis)

Marcia Davenport serves as a good example of a woman who flew coast-to-coast in early 1930s. The daughter of soprano Alma Gluck and the great-aunt of TV actress Stephanie Zimbalist, Davenport worked as a staff member of the *New Yorker* and published a biography of Mozart in 1932 before engaging in a long career of writing novels and screenplays. Her best-selling novel, *The Valley of Decision*, was made into a feature film in 1945, starring Gregory Peck.

A woman of means, Davenport had already traveled abroad extensively by 1932, when she and her husband, Russell, took an airline transcontinental journey. For her, the journey was more than a mere fast trip over variations in topography. She was looking for excitement: "I wanted adventure, or whatever semblance of it could be had in the year of 1932. So, of course, I flew."

After an uneventful trip from New York to Los Angeles, Davenport's flight departed for Salt Lake City just before 10 in the morning. She and her husband were the only passengers aboard, save for a man of 90 years who was, in Davenport's words, "so old and feeble that we could not seriously believe he intended to make the trip." Despite needing a crutch to walk and having some difficulty because of crippled hands, this spry gentleman overcame obstacles in stride, explaining that he had flown a round-trip between New York and Florida the previous year.

The three passengers braced for the notoriously rough flying over the mountains and deserts of southern California. The hot air rising from the deserts alternated with the cooler upper air, causing the airplane to oscillate between rising and sinking at an alarming rate. Although not posing any immediate danger to the aircraft or passengers, the experience could frighten the uninitiated. Davenport explained: "When a plane drops like a bullet, sometimes a hundred feet, your mouth flies open, your eyes goggle, you clutch the arm of your chair, and if you have time to watch your fellow passengers, you see them doing the same. Their faces blanch, and their knuckles, too, as they clench fingers over the chair arms. Your mental attitude is not helped much by the neat little cardboard ice-cream container fastened at each chair with the legend, 'Use in case of Air Sickness,' on its cover." Approximately 80 percent of passengers on the TWA flights over the Southwest succumbed to air sickness. Airline officials even joked that they pasted pictures of the Grand Canyon on the bottom of air sickness containers so that everyone could see the Grand Canyon. Even if only a minority of passengers became airsick during a flight, the view of people vomiting and the accompanying stench undoubtedly caused additional discomfort in those who were not airsick.[30]

Passengers aboard Western Air Express's Fokker F-10 trimotors between Los Angeles and San Francisco were quite grateful for windows that opened. Increased ventilation helped remove the stench. Yet when airsick passengers found the small sickness cups inconvenient, they often slid open an adjacent window and vomited into the airstream outside. Western warned its passengers against this because the airflow around the plane tended to reintroduce into opened rear windows whatever came out at the front.[31]

The same sort of thing could happen on the Ford Tri-Motor. On at least one occasion an airsick passenger near the front of the cabin emptied the contents of a motion discomfort container out of the nearest window. The slipstream around the aircraft sucked the putrid liquid back into the cabin and all over the front of an unlucky passenger seated near the rear of the aircraft. Sometimes airsick passengers, not using the cups provided, soiled the cabin's interior. In that case, airline personnel could use high-pressure water hoses to wash out cabins that airsick passengers had recently evacuated.[32]

Rapid changes in altitude could cause pain in passengers' ears. The lower air pressure at higher altitudes meant that travelers in an airplane climbing to elevations of many thousand feet needed to equalize the air pressure in the inner and outer ear. Airlines supplied chewing gum to help relieve the pressure difference. If that did not work, most passengers learned to pinch their noses and gently force air through the Eustachian tubes or to open their mouths very wide until their ears "popped."[33]

After refueling in Las Vegas, Davenport's flight continued toward Salt Lake City. Low clouds blocked the pilot's usual route following railroad tracks through the Iron Mountains of Utah, so he navigated the ponderous three-engine craft through another pass and up a canyon between sharp peaks and red bluffs. Just before breaking out of the confined spaces of the canyon, the airplane passed low over a woman with children who stood waving at the unexpected visitors passing over their small, lonely shack. The pilot soon picked up the railroad tracks again and overtook the train, which had left Los Angeles at about six the previous evening.[34]

In Salt Lake City, the Davenports and the elderly gentleman joined five more passengers aboard a United Air Lines flight bound for New York. Their a little band of "neo-Canterbury pilgrims," as Davenport called them, consisted of the three Los Angeles passengers; a man from Portland, Oregon; a very quiet young man; two male business executives from San Francisco; and a woman from Reno whom Davenport described as "a lively, pretty, chic young blonde, with a tiny red silk cap on the back of her shining head, and a smile for everybody."[35]

The motley group filed aboard a United Air Lines Boeing 80A. After the success of passenger service along the transcontinental route with the Boeing 40 mail plane, Boeing had developed this much larger three-engine biplane, designed primarily as a passenger airliner with space for mail. With a cruising speed of 120 miles per hour, the Boeing 80A boasted three-abreast seating for up to 18 passengers.[36]

The craft had a wingspan of about 80 feet with a gross takeoff weight of nearly nine tons when loaded. It carried, in the words of an awestruck passenger, "thirty meals, twenty-four blankets, twelve pillows, United States mail, baggage, one and a half million candlepower in parachute flares," plus passengers and airline personnel. This capacity was in stark contrast to that of the single-engine mail planes used only a few years earlier, with one passenger sharing an open cockpit with sacks of mail.[37]

Marcia Davenport likened the Boeing 80A interior to a "compact Pullman car"—comfortable, but crowded if full. A six-foot-tall passenger could easily stand erect in the five-foot-wide cabin. On Davenport's flight, the passengers left the middle seats vacant, giving them more room to stretch out.[38]

The interior was a work of art. Its decoration purposely mimicked that of a railroad car, giving a sense of the familiar to passengers accustomed to train travel. Metal fixtures featured a metallic bronze finish. Brown Leatheroid from the eight-inch-high mahogany baseboard to the windowsills, and black walnut paneling to the tops of the windows, graced the cabin walls, and a dark-colored fabric extended from above the windows to envelop the entire ceiling. Gray carpet covered the floor. At night a total of 27 electric lights illuminated the cabin, including a dome light in the center of the cabin and individual shaded lights with switches near passenger seats. The seats adjusted to four different positions, reclining so that passengers could sleep more easily. The three-ply wood paneling, with its wafer of balsa in the middle for noise reduction, and the gray fabric seat covers lent an air of calm and solidity to an experience that was utterly novel to many who took a seat therein.[39]

Davenport also commented that the passengers along either side of the cabin could control their own vents. The openings, according to Davenport, resembled "a minute copy of the mammoth ventilators that mount the decks of big steamships." Such vents in an enclosed aircraft cabin became all the more important because the windows on the Boeing 80A could not be opened. However, the ventilation system in this craft left much to be desired. Crudely constructed, it frequently injected exhaust fumes as well as heat into the cabin. Some of the first stewardesses had the choice either to let the cabin fill with toxins or to close off the system. They often chose the latter and then wrapped blankets around passengers already bundled up in their coats.[40]

The Davenports and the other six passengers settled in for the eastward flight toward Cheyenne, Wyoming. Soon darkness fell over the landscape below. At about 9:30 that night, fog shrouded the airway, and the pilot could no longer see the next light beacon. Not wanting to risk wandering from the airway, the pilot decided to touch down at an emergency landing field, also the location of a light beacon, not far from the notorious

Teapot Dome. The pilot refused to take off until the fog lifted. The airway beacon keeper, his wife, and daughter invited the passengers and crew to share their austere two-room shack. The daughter sat at the kitchen table, where she operated a wireless telegraph and a telephone located next to various airway charts, a barometer, and a clock. After a lengthy communication on the telephone, the pilot announced that the fog would probably not lift until morning. They were all to spend the night in this small house situated in the vast wilderness. But the passengers and crew were hungry. So the pilot commandeered the beacon keeper's car and drove six of the passengers into Parco, a little town about eight miles away. The plan was for the pilot and passengers to find an open restaurant, eat, and then return to the emergency field with enough food for everyone else.

Marcia Davenport vividly described what transpired: "All Parco offered was an all-night soda-fountain–dance-hall–restaurant–ice-cream-parlor staffed by a single young man, who nearly dropped dead when six stalwart, hungry, vociferous people, one in a flying suit, barged in and demanded all the food in the place." The young man hoped they wanted only sodas, but they insisted on cooked food. He fried what steaks and hamburgers he had and served them along with fried potatoes, coffee, and bread, enough to satisfy his seven demanding customers with some to spare.

Back at the beacon keeper's house, some folks attempted to sleep in the wee hours of the morning. One woman dozed on the couch, Marcia Davenport reclined in a chair, the 90-year-old man sat in a chair near the woodstove. Three of the men camped on the floor, as the others and the beacon keeper's family decided to play poker instead of sleep. At daybreak, the passengers trudged out of the little house and saw the pilots already preparing the airplane for departure. Davenport looked over the desolate Wyoming landscape. She was spellbound by the ruggedness, the primitiveness, and the romance of her surroundings. Her emotion of excitement and adventure could easily have turned to alarm. After all, she was a woman accustomed to the crowds and bustle of New York City. Still, she considered her airline journey a grand adventure. A train trip would not have offered such excitement, "where all I could see would be the neat rails engineers had laid where they fell most easily, and where, if I wanted a bottle of sparkling water or a filet mignon, I could wave my hand and get it." Davenport wrote that an automobile trip, "held to the conveniences of the moment by red-and-white filling-stations and hard white roads edged by tourist camps," would not have brought her this adventure either. A lifelong city dweller, Marcia Davenport fancied that, through her air travel experience, she had participated in a groundbreaking endeavor, mystically linked with the nineteenth-century overland pioneers. Upon arrival back home in New York, Davenport mused to her audience: "I, having traveled in many places and seen many things, looked gingerly down on the drab vastness of the Newark airport, and across at the towers of Manhattan

Dressed in fur coats and suits for the occasion, passengers wait
to board TWA's first all-air transcontinental service on October 25,
1930. Although a majority of airline passengers during this time were
men, this group of passengers had equal number of both sexes.
(From the TWA Archives of the St. Louis Mercantile Library at the
University of Missouri–St. Louis)

piercing the gray dawn rain, and as the field swooped up to meet us, and the motors died, thought to myself: 'It is possible. You *can* have adventure. You can find a frontier somewhere. *Oh, Susanna, and don't you cry for me . . .'*"[41]

In the early days of transcontinental air travel, women put much thought and planning into selecting the right clothes for their journey. While Maude Campbell, the first female passenger on Western Air Express, wore a leather flying suit to protect her from the discomforts of the open-cockpit mail plane, later female passengers wore more traditional dresses when they flew in enclosed cabins featuring more amenities. Yet proper apparel for air travel was important because temperatures varied and so did the accommodations. Women who had not yet flown asked those who had, "What did you wear?" Novelist Sophie Kerr answered that question in her account of transcontinental air travel. For her flight in the summer of 1932, she wore "a very light-weight checked cloth skirt, a soft crepe blouse and a dark gray cloth jacket which could be easily removed when the air was warm and put on again in the cold altitudes." Kerr kept a long coat close by "for the chilliest of moments." Upon her head she sported a hat with "brim enough to shade my eyes in front, and cut off in the back so that I could lean my head against my chair quite comfortably." Kerr understood that the varying altitudes and temperatures, in addition to the cramped quarters of air travel, required that passengers expect these conditions and dress accordingly.[42]

Ladies' Home Journal ran an insightful article in 1930, dispensing air travel fashion advice from a leading French designer. The author pointed out that there was no such thing as "'aviation clothes'—unless you are a pilot." Nevertheless, the female air passenger was to bear in mind that air travel was colder than rail travel. Thus, an overcoat and a tight-fitting hat would be in order, and well as wearing something around the neck to keep the cold draft away. Even though a woman would not be exposed to the soot and cinders of rail travel, she should wear a dark color that would not readily show stains. The primary goal for the female air traveler was to appear as stylish at the end of her journey as she had at the beginning. However, a woman should not dress conspicuously. Rather, she should avoid "elaborate fur coats, chiffon stockings and high heels" on the one extreme, as well as leather suits and helmets on the other extreme—unless in an open cockpit. Failure to follow such advice could result in the female passenger appearing "more like the heroine of a musical comedy dressed for her third act entrance than a well-turned out and experienced traveler."[43]

Baggage weight limitations, typically 30 pounds per passenger, also restricted the amount and type of clothing women could bring with them. Simplicity was the rule. The woman preparing for an air journey need pack only two blouses, a couple of skirts, a silk frock, and gloves to go with the hat and coat worn in flight, one pair of extra shoes, underwear, silk stockings, some handkerchiefs, and a select assortment of personal beauty products.

Food along the Way

Another consideration aloft was food. Novelist Sophie Kerr provided her readers with a detailed description of the complimentary food service she received aboard her transcontinental flight in the early 1930s. A couple of hours after leaving Newark in midmorning, she recalled, the United Air Lines copilot walked to the back of the Ford Tri-Motor, where he prepared the passengers' lunches at the kitchenette. He set before each passenger an elaborate meal on the trays attached to the side of the airplane beside each passenger. The menu, in its entirety, consisted of "chilled fruit salad served in a covered cup; three sandwiches—egg salad with brown bread, tongue, and cream cheese with pineapple—each wrapped in waxed paper; chocolate and coconut cakes; ripe plums; hot coffee in a paper cup; mints, cigarettes. There was a paper napkin and a paper spoon and fork." Airlines came to prefer paper dishes and utensils because they were lightweight, they made for rapid cleanup or disposal, and it did not matter if passengers took them as souvenirs.[44]

After transferring to a Boeing 80A in Chicago, Kerr noticed a few changes in the food service. Passengers held trays on their laps because the airliner lacked trays secured to the walls or chairs. However, the food was much the same as the lunch. Besides sandwiches and fruit salad, the attendant served hot coffee and soup from insulated metal flasks. During the trip, Kerr was thankful she had brought along a small bag containing chocolate and nuts when she wished for a snack along the way.

Sophie Kerr and the other passengers consumed a hearty breakfast of ham, eggs, toast, and coffee at the United Air Lines restaurant in the Cheyenne airport at the odd hour of two in the morning, when the Boeing arrived from Chicago. The travelers had moved their watches two hours ahead since leaving New York.

Cheyenne was an important center for United Air Lines' transcontinental operations. The company's managers had looked with envy at the Harvey House restaurants along the Atchison, Topeka, and Santa Fe Railroad system. Patterned after the Harvey House concept, United opened its own restaurant at the Cheyenne airport for its transcontinental passengers. One passenger marveled that "no matter what hour you land there, you are fed copiously, and with almost miraculous speed and efficiency." She found the food "delicious" and observed that passengers could order any item of choice and eat as much as desired, all included in the price of their airline ticket. The restaurant was particularly famous for its excellent beefsteaks. Even though transcontinental passengers ranked the food and service highly, many of them did not have enough time to sit down and enjoy a full meal. They tended to eat hurriedly while standing near their plane as they watched airline personnel refuel and restock the airliner. With few customers, the Cheyenne restaurant ceased business within a few years.[45]

As Kerr and others discovered, airlines standardized the food that they served aloft. According to a contemporary article on the subject, a typical airline meal in the early 1930s included "a cocktail of tomato or fruit juices; hot bouillon in winter months; three kinds of sandwiches (usually chicken, cheese and ham); a fruit or vegetable salad; fruit, pie or cake; and coffee." Airlines did not serve hot entrées during flight until the mid-1930s, because to install ovens aboard airliners such as the Boeing 80s and Ford Tri-Motors would have imposed an unacceptably high weight penalty and risk of fire.[46]

Passenger Pansy Bowen flew a transcontinental round-trip on United in 1932. While she admitted that it was not best to eat great quantities of food while traveling by air, she explained she had never before been "exposed to so much food in any single 30 hours of my life." She went on to write that the airlines spread before her at regular intervals "a dainty tray upon which is spread temptingly prepared sandwiches, delicious fruit cup, tomato or orange juice, hot coffee, small cakes, and after-dinner mints." Finished with the meal, the attendant invited her to select from a large basket of fruit and take whatever struck her fancy.[47]

Yet sometimes passengers did not receive the food service they expected. On one United Air Lines flight eastbound from Omaha in 1932, each passenger received only tomato juice and sweet buns. The airline apologized for the meager fare, explaining that because the flight had been delayed earlier in the day, an employee had forgotten to provide supplies at Omaha for the usual food service on the next leg. Upon their arrival in Chicago, the airline insisted on driving the passengers in a car to the restaurant of its catering service for a free meal to make up for the earlier oversight. The restaurant served up healthy portions of "bean soup, fried chicken, trimmings, dessert, coffee, and reassurance," sending the passengers off to New York, stomachs full.[48]

Aboard a TWA flight in 1933, a passenger described the lunch served after the airplane took off eastbound from Winslow. Using trays attached to the arms of the passengers' seats, the copilot placed before them "a picnic kind of lunch, but very good, with chicken sandwiches and hot coffee." But even in the mid-1930s the airlines served an unusual commodity: monotony. Airline patrons grew tired of chicken sandwiches, creamed chicken, and then fried chicken. Faced with chicken each time they flew, some frequent passengers "contended they had eaten so much of it, hot or cold, that they were sprouting wings and would soon be able to fly without the help of planes."[49]

In-Flight Smoking

Besides food, some airlines, such as United Air Lines, provided complimentary in-flight cigarettes. After finishing a meal, passengers passed around cartons of cigarettes and lit up as a way to help them relax.[50]

This was not always the case. Carriers had forbidden smoking aboard the earliest airliners. Wood, canvas, wire, and flammable sealant called dope constituted the primary aircraft building materials. Given those combustible materials, combined with large gasoline tanks, it was easy to understand why smoking of any kind was prohibited near airplanes. The advent of metal aircraft and enclosed cabins permitted the rules to be changed. Some airlines, such as TAT, allowed passengers to smoke if certain conditions were fulfilled—that is, the flight was not taking off or landing, and other passengers did not object to smoking around them.

Although European airlines as a rule allowed passengers to smoke during flight, U.S. airlines remained divided over the issue in the early 1930s. Airlines did not wish to have the enclosed cabins of their airplanes filled with cigarette smoke if the nonsmokers would not tolerate an environment filled with a blue haze. Many airlines were thus reluctant to lift the ban on smoking. Eastern Air Lines permitted in-flight smoking before most other domestic airlines but only aboard its Curtiss Condor sleeper aircraft. Even then, smokers could light up only in the forward compartment unless their number surpassed the compartment's capacity. Airline executives came to take the same view of smoking in airliners that railway executives held of smoking in dining cars.[51]

Airlines preferred smokers to light up in the forward section of enclosed cabin airliners such as Ford Tri-Motors. When windows in the rear and front areas of the cabin were opened slightly, cabin air moved from back to front pulling cigarette smoke from the cabin's anterior into the airplane's slipstream outside.[52]

At the request of its passengers who smoked, National Air Transport lifted the ban on in-flight cigarette smoking aboard its popular New York–Chicago-Dallas route early in 1932. NAT Ford Tri-Motors carried large numbers of smokers who were pleased to have the privilege at last.[53]

Sophie Kerr noticed that when she boarded her flight in Newark, a sign in the door window between the passenger cabin and the cockpit read: "No smoking, please, until this sign is removed." Just below the window beside each passenger seat were cigarette ash receptacles with lids. Beside each one, copies of another sign informed the seat's occupant: "You may enjoy a cigarette if your fellow passengers do not object." While United and other airlines allowed cigarette smoking aboard its airplanes, Western Air Express strictly prohibited smoking at all times.[54]

All cigarettes burned more slowly at high altitude in an unpressurized airplane than they did on the ground. Smoking passengers sometimes complained that their cigarettes did not taste the same in-flight as on the ground. Airline personnel explained that it was a natural phenomenon due to altitude changes.[55]

A TWA airline passenger watching the Mohave Desert drift by below her in the early 1930s suddenly felt a finger tap her shoulder to get her attention. It was the man in the seat behind her. He shouted an inquiry of whether she minded if he smoked. Being a smoker herself, she shook her head. The suggestion led the female passenger to take out her own cigarette and light up. She even offered one across the aisle to the nervous gentleman who was taking his first flight. Pointing to his queasy stomach, he declined.[56]

Later, between Winslow and Albuquerque, many passengers enjoyed an after-lunch smoke. With little to do besides look out the windows, the passengers had slowly eaten their food before savoring every inch of the smoldering cigarettes dangling from their mouths. Smoking gave passengers a form of recreation and also provided their bodies with the nicotine they craved, making flying more relaxing and enjoyable for them.

As in-flight smoking became more popular, the practice of tossing lit cigarettes out of aircraft windows became troublesome. The U.S. Department of Agriculture declared that smoldering cigarettes that passengers and aviators dropped from aircraft posed a significant fire threat to America's wilderness areas. In 1930, Department of Commerce official Clarence M. Young reminded aviators and airlines that to release objects, such as burning cigarettes or even cigars, "from aircraft which will endanger life or damage property" was against air commerce regulations. With seeming success, airlines posted signs warning passengers to dispose of all smoking material properly.[57]

Even on airlines that permitted smoking, passengers could not light up until the airplane had left the ground. During and after refueling, the danger of igniting lingering gasoline fumes was a fire hazard that no one wished to risk. Airline pilots and attendants strictly enforced the smoking ban until the flight was well on its way.[58]

The Introduction of Stewardesses

As previously described, male couriers, or stewards, had served various airlines in the United States. But the practice did not always endure at that time. TAT used male couriers from the line's start in July 1929 until February 1930, when copilots served in the cabin as well as in the cockpit.

The idea of putting young female attendants aboard airliners dawned on United Air Lines' district manager in San Francisco, Steve Stimpson. Copilots already had their

1956 TWA photograph featuring multiple sets of identical-twin stewardesses.

hands full in the cockpit without the added burden of looking after the needs of passengers, and the presence of female airline employees aboard commercial planes could serve notice to the nonflying public that if flying was safe for young women, it must be safe for all. Stimpson's idea gained acceptance when a nurse named Ellen Church stopped by his office one day, looking for a job with the airline. Although she wanted to be a copilot, a job that was denied her because of her gender, she explained that she could nonetheless help serve passengers in flight. As a registered nurse, she believed that she was an ideal candidate for such a task because she was trained to calm people and deal with emergency situations. In addition, Church argued, a female attendant would ease the minds of predominantly male passengers as to the safety of air travel.[59]

After his conversation with Ellen Church, Stimpson attempted to convince his superiors that the airline should hire stewardesses, but Boeing's management refused his request. Stimpson then turned to W. A. Patterson, who was soon to become president of the company. After discussing the idea with his wife, Patterson persuaded the line's current president to grant permission, however reluctantly, for a three-month trial along the transcontinental route between Oakland and Chicago.

Church chose seven other nurses from hospitals in Chicago and San Francisco to join her in the pioneering endeavor. Because of the airplane's restrictive cabin, the women could not weigh more than 115 pounds, stand taller than five foot four, be married, or be over 25 years of age. The airline consulted Ellen in the design of the stewardesses' uniforms—professional dark-colored suits with green capes and caps. While performing her duties in flight, a stewardess could remove her cape and wool suit to reveal a common, white nurse's uniform.[60]

Ellen Church became the first stewardess in history when she boarded a Boeing 80A for a United Air Lines flight along the transcontinental airway on May 15, 1930. Her tasks were not easy. She carried aboard all the luggage and checked the seats to ensure that they were fastened to the floor correctly. If they were not, she tightened the bolts by hand. She dusted the entire cabin and occasionally helped refuel the airplane and even push it from the hangar. In flight, her tasks included distributing cotton for passengers' ears, ensuring that passengers had fastened their seat belts for takeoff and landing, and watching that someone did not mistakenly open the exit door when seeking to use the nearby lavatory. She served meals, provided pillows and blankets, and handed out maps and magazines. If a parent with a young child was aboard, the stewardess had the additional duties of warming bottles and doing what she could to assist. When she was not busy serving the needs of her passengers, she could sit on a folding seat in front of the exit so as not to take a seat otherwise filled by a paying customer.[61]

In 1932, United stewardess Olette Hasle explained that women in her profession had multiple roles—"a saleswoman, an information bureau, a diplomat, an entertainment committee, a dietitian," and whatever else the job called for. The requirement for stewardesses to be registered nurses ensured that the women not only could deal with medical emergencies but also were "professional women, trained to meet and analyze and deal tactfully with all types, skilled in the diplomatic sciences, even tempered and well-disciplined." And medical situations did sometimes arise onboard. As an article reported in the early 1930s, an observant stewardess diagnosed a coast-to-coast passenger with acute appendicitis. The stewardess notified the pilot, who radioed a request for medical assistance to meet the flight at the next scheduled stop.[62] One writer perceptively noted that the in-flight stewardess was "a combination of nurse, ticket-puncher, baggage-master, guide ('The Grand Canyon and Boulder Dam must be pointed out to all passengers'), waitress, and little mother of all the world."[63]

The introduction of stewardesses in 1930 changed the psychology of air travel. The presence of a stewardess in the cabin meant that an airline employee was constantly with the passengers. Providing comfort and ensuring decorum, as well as representing their employer, stewardesses were "a traveling link" between the airline and its passengers. Passengers were no longer locked into compartments and left to fend for themselves—removed from the comfort of solid ground, as well as contact with an airline employee. Olette Hazel recalled what it was like before airlines placed female attendants aboard their aircraft: "In the early days of air travel, you were wished god speed by the field manager, then left to your own devices, until another field manager opened the cabin door at journey's end and shook hands with you and said, 'Well, well, glad to see you, Mr. Hassenpeffer, and how did you enjoy your trip?' But if you had developed a grouch in flight, if you had experienced a passing fear, or had been airsick with no one to hold your head, you weren't going to be fetched back a second time merely by polite good-byes!" If an issue involving passenger comfort arose during the flight with a stewardess aboard, she could address it immediately rather than let the passenger languish until landing.[64]

While United Air Lines enjoyed the public acceptance of their stewardesses, other airlines did not immediately pick up the practice. In fact, three years passed before American put stewardesses on its flights. And it was not until 1935 that TWA gave in and put stewardesses on its planes. Officially called hostesses in the hope that the title would convey a sense of domestic charm, TWA's female attendants each graduated from a hostess academy where they learned how to perform all of the functions of their job. TWA's requirements for flight attendants mirrored those of United. A cheerful disposition, a good sense of humor, and a good figure were among

them. One writer claimed that the stewardesses and hostesses "make Newark Airport on a busy day look something like a coed campus (there are men around too) or even more like the stage of the Roxy Theater, perhaps because all the girls are so lilting in movement, so crisply uniformed."[65]

A TWA coast-to-coast passenger named Elizabeth Bisgood would no doubt have appreciated a hostess aboard her 1933 flight. The only female among 11 male passengers on a flight east from Los Angeles, Bisgood endured without complaint the bumpy ride and airsick passengers as the flight crossed into Arizona. She enjoyed the chicken sandwiches the copilot served as the plane entered New Mexico. But after nightfall over the Great Plains of Oklahoma and Kansas, the cabin lights suddenly went dark for no apparent reason. No longer able to read her book, Bisgood found her mind racing. Bewilderment turned to apprehension, then outright fear and terror. She could not even see her hand when she raised it in front of her face. An airline representative, and another female at that, could have eased Bisgood's anxiety simply by being present and

Billing itself as "the Air Capital," Wichita, Kansas, was a stop for TWA planes flying passengers coast-to-coast. Even though Wichita did not become a major commercial airline hub, the city could boast in years to come that it was a center of aircraft manufacturing. Firms such as Beech, Cessna, and Boeing delivered thousands of airplanes that had been proudly made in Wichita. (From the TWA Archives of the St. Louis Mercantile Library at the University of Missouri–St. Louis)

providing matter-of-fact answers to Bisgood's questions about this strange and frightening environment in which she found herself. As it was, Bisgood sat with the other passengers literally and figuratively in the dark and full of fear. In her account of the flight, Bisgood wrote: "There is not one sign of familiar light to place us in this terrible void of time and space. Now all we know is the roaring of the engines and the wild white flame of the exhaust shooting past our ears. We are going faster and faster. We are hurtling into space, into the darkness, doomed by this desperate, suffocating speed. The night is a shell all around us, the blackness, a wall at which we are flying and against which we must inevitably crash. . . . I put my hand against my throat hoping to still the wild beat of its pulse." Bisgood's terror finally subsided when an airport beacon pierced the sky around her and the aircraft safely landed amid fog at the Wichita airport.[66]

Stewardesses could bring a sense of order and security to passengers who routinely flew but nevertheless found the experience frightening. Before each flight, one such frequent passenger prayed: "Please God, take me safely to where I'm going." Secure on the ground once again, he faithfully expressed a heartfelt "Thank you, Sir," to the Almighty. However, after stewardesses appeared aboard this passenger's flights, he no longer uttered such prayers. Stewardesses' professionalism and lack of fear boosted his confidence in air travel so that prayers for heavenly protection no longer seemed necessary. Clearly, the reassurance of frightened passengers by early stewardesses, metaphorically sent from heaven, was an important aspect of their job.[67]

Yet another important role of the stewardess was helping first-time passengers. When individuals took first flight, they exhibited traits that an experienced stewardess could easily spot. One stewardess claimed, "Usually I can read in your face before the take-off whether you have flown before. If you're young you can't sit still. If you're mature and filled with responsibilities your expression proclaims that you know you are to be killed and you've made up your mind to die bravely. You'll seldom admit to being a first-timer, but even if you're skillful enough to hide your emotions there is one infallible give-away. It's a curiously indirect question. I've never known a first-timer who didn't ask, first thing, what questions *other* people ask me!"[68]

A middle-aged woman in the early 1930s took her first flight out of necessity, and certainly not desire. She flew on United Air Lines from Omaha to Chicago at night. Before her flight's departure, she was hysterical with fear. Even though Jack Knight, the most famous of airmail pilots, had his steady hands on the controls, this woman refused comfort. The copilot and the ground crew, as well as the other passengers, did their best to calm the lady in the face of her "mounting terror," so that the flight could leave. To the rescue came a stewardess. Conveying confidence through her voice and movement, she sat beside the woman and answered her questions, all the while patting "the frightened creature's trembling hands." The woman soon fell asleep in-flight. She enjoyed the trip so much that she took the plane again on her return journey. And thus another person had joined the ranks of the air travel enthusiasts.[69]

Not all first-flighters were fortunate enough to have a patient stewardess on hand to calm their fears. First-flighters were on their own aboard airlines that had not yet hired stewardesses. A passenger flying out of Los Angeles aboard TWA in 1933 found herself across the aisle from a man who had never flown before. Writing of the experience, she observed: "At any other time he would look very undistinguished, but now his face is illuminated with fear. He screamed in my ear as we took off that he had never been up before. His knuckles on the arm of his chair are white, and he is watching the mountains slide away from under us with horror and fascination. . . . Already he is a little green, and I am afraid he may be sick." The first-time flyer did become ill. With no airline representative to come to the man's rescue, he gathered his courage and endured the flight to its conclusion. Upon landing, he kissed the ground in thankfulness, not wanting to set foot in an airplane ever again.[70]

The advent of stewardesses was a marketing coup for airlines wishing to attract female ridership. Until stewardesses rode with passengers in airliner cabins, a female passenger often traveled alone in the company of strange men sealed in a flying craft thousands of feet above the earth. Such an environment proved uncomfortable for many women and discouraged them from flying. The presence of another woman, who also happened to be a trained nurse, eased the minds of apprehensive female passengers. After the arrival of the stewardess, more women took to the skies in the less socially threatening environment. Even *National Geographic* magazine hailed the stewardess as "having done much to increase the number of women air passengers."[71]

Nevertheless, some women seemed to resent the presence of the beautiful young stewardesses, preferring instead to be reassured by male crew members. Actress Cornelia Otis Skinner flew transcontinental in the mid-1930s. She coolly accepted the hostess's offer of cotton for her ears while she explained to the lass that she was nervous about flying. The hostess attempted to calm her fearful passenger, yet Skinner only saw the hostess smile "scornfully" and make an "inane remark" about the safety of flying. In contrast, Skinner spied the handsome copilot coming down the aisle, asking passengers how they were doing. Skinner thought to herself: "He is so beautiful that he might ask you anything and it would be O.K. (I am convinced that the airlines choose their co-pilots for their beauty in order to encourage feminine patronage.)" Although terrified at the thought of the airliner crashing, Skinner found her "sense of fear suddenly diluted by an infusion of the gentler passion."[72]

Airlines needed to convince women of the safety of air travel for another reason as well. The airlines discovered that many women objected to their husbands boarding airliners. According to one study, women had "an instinctive dread about letting husbands and sons take any chance," and the airlines of the 1920s and early 1930s seemed quite unreliable in comparison with railways. Every air accident made headlines, reinforcing the idea that airplanes were inherently unsafe. Most wives in the 1930s did not work outside the home, and if their husbands, usually the only wage earner in the household, died, the loss of income could be devastating. Yet perhaps an even more compelling force prompting women to urge the men in their lives not to chance air travel was a maternal instinct to protect the objects of their affections. As a means of overcoming feminine objections, proponents of air travel devised a scheme to lure women aboard airliners with their husbands who wished to fly.[73]

Colonial Air Transport instituted a plan late in 1929 offering executives' wives free air passage when they flew with their husbands. The ploy worked. However, when the airline sent letters expressing its gratitude to the wives and hoping they would fly Colonial again soon, reply letters arrived from angry wives who indicated it was not they who had accompanied their husbands.[74]

The airline terminated the offer when it became clear that some of the "wives" were merely traveling companions, not spouses of the male passengers. Nonetheless, several airlines experimented with a wives-fly-free plan in an attempt "to educate wives to travel by air." Airline executives reasoned that if women came to view air travel as a normal part of their husbands' business, perhaps they would both object less to the men's flying and perhaps participate in air travel themselves. TWA, United, American, and a host of lesser airlines advertised some variation of the wives-fly-free offer. Although originally intended as a short-term offer, the increase in traffic it produced prompted some airlines to extend their campaigns.[75]

Hazel Cochran, the eighth stewardess that United had hired in 1930, confessed that she wearied of passengers' constant questions asking how high and how fast the airliner was traveling. Even though the passenger had no control over these factors, Cochran reported a nearly universal curiosity among the passengers. According to Cochran, if she told a passenger that the airplane had slowed from 180 to 160 miles per hour they "protest that they are not getting anywhere at all and groan over the possibility of being ten minutes late," only to later spend a quarter of an hour on the airport telephone "telling some one that they have arrived."[76]

The stewardess became an enduring feature of air travel. All major airlines had placed stewardesses aboard flights by the 1940s. However, the terms "stewardess" and "hostess" became history after the Civil Rights Act of 1964 forced airlines to hire males as well as females as flight attendants. Nevertheless, the function of onboard attendants remained basically the same for decades to come.

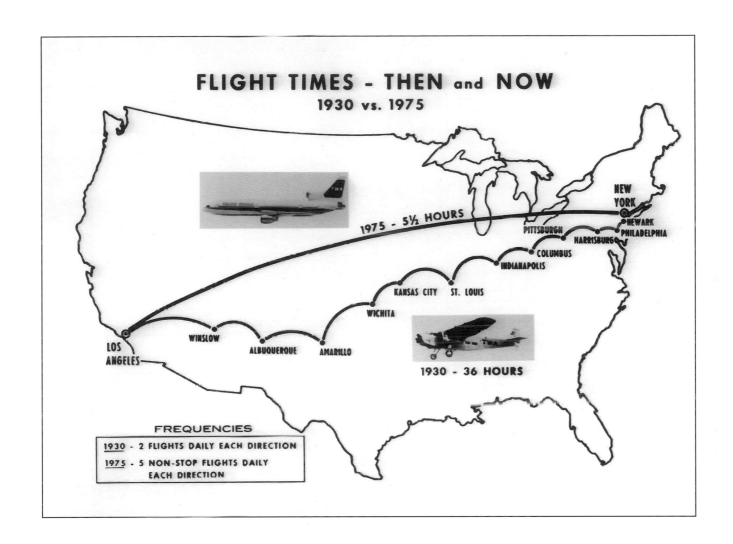

FLIGHT TIMES - THEN and NOW
1930 vs. 1975

1975 - 5½ HOURS

NEW YORK
NEWARK
PHILADELPHIA
PITTSBURGH
HARRISBURG
COLUMBUS
INDIANAPOLIS
KANSAS CITY   ST. LOUIS
WICHITA
LOS ANGELES
WINSLOW
ALBUQUERQUE
AMARILLO

1930 - 36 HOURS

FREQUENCIES

1930 - 2 FLIGHTS DAILY EACH DIRECTION
1975 - 5 NON-STOP FLIGHTS DAILY
       EACH DIRECTION

In 1930 a TWA transcontinental flight took 36 hours and stopped 11 times en route. Forty-five years later, Jumbo Jets carried passengers across the continent in under 6 hours nonstop. (From the TWA Archives of the St. Louis Mercantile Library at the University of Missouri–St. Louis)

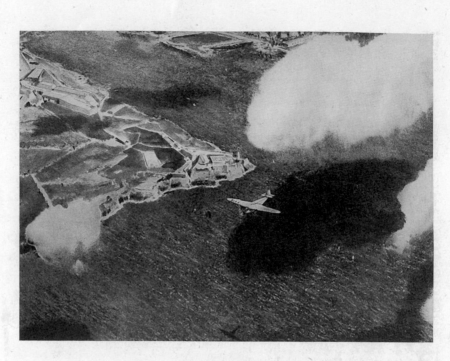

WE FLY...

YOU know the sudden breath-taking sense of exaltation when your car emerges on the crest of some magnificent headland from which you look for miles out to sea or over billowing rows of mountains below. What is that sensation? It is a sudden sense of power . . . a feeling that your human faculties have been miraculously extended . . . it is a slight taste of divinity!

How immeasurably greater this sense of divine exaltation is when gliding high in the heavens, looking serenely down upon the colorful, silent world below! It is a feeling known only to those who have learned from personal experience the tranquil glory of flight.

Those who know the freedom of the airways find in the old paths of earth something nerve-wracking . . . a sense of restraint, of suffocation almost . . . much as the pioneer motorists looked back on the days when they sat in clouds of dust behind plodding teams of horses. Each month they find increasing pleasure in the pathways of the sky . . . slipping down to bright Havana, to Panama or Peru.

Unless you are too old to readjust your habits to new aspects of life, some day you will fly. Fortunate are those men and women who today recognize that the realm of the skies is offering a fresh lease on life. The blithe spirit of a new renaissance is in the air. It is hard for those who feel it to interpret its significance, though we see the faces of men turning upward, and we see the far places of the earth brought nearer in friendly communication.

The great tri-motored, all-metal planes of 1931 are truly yachts that bring you safety not only as sure as the safety of your yachts upon the sea, but as luxurious and as restful. These new planes free your thoughts from mechanical limitations, just as you are today above the concerns of the engine-room of a steamship.

The pilot and mechanic in their forward control cabin have every mechanical device necessary for day or night flying in all seasons. Fundamentally the new plane is designed as close to mechanical perfection as possible, with all the strength and extraordinary performance ability for which Ford planes are famous. Beautiful as a jewel, it spreads its wings like burnished silver, to fly with the smooth grace of an albatross over sea, over land, over deserts or arctic wastes.

• FORD MOTOR COMPANY •

Addressing the issues of safety and the sensations of flight, this advertisement, circa 1931, from the Ford Motor Company extols the virtues of flying in a Ford Tri-Motor airliner. Calling air travel "a slight taste of divinity," the text chides the majority of Americans not yet taking advantage of it: "Unless you are too old to readjust your habits to new aspects of life, some day you will fly." (From the author's collection)

The View from the Sky

The novel aspect of air travel that most captured the attention of travelers was the view from their windows. Early passengers wrote comparatively more about what they saw from airliner windows than they did about airplane design details, in-flight food, or even stewardesses. Obviously intrigued with the fresh perspective that air travel afforded, passengers who published accounts of their transcontinental journeys, particularly in the 1920s and 1930s, emphasized the unique scenes passing below them.

For the traveler, observing the changing landscape served as endlessly fascinating entertainment. The panoramic view was unmatched in any other mode of commercial transportation. The world looked as if in miniature, as the patterns on the land – the course of rivers, main highways and railroad tracks, the symmetrical squares of midwestern farms, the seared desert of the Mojave, the smoke-shrouded cities of the Northeast, the layout of urban development, and many other sights—were revealed to airline passengers, holding them spellbound.

Noted research pilot and author Wolfgang Langewiesche once compared the view from an airplane to that of history. Just as the distance of time gives the historian a sweeping view of myriad events, the altitude of airline flight enables passengers to scan large geographic areas with a glance. The entire scene meets their eyes before they focus on the individual parts composing the scene.[77]

Another writer described the airborne view as unlike the "dead perspective" one had when looking down from a many-storied building. Rather, gazing at the ground from a 1920s airliner window was "more like standing in the center of a playroom with toy trains and cardboard villages laid out—standing in the center of a vast playroom that unrolls lazily and continuously under our feet." This writer saw more individual features of the land, as his flight was at an altitude of approximately 1,500 feet and at a speed of just over 100 miles per hour.[78]

The view from an airliner was unique, and some believed it to be even therapeutic. A magazine editorial from the summer of 1932, in the midst of dark economic news, prescribed air travel as medicine for the souls of Depression-weary Americans: "If you have not been up lately, take a ride in an airplane. It will stir your imagination and stimulate you to cheerful thoughts. There is tonic in the air." The writer explained that seeing the grid pattern of cities from the sky revealed the order and "reasonableness of purpose" hidden from a ground-based viewpoint. The large sweep of the American landscape, complete with roads, settlements, and fields, demonstrated a "long effort of thought and of triumph over difficulties." Literally expanding the passenger's horizons, the view from an airplane window could spark the imagination and bring hope into the gloomy mind of a person enduring the greatest economic depression in the nation's history. Clearly, the writer of this piece had found the view from the air nothing short of inspiring. Perhaps flying could provide not only a physical lift but an emotional one as well.[79]

Many early passengers expressed a sense of wonder at the sights played out far below their heavenly perch. While winging across the continent, Francis Vivian Drake wrote that he and his fellow passengers seemed "to be suspended in space while the country rolls slowly by below." Drake even asserted, "For a moment we are as gods, complacently surveying our world from a more splendid chariot than ever Phaethon drove." Surveying an unfolding aerial vista could lead passengers to believe that they had transcended their earthly existence and that the landscape below was their personal realm as they soared through the heavens on wings.[80]

At least one book published in the 1930s covered the topography of the central transcontinental air route. *Airways of America* traced the geographic and geologic features that passengers encountered while flying the United Air Lines route between New York and San Francisco. Section by section, the book provided details on the crops of farming regions, why agricultural regions in the Midwest followed various grid patterns, the geologic history, and a myriad of other facts of possible interest when flying United coast-to-coast.[81]

First Lady Eleanor Roosevelt enjoyed herself while flying around the United States. One of her main sources of pleasure was looking out of the window. She claimed to love flying primarily because the view from the sky allowed her to "see the country in a different way." Mountain peaks and threatening storm clouds outside an airplane window formed a scene not soon to be forgotten. Yet Mrs. Roosevelt also understood that repetition of even the most spectacular of scenery could jade the passengers to its natural glory: "It is true that if you fly over the same ground over and over again it becomes monotonous just as it does if you take the same trips by motor or by rail." She asserted that the very distance between the plane and the earth could cause the air traveler to lose interest in the view from the window more quickly than a view from the ground because the activities of humanity appeared so small from the sky.[82]

Not all sights proved beautiful from the air. A 1929 transcontinental passenger, M. de M. Porter, looked for something unique about Chicago from the air as she flew past, but she could not. The city was enveloped in haze. Porter commented: "It is so shrouded in its veil of smoke that I cannot escape the irony of comparing it to an Eastern woman. You must keep your beauty for your own men, O Lady of the Lake!" Chicago was not much of a spectacle during daylight hours if wind had not blown the sky clean of smog. Typically, night flyers witnessed more spectacular aerial views of cities that featured glowing fires at industrial plants and streetlights.[83]

Directly related to the view of the ground was the matter of aircraft speeds. While taking off could seem quite exciting—thundering along the ground, watching the airplane's wheels spin faster and faster, and then seeing the airport buildings and surrounding environs quickly recede in scale—the actual flight at cruising altitude produced yet another sensation. During flight, passengers wished to monitor their craft's speed and altitude. In the smaller one- to four-passenger mail planes, pilots often passed notes to passengers, telling them of the flight's altitude, speed, and estimated time of arrival. By the later 1930s, before the advent of onboard public address systems in the 1940s, airlines such as American gave pilots forms with blanks to fill in with current flight information to hand back through the cabin. But realizing that passengers wished to constantly monitor their altitude and keep an eye on the passing time, many airlines installed a clock, an altimeter, and an airspeed indicator on the front cabin wall of airliners. Passengers often glanced at the dials for accurate, real-time information. One firsthand account mentioned that when the airplane flew at more than 10,000 feet or went very fast, passengers watched the dials intently and looked away "only to exchange graphic gestures with their companions," because the noise in the cabin precluded audible communication. The instruments gave passengers a sense of knowing what was going on around them while in a strange environment, cut off from external reference points of time and space.[84]

Besides wishing to know the current time and the plane's current altitude and speed, passengers desired to identify the terrain passing below. Airlines provided maps, usually found in pockets in front of or beside passenger seats. Such maps allowed passengers to "follow every landmark" as the airplane made its way over the topography below.[85]

If so inclined, some passengers used the information from the dials at the front of the aircraft in conjunction with "strip maps" typically printed on the same piece of paper as a map giving the general outline of where the respective airline flew. Strip maps showed smaller sections of an airline's routes with greater detail. Using a strip map to find the flight's location, and knowing the plane's speed as well as the time of day, passengers could deduce information such as the estimated time of arrival at the next stop. Some passengers did this during the night, when the physical features of the ground remained hidden in darkness.[86]

The transcontinental air passengers of the late 1920s and early 1930s traveled at between 100 and 200 miles per hour. To them, the speed seemed incredible when considered against that of a train or a car. But during actual flight, passengers marveled that they felt as if they were moving quite slowly. For instance, one 1932 passenger knew she was flying at about 110 miles per hour, yet looking down from her window, she felt little sensation of going fast. Her senses told her she was not going 110 miles per hour, because the ground below appeared to pass ever so slowly. The author explained to her readers that in a cruising airplane "nothing whizzes past your bewildered senses. You may sit like Queen Victoria in

••• EFFECTIVE OCTOBER 1, 1932 •••

UNITED AIR LINES

Fly This Winter
In Heated, Comfortable Cabin Planes

LOW FARES
To 137 Cities in 38 States

Air Transportation at Its Best
Copyright 1931, United Air Lines, Inc.

BOEING AIR TRANSPORT   PACIFIC AIR TRANSPORT

UNITED AIR LINES

NATIONAL AIR TRANSPORT   VARNEY AIR LINES

SUBSIDIARY OF UNITED AIRCRAFT & TRANSPORT CORP.

A United Air Lines timetable from the fall of 1932 espouses the virtues of flying in the heated cabins of its Boeing 80 airliners. (Courtesy of the Washington State Historical Society, Tacoma)

her barouche, sedately watching a neat little farm approach beneath you, linger gracefully a few moments, and disappear. No matter what your air speed, it would not seem by comparison with automobiling to be greater than perhaps twenty to thirty miles per hour."[87]

A businessman from the New York area who flew transcontinental in a United Ford Tri-Motor in 1932, Francis Vivian Drake described how he perceived the motion from the passenger seat. At cruising altitude in a cloudless sky, Drake had no sense of how fast the airliner was traveling. However, when the airliner encountered storm clouds, Drake and his fellow passengers got their "first impression of speed as clouds flash[ed] by close overhead." As long as there was no reference point nearby, the airliner seemed to be standing still. Earlier in the flight, Drake noted that he seemed "to be suspended in space while the country rolls slowly by far below." Watching the airspeed indicator on the front wall of the cabin, Drake had clear proof that he was traveling at great speed. However, his downward gaze at the earth through a clear sky gave him the sense of virtually standing still on an aerial platform.[88]

Cruising over the sleepy fields of Iowa, a stewardess served dinner on Drake's flight. He marveled to his readers: "How strange it seems, sitting here in an armchair, traveling at a hundred and twenty miles an hour through pitch darkness, four thousand feet above the farms—and munching dinner! What an insane vision it would have seemed to the ancestors of these farmers! Momentarily, it seems insane to us." Drake and the others aboard the Tri-Motor were indeed doing something that people of many ages past had dreamed of experiencing. For air passengers in the early 1930s, only five years removed from the start of scheduled transcontinental passenger flight, it was truly an awe-inspiring experience.

Soon to be elected president of the National Education Association in 1933, Jessie Gray took an air journey from Los Angeles to Philadelphia and thoroughly enjoyed the trip. While she admitted to "intense emotion," it stemmed more from excitement than fear. She commented on the absence of smoke and dirt, so closely associated with rail travel. Gray also appreciated the airplane's combination of speed and altitude that enabled her to relish the view—"no tearing past beautiful scenery, wishing I could tarry a moment to see it." She added, "As if in the hollow of a great hand, I am upheld serenely to see the entire picture instead of tantalizing detail and unsatisfying incompleteness." How ironic that a train moving at about half the velocity of a contemporary airliner would give the passenger less opportunity to savor what passed by outside! The vertical distance from the passenger's vantage point to the earth below made all the difference, despite the airliner's significantly higher speed relative to that of trains.[89]

A passenger aboard a TWA flight traveling east from Los Angeles in 1933 recorded that her plane encountered a snowstorm as it crossed over the mountains. She looked out of the window and saw nothing but white. The airplane seemed to stand still, with no perceptible forward motion. She likened the sensation to being "suspended in a universe of cotton wool." The scene prompted her imagination to speculate, "Perhaps we are a toy aeroplane filled with stiff figures and packed in cotton for shipping."[90]

Her flight touched down at Winslow and Albuquerque. Mountains gave way to plains as the airliner continued eastward. She looked down from her window and wrote: "There it lies under our wings, the flat planet of the old maps. Over it the sky is a round blue bowl, empty of wind or cloud, in which we seem to hang. Only the slow progress of field following field gives us any sense of motion." The Tri-Motor cruised at more than 100 miles per hour, and yet the author felt merely suspended in the sky, waiting, "while the countryside slowly rolls past, for the time when the earth will begin to lift itself towards us and place its broad and substantial back under our wheels again."[91]

After sitting in an airliner seat for an extended period of time, not sensing the aircraft's speed, passengers emerging on the ground expressed amazement that they had come so far. Even tracking progress on a map during the flight did not mitigate this phenomenon. Passengers often commented that they seemed "unable to reconcile rationally the impossible facts" that they had arrived at their destination but had not actually experienced traversing the ground. Time and space had been compressed beyond their easy comprehension.

In the coming years, spatial disorientation among air travelers would only increase with the introduction of aircraft that flew hundreds of miles per hour faster than those of the early 1930s and effectively sealed off their passengers from the outside environment.

West with the Night

AMERICAN AIRLINES

The Modern Airliner

3

Vacationing near Miami on March 31, 1931, Bonnie Rockne received a stack of telegrams. On top was one her husband, famed Notre Dame University football coach, Knute Rockne, had sent before he stepped aboard TWA Flight 5 in Kansas City, bound for Los Angeles earlier that day: LEAVING RIGHT NOW STOP WILL BE AT BILTMORE STOP LOVE AND KISSES. Beneath that message was news that her husband's plane had crashed in eastern Kansas. Within hours Mrs. Rockne received an official telegram from the TWA traffic manager: WE REGRET IT BECOMES OUR PAINFUL DUTY TO NOTIFY YOU OF THE DEATH OF MR. KNUTE ROCKNE WHO WAS A PASSENGER ON OUR WESTBOUND PLANE LEAVING KANSAS CITY TODAY WHICH MET WITH AN ACCIDENT NEAR BAZAR KANSAS.[1]

The Aftermath of Knute Rockne's Plane Crash

The headline spread across the nation—"ROCKNE IS DEAD!" An American icon and the greatest sports figure of his time had perished, along with seven other passengers and crew members, when a Transcontinental and Western Airlines Fokker F-10A trimotor airliner crashed into a Kansas field.

Coach Rockne's "Fighting Irish" football team from Notre Dame University had just racked up two undefeated seasons, culminating in back-to-back national championships. More than a sports figure, Knute Rockne occupied a place in American culture that few attain. As the Great Depression tightened its grip on the nation, Rockne became a symbol of success in the face of hardship. His coaching prowess turned Americans' minds from economic tragedy to the triumph of the nation's ideals, and his achievements

The death of Notre Dame University football coach and cultural icon Knute Rockne aboard a TWA flight over Kansas shocked Americans and led to the end of the wooden airliner in U.S. commercial service. (Courtesy of the University of Notre Dame Archives)

even caught the attention of Hollywood producers. Reportedly, the 43-year-old Rockne had a $50,000 movie deal waiting for him in California when he boarded the airliner in Kansas City that fateful morning. Any premature death is tragic, but Rockne's loss struck the nation and the airline industry particularly hard.[2]

In the midst of a public outpouring of grief and sympathy, the question on everyone's lips was, "Why did the plane crash?" A Kansas farmer had been feeding his cattle when he heard the familiar drone of a TWA plane, invisible to his eyes because of low-hanging clouds. A change in the sound caught his attention. And then to his horror, he saw the aircraft drop from the sky, engines still revving, followed by one of its wings.[3]

The Air Commerce Act of 1926 required the secretary of commerce "to investigate, record, and make public the causes of accidents in civil air navigation in the United States." Lacking additional instruction, the secretary had considerable latitude in carrying out this mandate. The science of air accident investigation was in its infancy; sophisticated methods and tools for determining the cause of aviation disasters lay in the future. When Commerce officials arrived on the scene of the Rockne crash, they were keenly aware that the public demanded a swift answer as to the accident's cause. A rushed investigation would produce half-baked conclusions that left the American people wondering as to the competency of the investigators.

Before investigators left the accident site, the Department of Commerce announced that pilot error was the reason the aircraft had crashed. Encountering turbulent conditions, the pilot had evidently sent the aircraft into a steep dive and tried to recover, but the stress on the craft ripped off a wing. Looking for more clues, investigators discovered one of the three engines lacked its propeller. They also found ice nearby. In light of the new information, the department declared that a piece of ice had broken loose from a hub and struck a propeller, fracturing it, resulting in severe engine-mount vibration that had ripped the wing from the fuselage. However, another theory soon emerged when investigators found the missing propeller buried near the location of engine impact. Investigators had missed it during their initial search. The Commerce Department changed its explanation yet again, announcing that ice

Husted Photo
Cottonwood Falls, Ks

The twisted remnants of the TWA trimotor in which Rockne
and his fellow passengers perished lie scattered in a field near
Bazaar, Kansas. A monument was later erected on this sight to
commemorate those who lost their lives in the crash. (Courtesy of
the Chase County Historical Society)

Onlookers view the tail of the crashed TWA Fokker F-10 trimotor. The mangled airframe gave witness to the violent nature of the crash and convinced many people that air travel was inherently dangerous. (Courtesy of the Chase County Historical Society)

buildup on the aircraft had "rendered inoperative certain of its instruments," and thus weather conditions were the primary cause of the accident. This explanation, too, was soon discarded.[4]

The truth finally emerged when investigators examined pieces of wood from the Fokker's wing. Fokker had constructed the F-10's fuselage from welded steel tubes covered with cloth and had crafted its wings of wood covered with a plywood skin. Penetrating moisture had rotted the wood and weakened the glue holding together the wing's components. Because the manufacturer had made no provision for accessing the inside of the wing root, the wing's sound exterior hid a deadly secret lurking within. Investigators finally concluded that the pilot of Rockne's flight had encountered some rough air and attempted to gain more altitude, but the aircraft's weakened wing root gave way under the strain of the turbulence.

In light of its findings, the Commerce Department grounded all 35 Fokker F-10s in commercial service until each could undergo wing inspections immediately and on a scheduled basis in future—a costly and time-consuming requirement. Most F-10s did return to service briefly, but the Rockne crash spelled the end of wooden airliners in the United States. However, de Havilland in England continued building aircraft with wooden wings, most notably the Mosquito bomber of Second World War fame. And Howard Hughes constructed the wings of his giant HK-1 flying boat, dubbed the Spruce Goose, from wood. But in the wake of the Rockne tragedy, the American public lost confidence in the technology. Considering its remaining F-10s worthless, TWA removed their engines and destroyed the airframes by fire.[5]

Promoting Air-mindedness

Rockne's death compounded the airlines' perennial problem of attracting riders. Unlike most of his contemporaries, Rockne booked a ticket on an airliner rather than on a train whenever possible. He enjoyed air travel and was, to use a popular term from the day, air-minded. His demise in a plane crash had personalized the terrors that possibly awaited the airline passenger and had prompted many Americans to conclude that air travel was not for them. No matter how loudly air travel proponents proclaimed the good overall airline safety record, the proverbial man on the street paid no heed to such evidence. As one observer pointed out, "It is useless to tell such a man that his feelings of skepticism about commercial aviation [are] unjust." Nothing could change his opinion "that Rockne's death proves airplane travel to be dangerous." The fledgling air travel industry could scarcely afford the negative press following Rockne's death.[6]

Despite money spent on advertising and many news stories expounding the wonders of air travel, airlines in the 1920s and early 1930s faced an uphill battle to make Americans "air-minded." Many people confused the more dangerous military flying with routine commercial flying. The public also tended to overlook the number of annual deaths due to auto accidents. Although more than 25,000 Americans lost their lives in automobile accidents in 1929 and only 178 died in airplane crashes, Americans did not abandon the automobile and rush to embrace air travel. The comparison between the two was not valid in most minds, because of what people witnessed personally. As a commentator noted in 1931, "The death-rate becomes really insignificant, not by virtue of the available statistics, but purely as a result of personal experience. It is because people generally lack personal experience in aircraft that . . . a serious accident of a single plane convinces them that flying is dangerous." Another writer put the number of airline accident fatalities in 1938, a total of 25, into perspective by pointing out that six times that number had been murdered in the city of Chicago that year.[7]

Before the widespread operation of modern airliners, the federal government and the airlines invested millions of dollars, only to see annual passenger boardings hover around 500,000 in the early 1930s. The Great Depression took a toll. In response, the airlines reduced fares. It was not a price war; rather, the lines needed passenger volume any way they could get it. As one industry observer succinctly pointed out, "In the main, the airlines are pulling harmoniously, working together against a stubborn prospect, the Unsold Public." While lowered prices lured some passengers, aircraft still flew with many seats unfilled.[8]

"The general public does not want to fly and probably never will want to," famous test pilot Captain Frank T. Courtney bluntly stated in 1931. Flying, the act of hurtling through the sky in a wooden or metal box at high velocity still appealed to few people in the early 1930s. How then could airlines attract large numbers of people to step aboard their airliners on a regular basis? In response to that vexing question, Courtney had pointed out that "nobody wants to go for a train ride, but millions travel by trains as a means of getting somewhere." Therein lay the answer: make air travel "so efficient as to become a necessity" for anyone who wished for rapid transportation. Merely educating the public as to the various aspects of air travel was not enough. Air travel had to prove its value before large numbers of people would come aboard.[9]

Airlines needed to provide efficient, fast transportation instead of merely promoting the idea of flying. Courtney had pointed to airline advertising circa 1930, observing that it was filled with "pseudo-technical bunk" of no particular interest to the passengers. Such "mental fodder" served only to give the passenger a case of "aeronautical indigestion": "The So-and-so Airline informs him directly or indirectly, that he will travel on a famous plane; that it is a tri-engined; that the engines are the famous Whatnots with which Captain Whoosit flew nonstop from Patagonia to Zanzibar; and that the pilots are personally selected by Captain Whoosit. These are matters purely for the concern of the operator and have nothing to do with the passenger." The passenger would be best left in the proverbial dark about such details.

When Courtney took a rail journey, he knew that he would "get there in a certain time at a certain cost with certain comfort and conveniences." Courtney could not care in the least who manufactured the components of the train or what materials were used in the train's construction or who selected the personnel running the operation. "Probably if I knew a little about those matters," he stated, "I should be less happy when I knew the train was traveling fast, but the railroad company does not confuse me with these things, because it is not trying to sell me a train ride." The railroad company was selling efficient transportation with acceptable comfort and safety standards. The airlines needed to follow the railroad strategy.

Yet the best advertising strategy made little difference in the face of well-publicized airline accidents. Bold newspaper headlines heralding the latest fatal crash of an airliner reinforced the stereotype of airline travel as inherently unsafe. Air crashes inevitably brought a temporary reduction in airline ridership. Crashes shook people's confidence in air travel, prompting the federal government, the aircraft manufacturers, and the airlines to decrease the likelihood that a similar accident would occur again.

A Revolution in Airliner Design

Knute Rockne's death triggered events leading to nothing less than a revolution in air transportation. Fokker, a well-respected aircraft manufacturer, left the American commercial airliner business in disgrace. Yet Fokker continued making airliners for the European market right into the jet age. American passengers shunned wooden airliners, leaving company executives scrambling for suitable replacements. Suddenly deprived of a key aircraft type in their fleets, airlines eagerly sought new planes that pushed the limits of aviation technology. Their quest led to the introduction of the modern airliner and culminated in one of the greatest aircraft of all time, the Douglas DC-3.[10]

Born in 1892, Donald Wills Douglas earned a bachelor's degree in mechanical engineering from the Massachusetts Institute of Technology after three years as a student at the U.S. Naval Academy. He worked as an aeronautical engineer for the Glenn L. Martin

Donald W. Douglas, president of Douglas Aircraft Company, poses beside the experimental Cloudster II in the late 1940s. Featuring a rear-mounted propeller, the plane flew only twice before Douglas donated it as a training aid for Boy Scouts. (From the Library of Congress, reproduction no. LC-USZ62-98158)

Company in Los Angeles and Cleveland before returning to California to found his own business in 1920. The inaugural Douglas design, a single-engine biplane called the Cloudster, was the first airplane in the world capable of carrying a payload greater than its own weight. Douglas's reputation as an aircraft designer and builder was established after the U.S. Navy's highly publicized 1924 around-the-world flight of Douglas torpedo planes modified with extra fuel capacity. Military orders kept the Douglas factory busy and the company profitable even amid the bleakest days of the Great Depression.[11]

During the normal course of a workday on August 5, 1932, Donald Douglas read a stack of letters that had been delivered to his office. One of them was from Jack Frye, vice president of TWA. Frye wrote that he wished to purchase 10 or more commercial trimotors capable of flying nonstop between Chicago and New York with "at least 12 passengers." TWA desperately needed a replacement for the Ford Tri-Motors it was using instead of the discredited Fokkers. And the airline had given up the hope of purchasing the revolutionary twin-engine Boeing 247, then in development in Seattle.

With the introduction of the Boeing 247, the first modern airliner, United Air Lines offered 20-hour transcontinental flights. Within less than two years after its introduction, this sleek aircraft was eclipsed by the Douglas DC-2. (From the collection of Dr. Charles C. Quarles.)

Douglas Aircraft Company

With financial backing from David R. Davis, Donald Douglas founded the Davis-Douglas Company in Santa Monica, California, in 1920. The firm's initial design, dubbed the Cloudster, flew in 1921. That same year Davis sold his portion of the business to Douglas, who renamed it the Douglas Company. The company soon established a firm reputation as a builder of military aircraft. Donald Douglas made several key hiring decisions in those early years, including John K. "Jack" Northrop in 1923, James Howard "Dutch" Kindelberger in 1925, and Edward H. Heinemann in 1926. Each of these men made significant contributions to the advancement of aviation technology in ensuing decades.

The renamed Douglas Aircraft Company turned out hundreds of military airplanes during the dark days of the Great Depression. Douglas also developed the Douglas Commercial 1 (DC-1) for TWA in answer to the Boeing 247. The production model DC-2 first flew in 1934. The next December a larger version called the DC-3 took off, becoming one of the most famous airliners in history. At the initiative of United Air Lines, Douglas developed the DC-4E, which first flew in 1938. The four-engine airliner proved uneconomical and difficult to maintain. A simplified version, the DC-4, emerged at the start of the Second World War and became the military C-54.

Douglas produced over 29,000 aircraft between 1942 and 1945. Among its products of the war were the DB-7/A-20 attack bomber, the military version of the DC-3 (designated the C-47), and the SBD Dauntless dive bomber, which served with distinction in the Pacific Theater.

After a peak employment of 160,000, the company cut approximately 100,000 jobs immediately after the war. In 1946 the DC-6 four-engine airliner flew for the first time. Seven years later the company's last piston-powered airliner, the DC-7, made its maiden flight. Douglas pioneered in military jet aircraft, such as the F3D Skyknight of 1948 and the F4D Skyray in 1951. Even though it had first flown in 1945, the company's propeller-driven single-engine bomber, the AD/A-1 Skyraider, served in large numbers in both the Korean and Vietnam wars. The company also built missiles and missile systems in the 1950s and beyond.

Donald Douglas, Jr., assumed the firm's helm as president in 1957, but his father remained chairman of the board until his retirement 10 years later. Douglas developed the four-engine DC-8 (first flight 1958), directly competing against the Boeing 707 jetliner. In 1965 the short-range twin-engine DC-9 flew for the first time. It proved to be the most popular Douglas commercial aircraft since the DC-3. Struggling under the costs of developing and producing its line of commercial jets, Douglas merged with the McDonnell Aircraft Company in 1967. Three years later the merged company's large, three-engine DC-10 jetliner left the ground for the first time. A modified DC-9, called the MD-80, signaled the start of a new series of successful jetliners when it flew in 1979. McDonnell Douglas developed many of the most recognizable military fighters, helicopters, and transport aircraft in the 1970s and 1980s. In 1997 the company merged with Boeing.

A female passenger steps from the door of a United Air Lines Boeing 247 in the 1930s. The rivets used to construct the aircraft are clearly visible. (Courtesy of the Northwest Museum of Arts and Culture/ Eastern Washington State Historical Society, Spokane, L87-1.4237-34)

Credited by aviation historians as the first modern airliner, the Boeing 247 monoplane boasted all-metal construction, a comfortable passenger cabin with a six-foot-high ceiling, two 500-horsepower air-cooled engines wrapped in cowlings blended into the wing to reduce drag, retractable landing gear, an autopilot, and state-of-the-art deicing equipment. Based on the Boeing B-9 bomber, the 10-passenger airliner represented a leap in technology. It cruised at more than 160 miles per hour, making it the fastest plane in its class worldwide. Its introduction would outmode all other airliners. The newly formed United Air Lines stood to receive the first 60 copies from Boeing's Seattle factory. The same holding company, United Aircraft and Transportation Company, owned both United Air Lines and Boeing Aircraft. Any additional customers could only wait until United obtained its fleet of the planes, because Boeing refused to expand production capacity. No competitors were to share in United's initial glory of flying the first modern airliners. But TWA could not wait two additional years while United put the 247 into transcontinental service. It needed an immediate replacement for its Fords. After seeking advice from TWA pilots and executives, Jack Frye sent a letter to several manufacturers, including Douglas, outlining his requirements for a new airliner, designed to equal the 247.[12]

The idea of designing an airliner even better than the Boeing 247 intrigued Donald Douglas. Although his small Santa Monica–based company built military aircraft,

Douglas himself wanted also to build large commercial airliners. Douglas consulted with his colleagues, who agreed they could build an airliner capable of meeting all of the TWA requirements, except that it would be a twin-engine plane. The Douglas design would not meet Frye's stipulation for three engines, but dispensing with the fuselage-mounted center engine lessened much of the cabin noise. Ten days after receiving the letter from Frye, Douglas sent two of his employees to New York, where they met with TWA officials for three weeks of discussions. The men took the train instead of flying, because they needed the additional time to prepare a proposal outlining the specifications of what they named the DC-1 (with "DC" standing for "Douglas Commercial"). The meetings went well. TWA officials liked that the Douglas airliner would have 12 passenger seats—two more than the 247. But TWA's chief technical adviser, Charles Lindbergh, added another performance requirement for the proposed aircraft. Besides requiring that the fully loaded airliner be able to take off with only one engine from the highest airport in the TWA system—the Winslow airport, at an elevation of 4,500 feet—Lindbergh said the plane must also be able to continue flying, with only one engine, up over the highest point that TWA planes regularly traversed. The Douglas team believed their design could meet or exceed these requirements, and TWA ordered a prototype for $125,000 in gold.[13]

Less than one year after Frye's letter to Douglas, the company rolled out the only DC-1 ever built. The aircraft incorporated many innovative features. Its fuselage gave taller passengers room to stand erect in the aisle of the 12-passenger cabin. The airplane's all-metal, stressed-skin cantilever wings, inspired by designs of John K. Northrop and Adolf K. Rohrbach, provided exceptional strength without the need for a wing spar obstructing the passenger cabin, unlike the Boeing 247. Two supercharged 700-horsepower Wright air-cooled radial engines each drove a three-blade adjustable pitch propeller. A mechanism in the propeller's hub allowed the pilot to adjust the blade's angle of attack for optimum performance during takeoff, cruising, and landing. The DC-1's retractable landing gear improved the plane's aerodynamic efficiency in flight. Wing flaps, not found on the Boeing 247, permitted the DC-1 to land at unusually low speeds. In fact, it could fly as slowly as 60 miles per hour before stalling.[14]

The elegant craft flew for the first time on July 1, 1933. With a cruise speed of 170 miles per hour, the plane subsequently passed all TWA performance requirements. In September 1933 the fully loaded DC-1 took off from Winslow and successfully flew the 280 miles to Albuquerque on a single engine. Jack Frye and Eastern Air Transport's vice president, Eddie Rickenbacker, demonstrated the plane's capabilities in February 1934. They flew the DC-1 with a full mail load from Glendale, California, to Newark, New Jersey, in just over 13 hours—shattering the previous transcontinental speed record by 5 hours. One reporter marveled: "This plane has made obsolete all other air transport equipment in this country or any other."[15]

TWA

Western Air Express started mail and passenger service between Los Angeles and Salt Lake City in 1926. Led by Harris "Pop" Hanshue, the line merged with Transcontinental Air Transport (a combination air-rail service from New York to Los Angeles) in 1930, resulting in the formation of Transcontinental and Western Air (TWA). Later that year TWA offered all-air flights coast-to-coast, with an overnight stop in Kansas City. The airline nearly failed after one of its airliners crashed near Bazaar, Kansas, in 1931, killing all aboard, including the famous Notre Dame University football coach, Knute Rockne. First to put the revolutionary Douglas DC-2 into service, TWA was operating a fleet of Douglas DC-3s when Howard Hughes bought controlling interest in TWA in 1939. The following year TWA introduced the pressurized Boeing 307 Stratoliner in 14-hour transcontinental service capable of cruising at over 20,000 feet elevation.

After the Second World War, the airline started transatlantic service in 1946 and, reflecting its global aspirations, officially changed its name to Trans World Airlines in 1950. TWA flew ever-improved and expanded Lockheed Constellation airliners until introducing the Boeing 707 jetliner for transcontinental service in 1959, just before Howard Hughes lost control of the airline. Two years later TWA installed the first permanent in-flight movie system. The company added the Hilton Hotel chain to its holdings in 1967, as the airline continued to expand its domestic and international routes, adding the Boeing 727, the jumbo 747, the Lockheed L-1011 TriStar, as well as the Douglas DC-9 to its fleet. By 1967, TWA had become the first major U.S. airline to possess an all-jet fleet. Businessman Carl Icahn gained control of the airline in 1985 at a time when TWA struggled for survival following airline deregulation. The following year, Ozark Air Lines merged with TWA.

Continuing financial difficulties resulted in TWA's filing for bankruptcy in 1992. The following year, Icahn gave up control of the airline, and it exited bankruptcy protection. Just as it was emerging from the shadow of a second bankruptcy filing in 1995, TWA experienced another setback when its Flight 800 exploded soon after takeoff from New York's JFK Airport in July 1996. The airline briefly recovered. It ordered more than 100 new aircraft and focused its domestic routes on a hub at St. Louis. Still struggling financially, TWA was sold to American Airlines in 2001 and ceased to exist as of December 1, 2001.

TWA ordered more copies of the plane, but the DC-2 was slightly larger, with more powerful engines and accommodation for 14 instead of 12 passengers. The type entered TWA coast-to-coast service in May 1934, immediately after the greatest upheaval the airline industry would know until the Airline Deregulation Act of 1978.

The Airmail Crisis

In the late 1920s and early 1930s, Postmaster General Walter Folger Brown had wielded an altered mail payment system to encourage fledgling airmail contractors to carry passengers. At the series of meetings later derided as the "spoils conferences," he had awarded choice mail contracts to his chosen air carriers effectively fostering the creation of the Big Four airlines: United, American, TWA, and Eastern.

When news of the spoils conferences became public in 1933, during the darkest days of the Great Depression when Americans sought someone to blame for their economic misery, the U.S. Senate established a committee to look into the matter of airmail contracts. Federal investigators seized documents from airline corporate offices around the nation, and hearings in Washington soon followed. Senator Hugo Black of Alabama, presiding over the hearings, criticized the airline executives for making excessive stock market profits during the 1920s. With long bread lines in the nation's cities, the millions of dollars that the large aviation holding companies, such as United Aircraft, reaped in the 1920s appeared unseemly. A public backlash against big business and anything resembling monopoly fueled the investigation into airmail contracts. A long parade of witnesses painted a picture of an infant industry grown suddenly large through government contracts at the expense of American taxpayers.

Accused of collusion with the large airlines, Brown defended himself by claiming he had acted in the public interest. The committee was unmoved. Its members cared little that passenger service, aircraft development, and safety had made great strides during Brown's tenure. Brown had used his power to shape the airline industry to his will, and it cost him his political career. The committee accused the airlines of going along with Brown's high-handed machinations, even though they had little choice at the time.[16]

Under tremendous political pressure and armed with a report claiming that the airmail contracts had been "procured as a result of fraud, conspiracy, and collusion between post office officials and the holders of such contracts," President Roosevelt issued Executive Order 6591 on February 9, 1934, canceling all domestic airmail contracts. He then directed the Army Air Corps to fly the mail. The military was unprepared for such a task, and disaster ensued. Within the first five weeks of flying the mail, 12 army aviators had died in training and in carrying mail during bitter winter conditions over unfamiliar terrain. Public opinion quickly turned against Roosevelt as the army death toll increased. Sensing an impending political crisis, Roosevelt called for new airmail contract bids and ordered the army to carry mail only during daylight hours.[17]

Federal legislation emerged, decreeing that airlines must sever direct ties with companies manufacturing aircraft or parts of airplanes and that no airline represented at the spoils conferences could bid on new airmail contracts. Yet Postmaster General James Farley understood that he could ill afford to alienate the large airlines that Brown had created four years earlier. Obeying the letter but not the spirit of the law, Farley allowed bids from the airlines after minor alterations in their names. American Airways became American Airlines, Eastern Air Transport became Eastern Air Lines, and Transcontinental and Western Airlines added "Inc." to the end of its name. United Air Lines remained unchanged because its component airlines had technically represented themselves at the 1930 meetings and did not need more routes anyway. Another, more damaging decree from Capitol Hill insisted that the bidding airlines must fire all executives who had participated in the spoils conferences. Harris "Pop" Hanshue of Western Air Express, who bitterly opposed the creation of Transcontinental and Western Airlines, left the airline business for good. And the whole ordeal prompted William Boeing to retire from any further direct involvement in the companies he had helped create.[18]

New bids revealed few changes from what Brown had created. Two companies not in attendance at the spoils conferences, Braniff and Delta, now won mail contracts. Yet the map of transcontinental air routes remained much the same as in 1930. The airlines once again went about their business, but now on the wings of an airliner unlike any that had come before.

Flying in a Douglas DC-2

Cruising at about 170 miles per hour, the DC-2 could speed passengers across the country in only 18 hours. One of commercial aviation's greatest journalists, Wayne Parrish, experienced this service firsthand as a guest of TWA in 1934. Parrish swam in the Atlantic Ocean in the afternoon, a few hours before leaving Newark aboard one of three daily transcontinental TWA flights. He relished the flight aboard the DC-2, "riding the skies as smoothly as a fast train" and marveling at the comfortable reclining passenger seats and the cool, air-conditioned cabin.[19]

Darkness enveloped the plane as it passed over Ohio. Brief stops in Chicago, Kansas City, and Albuquerque broke Parrish's restful sleep, and then he watched the sun

The only DC-1 ever produced is pictured here at the Burbank, California, airport in the markings of TWA. The elegant aircraft heralded a new era of swifter and more comfortable air transportation. (From the TWA Archives of the St. Louis Mercantile Library at the University of Missouri–St. Louis)

A TWA timetable from the summer of 1935 depicts the Douglas DC-2 and boasts that the line was now the "fastest coast to coast." (From the collection of Dr. Charles C. Quarles)

begin to light the wilderness of northern Arizona and shed its full glory on the parched Mojave Desert. Typically cruising at over 8,000 feet elevation in the DC-2, Parrish gained a new perspective on the nation's topography. He could not see individual people, and even cars were nearly lost from sight. Patchworks of fields and thin strings of roads cut across an ever-changing landscape. A similar TWA flight in the 1930s prompted a visitor from England to muse: "To see a country properly, we must fly over it. To pass comfortably through it, we can take a train. But to know it in passing, we need a car. And really to live in it, we still ride horses or walk." The modern airliner effectively removed from perception all but the most obvious features upon the earth.[20]

Parrish's DC-2 touched down in Glendale, California, at 7 A.M. local time. A refreshing swim in the Pacific Ocean less than 24 hours after dipping in the Atlantic completed his experience. TWA hoped that Parrish's positive article, and others like it, would prompt more people to fly on the airline and experience the wonders of air transportation for themselves.[21]

Author George R. Reiss recounted in *Popular Science* a flight he took aboard a TWA DC-2 in 1935 from New York to Los Angeles. The article read like one long airline advertisement, declaring that "the air lines' utopia is almost within grasp." Reiss spent $161.50 on his trip—including the expense of taxis. The author contrasted this price with that of making the same trip via rail. If he paid for a lower berth, ate three meals a day for the four days he would spend on the train, and tipped appropriately, the journey could cost him $134.50. Technological advances had dramatically improved airline safety and enabled transcontinental transit times of 16 hours. Whereas the fastest railroad left New York on Sunday afternoon and arrived at Los Angeles the next Thursday, Reiss's TWA flight had left New York on a Sunday afternoon and delivered him to Los Angeles the following morning. Reiss marveled: "For $27 extra I have saved four days."[22]

Making Air Travel Safer

Yet another air accident brought more bad news for TWA and the commercial aviation industry. A modern DC-2 crashed into a fog-shrouded Missouri landscape on May 6, 1935. The TWA accident attracted great attention because Senator Bronson Cutting of New Mexico was among its victims. Multiple investigations, including congressional hearings, pointed fingers at the federal government for not doing enough to ensure the safety of air passengers. The Weather Bureau, charged with accurately forecasting dangerous flying conditions, had failed to predict the hazard that the DC-2 encountered. Critics also placed blame at the feet of the deceased pilot and the airline. With TWA's permission, he had departed from Albuquerque, knowing that the airplane's two-way radio was not functioning properly. The aircrew may or may not have received a message from airline personnel in Kansas City that the weather was below minimums for landing there. The pilot wasted valuable fuel attempting to land at Kansas City before dropping down to get below the fog layer so that he could fly visually toward Kirksville, Missouri. Flying just above the treetops in the dark, the DC-2 crashed only 16 miles from the Kirksville airport. The Cutting crash, the first in a subsequent rash of air accidents, undermined American's fragile confidence in air travel. Ironically, after all the rightly deserved criticism of pre-1934 safety, 1935 and 1936 witnessed several more accidents—involving 247s and DC-2s.

Federal authorities and the airline industry itself demanded more regulation. The landmark Civil Aeronautics Act of 1938, a response to the Cutting crash, set the course of commercial aviation in the United States for decades to come. The act created a five-member Civil Aeronautics Authority to oversee all aspects of airlines' economic development and safety. A separate body, the Air Safety Board, investigated all commercial air accidents. In 1940 the two bodies combined as the Civil Aeronautics Board—an independent federal agency. Under the Civil Aeronautics Act of 1938 and its amendments, the federal government took greater responsibility for passengers' safety, assuring the public that flying was a safe means of transportation.[23]

Despite the government's actions, most Americans still avoided air travel. *Fortune* magazine conducted a survey in 1936 asking a sample of men and women the following question: "If you had to travel a distance of 500 miles or more and were given a choice of train or airplane, which would you take?" More than 75 percent declared they would rather take a train than an airplane. The overwhelming reason the majority did not want to take an airplane was safety. Other reasons given for preferring train travel included lower prices, greater comfort, and reliability. But fear for their personal safety outweighed all the other factors. Half of all respondents would not ride in an airliner out of fear for their safety. The magazine's analysis bluntly stated that because the American public mistrusted airplanes, "it will be many a year before the airlines will be able to persuade a large part of the American public aboard one of their passenger planes." Even though airline ridership increased greatly in the 1930s, the total number of air passengers was minuscule in comparison with other modes of transportation. The half million air passengers looked very small beside 400 to 700 million train passengers.[24]

Human error, mechanical failure, and poor weather conditions led to most of the aviation accidents of the late 1920s and 1930s. More reliable engines, multiple engines, better aircraft maintenance, deicing equipment, improved weather prediction, trailing wire to release static that otherwise interfered with radio operation, and increased cautiousness of pilots led to a dramatic reduction in the number of accidents. In 1939 the airline industry recorded a mere 0.024 fatal accidents per million miles flown.[25]

Another advance, radio navigation, also proved invaluable for in-flight navigation. For a quarter of a century, airlines in the United States had used visual cues from the ground to guide their planes across the nation's skies. During the day, even in the 1930s, commercial airline pilots followed railroad tracks to navigate from one city to another. This was called contact flying. The Post Office issued a book in 1921 entitled *Pilots' Directions: New York–San Francisco Route*, which contained the collective navigational wisdom of airmail pilots who flew according to landmarks on the ground across the continent. All airmail pilots flying the route benefited from the book's practical advice, guiding them from town to town along the railroad lines. By the late 1920s, some stretches of railroad tracks, such as the Union Pacific line through Nebraska, fostered a busy airway overhead. Pilots learned to keep right of the tracks to avoid colliding with oncoming aircraft. But after nightfall, such visual cues disappeared. The extensive network of airway light beacons installed by the federal government in the 1920s and 1930s, though helpful for nighttime air navigation, was of limited use in fog or storms.[26]

Invisible radio waves, not light beacons, were the navigational aid of the future. Radio navigation enabled aircrews to confidently fly without having to see the ground. During the 1920s the National Bureau of Standards and the U.S. Army Signal Corps had developed what became the four-course radio range. Radio transmitters, arranged in a square on the ground, broadcast a Morse code signal pattern, producing a constant tone in a pilot's earphones when he flew along one of four beams. If a pilot stayed "on the beam," a steady dash, or letter "T" sounded in the headset. Straying to the left or right of the proper course produced an "N" or an "A." Without visual reference to the ground, the pilot passed from one radio transmitter beacon to another, located approximately 200 miles from each other, along the airway to his destination. Weather reports interrupted the tone every 15 minutes, keeping aircrews informed of conditions. On the eve of the modern airliner's introduction in the early 1930s, the federal government required all commercial pilots to master radio navigation. No longer reliant upon railroad tracks or flashing light beacons, pilots now safely traversed thousands of miles of airway in good or poor visibility conditions. With the advent of radio navigation, the airlines now had the tools to fly by day or by night, in pleasant or adverse weather. The radio range beacons guided the planes, in the words of one passenger, "as unerringly as the two steel rails guide the railroad train." Radio also meant that airlines could keep a reliable schedule much like the railroads. Reliable air schedules, with timetables designed like railroad schedules, helped draw people to air service.[27]

While invisible radio waves represented a leap in air navigation technology, they remained unseen. Night passengers in the late 1930s and onward did not have immediate visual assurance that their airliners were on course. No longer could air travelers glance out their windows and see flashes of light to indicate that all was well. Such passengers had an increasingly evident visual and psychological separation from the world below them.[28]

Expanding the Appeal of Air Travel

Airlines knew that time was on their side with regard to persuading Americans to fly.
Although the middle-aged only reluctantly took to the skies as airline passengers, a younger
generation familiar with airplanes from childhood viewed the flying experience with much
less trepidation. As one writer pointed out in 1933, "Those under thirty take to the air as
naturally as the youth of 1840 took to the railroads or the youth of 1908 to the automobile."
Even First Lady Eleanor Roosevelt believed that air-mindedness was inevitable: "I think
more and more we are going to find the younger generation taking to the air, just as they
have taken to automobiles." Yet it would not happen overnight. Besides improving safety and
reliability, the airlines attracted ridership through lowered fare prices.[29]

The 1930s witnessed a dramatic reduction in the price of airline tickets, in
response to the toll the Great Depression was taking. The average passenger fare dropped
from 12 cents per mile in 1929 to 8 cents in 1930 and then leveled off at six cents a year
later. In the opening weeks of 1932, United, TWA, and American Airlines announced fare
reductions as great as 28 percent. The basic transcontinental rate dropped to $160 one-
way—an immediate $40 reduction. Round-trip tickets were subject to another 10 percent
reduction.[30] The lower prices brought airfares into the range of the price of Pullman travel.
Early in 1932, a passenger spent $288 for a round-trip ticket between Newark and Oakland,
including all en route meals. If a passenger took a Pullman car, then, adding 22 meals with a
lower berth, the trip would cost $317.[31]

Lower fares did not change the composition of the airlines' clientele in the
1930s from what it had been in the late 1920s. Men still constituted approximately 95 percent
of airline passengers, and the vast majority of them flew for business and had expense
accounts. A second, but less numerous, group was people who needed fast transport because
of an emergency. A required court appearance on short notice or a loved one's death on the
continent's opposite coast often necessitated the speed that only air travel offered. Celebrities
and politicians also valued the time savings.

Traveling with Children

Air travel held special appeal to passengers traveling with children, especially over great
distances. The speed of air travel meant that mothers no longer had to endure long hours
or days with their youngsters aboard trains, ships, buses, or even private cars. Air travel
simplified a mother's planning for entertainment and food for her children along the
journey. Gone were the days of lugging bags full of diapers, toys, formula, and other supplies

vital to a baby's well-being—now major airlines equipped their planes with baby kits, ready at a moment's notice. When a mother and infant boarded, they were handed a kit containing an assortment of items for the trip, typically including two bibs, a crib sheet, safety pins, more than a dozen diapers, soap, towels and washcloths, jars of baby food, formula, a spoon and a bowl, nursing bottles, and a box of tissues. The kit was necessary because passengers could not open their checked luggage in flight, and carry-on baggage could include little more than a woman's purse. Even though the airlines had raised the baggage weight limitation for each passenger from 35 to 40 pounds—with an additional charge for each pound over 40—all air travelers packed with economy in mind.[32]

In 1935, United Air Lines featured a series of advertisements with the heading: "Sky Travel News, by Edwin C. Hill, the Flying Reporter." One installment pictured a pert young mother from Cleveland seated in an airliner with her baby son in her arms. The mother, Mrs. Arthur Lybarger, was flying by United to Chicago to visit Tommy's grandmother. Mrs. Lybarger exclaimed: "Oh, he likes flying. Sleeps in a basket beside me. The United stewardesses fix his bottle—they're nurses, you know." Mother and son had flown repeatedly even though he was only five months old.[33]

Airlines marketed the advantages of flying to mothers of small children. This publicity photo depicts a TWA hostess helping a female passenger care for an infant aboard a transcontinental sleeper aircraft. (From the TWA Archives of the St. Louis Mercantile Library at the University of Missouri–St. Louis)

FLYING ACROSS AMERICA

United advertising also showcased the flight of another infant. On a transcontinental United flight circa 1933, a boy only six weeks old flew across the continent in 31 hours "and seemed to enjoy his sky ride." The same ad noted, "When another infant was being flown east from Los Angeles, the pilot kindly sent radio calls to stations ahead to have special baby food ready when the plane halted." Airline personnel did all they could to ensure that women and children had a pleasant experience.[34]

Despite the advantages of air travel, babies seemed a rarity on U.S. airlines until the late 1930s. Whenever a child under six years old took to the skies before 1930, the event was front-page news in the local papers. By the mid-1930s, only children under age two were worthy fodder for pictures in the newspapers. In the late 1930s, children flying on scheduled airlines did not make news unless they were under two weeks old or were already famous, such as Shirley Temple.[35]

The airlines paid special attention to their young passengers in order to attract women with families. Many mothers, as well as fathers, were reluctant to take their children aboard airliners out of fear of their safety. Flying babies elicited reactions from other passengers ranging from astonishment at their presence in an airplane to disapproval of the parents for bringing young children aboard an airliner fraught with danger. On the other hand, babies and youngsters attracted some passengers and even helped to promote friendships. Once airlines began to build a respectable safety record and widely advertised it, more parents brought their babies along for flights. More than three thousand children, ranging in age between 2 and 12, flew on a transcontinental airline in 1940.[36]

Another reason for increasing numbers of children aboard the airlines was the advent of reduced-rate fares for children under 12 years of age. By 1938 most of the major airlines in the United States had a policy of carrying children between the ages of 2 and 12 at half price. American Airlines, TWA, Northwest Airlines, and United Air Lines pushed the age limit up to 15. Previously, children over two years old required a full-fare ticket. Under the new rules, fare-paying parents could bring along children under two years old, lap babies, for no additional fee, as they did not require an additional seat.[37]

The effect of changes in altitude upon babies concerned many parents. They feared possible inner-ear damage to their children because of the change of pressure as the planes ascended and descended. Although increased air pressure in a child's inner ear could produce pain, the simple remedy of sucking or of chewing and swallowing could relieve any discomfort by equalizing the pressure in the inner ear and the air pressure outside.[38]

Sometimes children could fly without a parent or guardian. Airlines required a child be at least six to eight years old if traveling alone. A solitary child remained under the supervision of airline personnel for the entire journey. Stewardesses paid special attention to these underage passengers, pointing out interesting sights outside the window, playing

A young boy finds the view from an airliner window in the late 1930s exhilarating. (From the Farm Security Administration–Office of War Information Photograph Collection, Library of Congress reproduction no. LC-USF34-081900-E)

table games, and doing whatever it took to keep their young minds and hands busy. Even one child traveling alone could place significant demands on a stewardess's time. For this reason, airlines preferred that no very young children travel alone.[39]

Women in the later stages of pregnancy were discouraged from air travel. Airlines recommended that expectant mothers obtain their doctor's permission before boarding a commercial flight. The airlines earnestly wished to avoid an emergency delivery in flight. However, when it did happen, the airlines' public relations departments ensured that the news media learned of the incident. Yet not every in-flight delivery appeared in newspapers. In the 1940s there was at least one case in which the new mother, 17 years of age, was not married. The story never reached the press.[40]

Wealthy passengers and their young children gladly paid more for air travel rather than rail when they wished for speed. Along with the businessmen and emergency passengers, they paid fares that most Americans could not afford. On the eve of the Second World War, a one-way ticket for a coast-to-coast flight cost as much money as the average wage earner brought home for three months' work. It was little wonder that scheduled airliners in the United States flew with an average of only 6 in 10 seats filled, soon to be referred to as the load factor—in this case, 60 percent.[41]

Extending the Range of Airliners

As TWA and American Airlines carried transcontinental passengers along the southern portion of the continental United States, United Air Lines operated the central route between New York and San Francisco. Northwest Airlines had started service on a fourth major air route across the northern tier, linking Seattle with Chicago via Minneapolis–St. Paul. Nick Mamer, an aviation pioneer from Spokane, Washington, had blazed the route in 1929 with the record-breaking flight of the *Spokane Sun God*. Mamer and his copilot, Art Walker, had flown nonstop from Spokane to San Francisco and on to New York City, then back to Spokane by way of the Twin Cities. The single-engine *Sun God* stayed airborne for nearly 116 hours and set a world record for the longest nonstop flight, covering a distance of 7,200 miles. Air-to-air refueling, using hoses to transfer gasoline from modified tanker airplanes, made the flight possible. On 49 occasions, some of them at night, the *Sun God* received fuel from tanker aircraft. A primary sponsor of the flight, Texaco, planned to capitalize on Mamer and Walker's feat by keeping its air-to-air refueling operations in place across the continent, envisioning that scheduled airliners would accept gasoline and oil, in addition to food, at prearranged times from its tanker planes. Texaco hoped that the transcontinental airlines would use its aerial services to extend their range and thereby reduce coast-to-coast travel times.[42]

Although air-to-air refueling would become an everyday operation for the U.S. military around the world during the cold war, demand for Texaco's aerial gas stations did not materialize. The inherent dangers of the practice prevented its commercial acceptance. Boeing Air Transport and the U.S. Army Air Corps sponsored several nonstop transcontinental attempts in a modified Boeing mail plane named the *Boeing Hornet Shuttle*. A series of accidents prevented the *Shuttle* from ever flying coast-to-coast without stopping. In one of the accidents, a tanker aircraft dropped a can of oil during an aerial transfer, punching a hole through the *Shuttle's* wing. The public already perceived air travel as dangerous. Aerial refueling only compounded such opinions.[43]

Additionally, transcontinental air passengers needed some reprieve from the aircraft cabin environment. Passengers aboard Ford and Fokker trimotors endured noise levels of more than 115 decibels, bumpy rides at altitudes under 10,000 feet elevation, temperature variations, and cold food. Frequent stops gave beleaguered passengers the opportunity to refresh themselves. Spending 24 hours in 1929-era airliners while crossing the continent nonstop would have been nearly unbearable.[44]

Ultimately, the concept of refueling passenger airliners in the sky faded with the advent of the modern airliner. Aircraft manufacturers found other means to extend the range and efficiency of aircraft: retractable landing gear, more powerful engines, variable pitch propellers, improved aerodynamics, and bigger fuel tanks in larger airplanes. For instance, the nonstop range of the DC-2, first flown in 1934, was twice that of the other airliners plying transcontinental routes in 1929.[45]

Promise and Tragedy of the *Zephyr*

After establishing the northern transcontinental air route in 1933, Northwest Airlines put the Lockheed L-10 Electra into service. A twin-engine, all-metal, low-wing monoplane seating 10 passengers, this was Lockheed's answer to the Boeing 247 and the Douglas DC-2. In 1937, Northwest bought a modified version, the Lockheed L-14 Super Electra. It was the fastest airliner in the United States, with a top speed of nearly 255 miles per hour, far surpassing the DC-2. With its L-14 Super Electra, *Zephyr*, Northwest offered the swiftest transcontinental passenger service—just over 15 hours coast-to-coast. Yet over the course of one year the design experienced 10 crashes, four of them in Northwest service. In January 1938, Nick Mamer, at this point a senior Northwest pilot, was at the controls of a Super Electra on a scheduled flight with eight passengers when the plane's tail separated from the rest of the craft, sending all aboard to their deaths on a snowy Montana mountainside.

The federal government grounded all Super Electras until crash investigators discovered that the tail had come off because of severe harmonic vibration called rudder flutter. A minor modification to the remaining Super Electras prevented that from happening again. But the past crashes and bad publicity doomed the speedy Super Electra from continued widespread airline service, although Howard Hughes used a specially modified L-14 for his record-breaking, round-the-world flight in 1938.[46]

Although technologically outmoded, American Airlines' Curtiss Condor biplanes offered transcontinental passengers sleeping accommodations similar to those found on Pullman cars. When American's C. R. Smith asked Donald Douglas to design a replacement for them, the result was the Douglas DC-3, one of the most famous airliners in history. (From the collection of Dr. Charles C. Quarles)

The Douglas DC-3

As United, TWA, and Northwest competed with each other for the fastest transcontinental air service, American Airlines took a different approach, offering coast-to-coast airborne sleeper accommodations. The line outfitted nine Curtiss Condor biplanes with 14 Pullman-style sleeping berths, creating the first sleeper planes in the United States. Starting in May 1933, American's Condors pampered travelers with plush surroundings, much like those found in a Pullman car, and carried the line's first stewardesses. Introduced at the same time as United's Boeing 247s, the Condor struggled to cruise at even 120 miles per hour and performed poorly in icing conditions. The lumbering biplane did not last long in transcontinental service. It was simply too slow and the pilots disliked it.

But American's president, C. R. Smith, liked the sleeper concept because it attracted luxury passengers. He called Donald Douglas in 1935, asking for a sleeper version of the highly successful DC-2. Douglas had abundant orders for the DC-2 and initially refused Smith's request. After a two-hour long-distance telephone call, costing more than $300, Smith finally persuaded Douglas to modify 10 DC-2s into sleepers with accommodations similar to those of the Condors. Engineers at Douglas widened and lengthened the DC-2 fuselage to hold 14 sleeping berths. Changing the fuselage required a new wing and tail design, stronger landing gear, and more powerful engines — essentially a new aircraft.

The finished plane took to the sky for the first time on December 17, 1935—exactly 32 years after Orville and Wilbur Wright first took off at Kitty Hawk. Douglas delivered 40 of the planes, which were designated as Douglas Sleeper Transports (DSTs). American put the first DST into transcontinental service in September 1936. Stopping for fuel at Tucson, Dallas, and Memphis, the airplane completed the inaugural eastbound trip in less than 16 hours and the westbound trip in less than 18. The flights proved immediately popular, selling out two weeks in advance, even though airline passengers in the 1930s typically purchased tickets the day before departure. But the popularity of DST flights quickly faded. With so many intermediate stops, passengers discovered there was little quiet time to sleep.[47]

A TWA DC-3 flies over New York Harbor and the liner *SS Normandie* in the late 1930s. The New York skyline and the Brooklyn Bridge are visible in the background. (From the TWA Archives of the St. Louis Mercantile Library at the University of Missouri–St. Louis)

The desert Southwest reverberated with the roar of this TWA DC-3's 1000-horsepower engines as it took off in 1939. The sleek lines of this classic airliner epitomize the amazing technological progress of the 1930s. (From the Library of Congress, reproduction no. LC-USZ62-95489)

Douglas developed a day version of the DST and named it the DC-3. Fitted with 21 three-abreast seats instead of sleeping berths, the DC-3 transformed the airline business. The DC-3 hauled 50 percent more passengers than the DC-2 yet cost only 3 percent more to operate. Thus airlines could earn a profit even when the plane carried only a capacity load of full-fare passengers without any contract airmail. Passengers had enjoyed sleeper flights aboard the DST and willingly paid more for the convenience of a bed in flight, but those fares could never equal the additional revenue from seven extra passengers. TWA briefly offered transcontinental DST service, starting in July 1937. United Air Lines competed directly with TWA, flying DSTs between New York and California on its 15-hour Mainliner Sleeper Service. But, for economic reasons, both airlines soon abandoned sleeper service in favor of day planes. Douglas built only 40 DSTs. Amazingly, almost half of them were still flying in 1989.[48]

United Air Lines received from Douglas several DC-3 Club models equipped with only 14 passenger chairs. Similar to seats in railroad parlor cars, the overstuffed reclining chairs swiveled 225 degrees to face the aisle, the window, or a neighboring chair. The exceptionally wide aisle could accommodate a card table. Dubbed Skylounge Mainliners, the airplanes attracted executives and women along the New York–Chicago route who were willing to pay the additional $2.05 for the service. Every female passenger on a Skylounge flight received a complimentary "overnight kit" containing various toiletry and makeup essentials. United reported that one-third of the passengers it carried in 1936 were women, due in large measure to the popular Skylounge.[49]

Even in 1938, United Air Lines' route system still centered on the transcontinental line between New York and San Francisco. (From the author's collection)

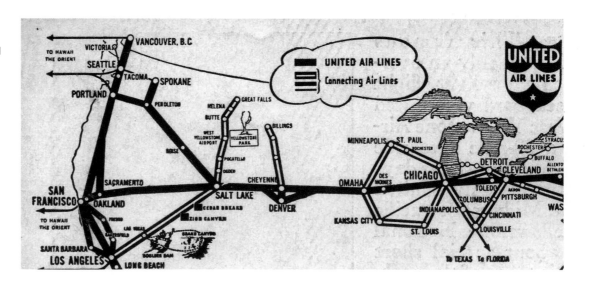

United Airlines

United Airlines traces its earliest roots to the contract airmail route between Elko, Nevada, and Pasco, Washington. Walter T. Varney's airline started mail service over that route in April 1926. By 1930 a holding company called United Aircraft and Transport Corporation (UATC) possessed many aircraft manufacturing firms and several airlines, including Boeing Air Transport, Pacific Air Transport, Varney Airlines, and National Air Transport. The following year, UATC incorporated a management company named United Air Lines Inc. to coordinate the services of UATC's subsidiary airlines. Known collectively as United Air Lines, the subsidiary lines nevertheless continued operating under their individual names. In the wake of the airmail crisis in the early 1930s, the U.S. government enacted new antitrust laws, forcing the breakup of the UATC. United Air Lines Inc. emerged as an independent company in 1934 under the direction a new president, William Allen "Pat" Patterson.

In 1930 United hired Ellen Church as the first airline stewardess, and in 1933 the air line became the initial operator of the Boeing 247, the first modern airliner. Three years later United was the first airline to open a flight kitchen. In 1947 the airline introduced the pressurized Douglas DC-6 in transcontinental service. United Airlines inaugurated nonstop coast-to-coast flights aboard Douglas DC-7s in 1954. The flights lasted less than eight hours one-way. United entered the jet age in 1959, when it put the Douglas DC-8 jetliner into transcontinental service. Two years later United merged with Capital Airlines, creating the world's largest airline. In 1965 United launched a new marketing campaign around the most enduring airline slogan, "Fly the Friendly Skies." During the growth years of the 1960s, United reorganized as UAL Corporation, with United Air Lines as a subsidiary in 1969. One year earlier, United offered the first domestic air service aboard a Boeing 737 jetliner. In 1974 the airline adopted its famous U-shaped logo and began marketing itself as United Airlines, rather than the three-word signature "United Air Lines."

During the turbulent 1970s and 1980s, United had a succession of six presidents as the company grappled with a combination of factors, including higher costs, the greatly increased passenger capacity with the introduction of the Boeing 747 Jumbo Jet followed by a period of lower fares and stagnant ridership levels, and the deregulation of the airline industry. Following American Airlines' lead, United launched its own frequent flyer program, Mileage Plus, in 1981. Three years later the airline could boast that it was the first to serve all 50 states. Rising fuel prices and low-cost competition resulted in a loss of $957 million for United in 1992. As a result of this crisis, United became the world's largest employee-owned corporation in 1994. United formed a global partnership called the Star Alliance with four international carriers in 1997.

Teams of terrorists hijacked two transcontinental flights on September 11, 2001, ramming one aircraft into the World Trade Center in New York City. Passengers thwarted the hijackers aboard the other aircraft, Flight 93, which crashed into the Pennsylvania countryside near Shanksville. Economic hardship and the results following the 9/11 attacks led United to furlough 20,000 employees and file for bankruptcy in 2002. Before emerging from the industry's longest bankruptcy in 2006, United reduced its mainline fleet by 97 aircraft, closed ticket offices and maintenance hubs, launched its own low-cost carrier—Ted, won concessions suppliers and employees, and cancelled its employee pension plan. As of 2007, United was the second largest airline in the world, after American Airlines.

The "Aristocracy of the Flying Profession"

Despite the advanced technology of the DC-3 and the airway infrastructure on the ground, air travel's most vital component was still the pilot. The airline system, composed of airplanes, mechanics, weather observers, airway beacons, airports, and a myriad of other no less important items, hinged on the skill and professionalism of those in the cockpit. One passenger in the 1930s described the captain of his flight as a "clean, well-built, military-looking man about thirty-five years old" who had earned his wings in the armed services and had flown for the airmail service. He was a true professional; piloting was his sole career. Such men obviously commanded attention and respect.[50]

During the 1930s the major airlines standardized their flight crews' clothing with the adoption of smart-looking uniforms and caps. Military-style dress, combined with the title "captain," prompted added respect from passengers. As one industry observer pointed out, people in the air or on the ground were "apt to resent advice from a pilot whom they [could not] distinguish from any other individual." Even for the nonflying public, pilots had an image to project. By having their pilots convey professionalism and competence, airlines hoped that they could persuade more people to board their planes.[51]

Commercial airline pilots in the early 1930s remained a highly select, almost fraternal group. In 1931 the number of pilots engaged in scheduled, commercial mail and/or passenger air transportation in the continental United States totaled only 460, plus 138 copilots. The flying public recognized famous pilots such as Jack Knight and Hamilton "Ham" Lee, who flew with major transcontinental airlines and interacted with passengers on a personal basis. When Francis Vivian Drake, a businessman flying coast-to-coast on United in 1932, boarded in Omaha with a living legend at the controls, he could scarcely contain his excitement: "To-night we happen to strike the granddaddy of them all, Ham Lee." Lee had started flying in 1913, his pilots' license signed by none other than Orville Wright. He performed aerial stunts at county fairs before the United States entered the First World War, when Uncle Sam hired him to teach army flying instructors. One of seven original U.S. airmail pilots hired in 1918, Lee assisted in blazing the route between New York and San Francisco. Including Lee, only 9 of the first 40 airmail pilots lived beyond that job. Surviving several accidents, Lee far exceeded the airmail pilot's three-year life expectancy, racking up over 4,000 hours in the cockpit for the Air Mail Service. Boeing Air Transport hired him soon after it assumed the San Francisco–Chicago route in 1927, and Lee remained with the line after it became part of United Air Lines. At the time Drake flew as Lee's passenger, Lee had accumulated more air miles than any other pilot worldwide—more than 1 million. Upon Lee's retirement in 1949, his logbook showed nearly 28,000 hours in flight, covering more than 4.4 million miles.[52]

Flyers such as Ham Lee made up the "aristocracy of the flying profession"—veterans of the First World War who also had barnstorming and airmail experience. By the late 1930s, this first generation of airline pilots had given way to younger men who held college degrees and were willing to rely more on instruments and radio beams than instinct. These pilots flew some of the fastest craft on the planet, and children wished to emulate them, in the same way that a previous generation had idolized locomotive engineers.[53]

The relationship between pilot and passenger had evolved over time. In early mail planes with two open cockpits, the rear one was for the pilot and the forward one was for the occasional passenger who rode amid the sacks of mail. The passenger sensed a personal connection with the pilot. The pilot knew the passengers and the passengers knew the pilot at a level that was rare on later commercial airline flights. Sometimes on a first-name basis, pilot and passengers sometimes ate together and talked during refueling stops. In flight, the pilot frequently passed notes to the passengers. The primitive nature of the experience brought pilot and passenger together physically, as well as emotionally.

In the 1920s, Boeing 40As and the aging mail planes carried at the most four passengers. At this stage in the evolution of passenger air travel, the pilot was still readily accessible to passengers. As the number of passengers per plane increased during the late 1920s, however, the level of cockpit-cabin intimacy declined. Fokker and Ford trimotors held up to 17 passengers as they winged their way coast-to-coast. Starting in 1930, Boeing Air Transport operated Boeing 80s, with seating for 12 to 18 passengers. The ubiquitous DC-3s that came to dominate domestic air transport in the later 1930s had 21 available seats. Even with that many riders, there was still a particular closeness, though short of intimacy, between cockpit and cabin. The DC-3 was one of the last commercial airliners in which passengers could experience such closeness with the cockpit. The introduction of even larger aircraft after the Second World War, with many dozens of seats, created greater physical and psychological distance between those in the cabin and the crew in the cockpit. Unlike travel by ocean liner, flying provided no seat at the captain's table.[54]

Besides passengers, others among the general public longed to be part of the emerging age of air travel. Many people who did not have opportunity to fly came to airports for no other reason than to watch the sleek silver planes land and take off, the handsome pilots and beautiful stewardesses going to work, delivering well-dressed people hurrying from one place to another. In 1930, Love Field in Dallas recorded 15,000 to 25,000 airport visitors during a typical summer weekend. The Kansas City Airport reported 10,000 to 30,000 weekend visitors. Yet both airports averaged only five or six daily arrivals and an equal number of departures, with a combined total of fewer than 100 seats available. Obviously, only a tiny percentage of the thousands of people coming onto airport property were taking flights.[55]

Broad observation decks graced the upper levels of airports, giving the public a better view of the intriguing activities on the ramp below. Anxious for a better view, the curious sometimes stood along runway fence lines designed to keep livestock from wandering into the path of aircraft. One woman, Margaret Macphail, recorded her experience as a casual observer at the Salt Lake City Airport in the 1930s. She and her male companion drove a car to the airport after work for the expressed purpose of watching, wishing, and wondering. With only their coats to block the sharp breeze off the Great Salt Lake, they ascended the stairs leading to the observation deck over the terminal but then retreated back to the ground. They stood in the night, arms draped over a fence near the runway, along with nearly 75 other like-minded people, watching a fascinating scene play before them under the bright airport lights. The public address system boomed: "West-bound plane from New York and Chicago, trip one, approaching the field." A sleek DC-3 swooped down from the sky and rolled to a stop before the terminal. Self-conscious under the gaze of so many eager witnesses, eight passengers descended the steps that had been wheeled up to the aircraft. Macphail wrote: "These passengers were having the grand experience we, of the sidelines, were all wishing we might share. That they were surviving at all and could walk to the station was a source of wonder to us. Each scrap of conversation among us landlubbers, thus far overheard, had contained both 'I wish' and 'I wonder.'" Macphail and the others watched the pilot, copilot, and stewardess, "attractive people, self-possessed, and neat-looking," walk from the airplane. A connecting flight for Las Vegas and Los Angeles soon welcomed aboard a near-capacity load of passengers before the plane made its way to the end of the runway and soared into the dark sky. Blue flames glowed from its engines. Before trudging back to their car for the ride home, Macphail and her companion remained at the fence, pensively scanning the black horizon long after the night's last departure.[56]

America's airports, such as the one in Salt Lake City, welcomed onlookers such as Macphail and her companion. They were free to wander around the terminal while their car occupied a free parking space, close to where passengers arrived or departed. Until the mid-1940s, all parking at airports in the United States was free of charge. Carl Magee invented the parking meter and approached the city manager of Oklahoma City in 1935 with the device he promised would put money in the city's coffers. The city manager agreed to try out the new device on an experimental basis. The parking meter soon appeared not only on city curbs, but also at airports across the nation.[57]

In the mid-1940s, patrons of Washington, D.C.'s National Airport encountered parking meters in front of the main terminal. They complained when required to pay for parking while delivering or picking up passengers, taking an air trip themselves, or simply coming to observe the excitement surrounding air travel. Despite their protests, the airport manager defended the meters. His justification was that some people left their cars near the terminal entrance for days on end, blocking access to short-term parking.[58]

Evolving In-flight Amenities

The speed of modern airliners altered the number of in-flight meals served coast-to-coast. Whereas the Boeing 80 and the Ford Tri-Motor aircraft flew, at best, just over 100 miles per hour, with fairly short stage lengths, the first modern airliners clicked off miles more quickly. The Douglas DC-2 cruised at 170 miles per hour. Because it could therefore fly coast-to-coast in less than 24 hours, the airline needed to serve fewer meals on the ground and less food in flight. On his 1934 flight across the continent aboard a DC-2, Wayne Parrish enjoyed dinner as he cruised westward over Pittsburgh, and arrived in Los Angeles in time for breakfast.[59]

George Reiss's dusk-to-dawn DC-2 flight between Newark and Los Angeles on TWA mirrored Parrish's. Reiss portrayed the evening meal as a "luncheon—fruit salad, sandwiches, cake, fruit, and coffee." The copilot served the food and removed the tables after people were finished eating. Before returning to the cockpit, he handed out pillows and adjusted seats so that passengers could sleep comfortably.[60]

Denied access to jobs aboard airliners until the civil rights movement of the 1960s, African Americans worked at airports in many roles. This man was a skycap at the municipal airport in Washington, D.C., circa 1940. (From the Farm Security Administration–Office of War Information Photograph Collection, Library of Congress reproduction no. LC-USF34-045038-D)

A pillow and a soft chair with room to stretch his legs was all that this passenger needed to sleep comfortably aboard a DC-3. (From the Farm Security Administration–Office of War Information Photograph Collection, Library of Congress reproduction no. LC-USF34-081904-E)

Airborne food service was no small expense for airlines. In 1936 the eleven airlines providing in-flight meals paid a total of almost $500,000 so that passengers could munch on chicken and other snacks. In the 1930s, airline executives debated the issue of serving complimentary meals aloft. Immediately before the introduction of the DST on American Airlines' routes, some in management suggested charging passengers directly for in-flight meal service. After reviewing the issue, the airline concluded that it could not afford to keep up the accounting necessary for such an operation, and that, if passengers were forced to pay out-of-pocket for food served on flights, they would soon demand more choices and even ask for refunds if they became airsick. However, the determining factor in American's decision to keep serving complimentary meals was the business that would be lost if the company began charging for meals and its competition did not.[61]

When American Airlines introduced the DST on its transcontinental service, it offered the first hot in-flight meals in the United States. The German airline Deutsche Luft Hansa had pioneered the concept of serving preheated meals aboard its planes in 1928. The DST boasted a galley in the rear where large Thermos jugs and preheated meals in aluminum cases, direct from a caterer, were kept hot for in-flight service. For breakfast, passengers could expect omelets or wild rice pancakes stylishly presented on china dishes. Lunch was fried chicken with mashed potatoes and a serving of other vegetables. Passengers selected dinner entrées from an elegant menu that listed, among other delicacies, chicken Kiev, Long Island duckling, filet mignon, or lamb chops, with sides of vegetables and salads. A choice of an ice cream scoop or a chocolate sundae completed the culinary fare. The selection of hot drinks (also stored in Thermos jugs) included coffee, Ovaltine, and water for tea.[62]

A *Good Housekeeping* article in 1937 admonished its readers to "come dine with us in the air while there is still some novelty and glamour." Airline passengers on one of United's westbound transcontinental flights typically enjoyed breakfast over Pennsylvania, lunch near Chicago, and afternoon tea far above the Great Plains of Nebraska, followed by a hot dinner over Denver and a late evening snack before gliding into San Francisco.[63]

Aboard a United flight from Newark to the West Coast in the late 1930s, one woman experienced the novelty and glamour of eating aloft. She was genuinely surprised when the stewardess placed a turkey dinner with all the trimmings on the table before her. The stewardess explained that sometimes the menu included filet mignon or even grilled lamb chops with vegetables. Along United's transcontinental line, the passengers "ate as kings in these silver castles in the air." To accomplish this, United was a forerunner in developing its own kitchens at strategic points along its coast-to-coast route: New York, Chicago, Iowa City, Cheyenne, and San Francisco.[64]

Like most other airlines, United had contracted with caterers whose kitchens most often were a great distance from the airports. By the time the food jostled its way from a downtown kitchen to an airport runway for loading into an airliner, it was in less than ideal condition. With the creation of airline-operated kitchens at key airports, United led the way in better meal service. The company hired a staff of highly trained Swiss chefs to oversee the food preparation. Because the chefs submitted each menu to the airline's dietitians for approval a month before preparing the food, the airline knew what passengers would be eating and its dietitians ensured that it was healthy for them.[65]

By and large, airlines offered only easily digested foods, avoiding fatty or greasy entrées. The variety of foods served had to be limited because of space restrictions,. Menu choices reflected careful airline studies of people's tastes. Airlines typically served American favorites appealing to a wide audience. By the end of the 1930s, passengers commonly found ham, lamb chops, turkey, and the ubiquitous chicken on in-flight menus. Decades later, U.S. trunk airlines still served similar entrées, such as Yankee pot roast and country-fried chicken. Alongside a portion of meat, green vegetables frequently embellished passengers' plates. Airlines found great success in serving high-moisture breads, such as raisin or rye. Desserts proved ever popular. A 1938 article cited "ice cream with cookies, Bavarian cream pudding, apple pie, and assorted cheese" as the favorites of most passengers. A United Air Lines poll revealed that the most popular meal consisted of filet mignon with a lettuce salad, mashed potatoes, asparagus, and lima beans on the side, finished with coffee and ice cream for dessert.[66]

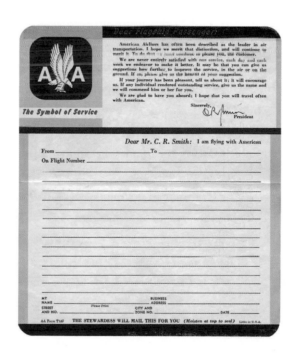

American Airlines invited its passengers to write suggestions for how the company could improve its service in the air and on the ground. Stewardesses collected completed forms from passengers at the conclusion of each flight. (From the author's collection)

This illustration graced the cover of an American Airlines map given to passengers in 1939. A stewardess helps curious passengers identify geographic features on maps while flying across the country. (From the author's collection)

While simple American-style foods seemed to satisfy the majority of passengers, approximately one in four passengers flying in the 1930s era did not eat meat on Fridays or during Lent for religious reasons. Attempts to accommodate them with fish posed unique problems for the airlines. The strong odor of fish seemed more intense aboard the enclosed cabins of airliners at altitude. However, airlines discovered that halibut, cod, or haddock could be cooked and sealed in glassine bags before loading, to preserve the entrée until served in the air. Although reduced by this practice, the fish odor remained. And the fish had to be fresh—if not, the few passengers who requested it would reject it. By the late 1940s, some airlines, such as Delta and National Airlines, discontinued serving fish. Others, including American, gave passengers on longer flights the choice of fish or meat. American found that salmon and swordfish fillets were best suited to in-flight meal service. United served fish on all flights, seemingly with few complaints. TWA stopped serving fish for a time, only to reinstate it when large numbers of its Catholic passengers protested.[67]

While United Air Lines built its own kitchens at airports, American Airlines took a different approach. President C. R. Smith realized that passengers endured poor food service at airport eateries, and even those were few and far between. Of the 30 major American airports in 1940, only 12 had some kind of meal service for passengers on-site. Smith's resolution to rectify the lack of good food at airports resulted in the launch of an American Airlines subsidiary called Sky Chefs in 1942. Sky Chefs not only operated airport restaurants for patrons to eat good food at reasonable prices but also provided food for in-flight service. Airport gift shops soon opened under the management of Sky Chefs.[68]

Food service was not the only improvement in air travel on the eve of the Second World War. Until the advent of pressurized cabins in commercial airliners, air passengers were subject to the whims of weather at the turbulent lower altitudes. Weather reports via radio certainly aided pilots in their quest for finding calm air that would not produce undue discomfort to the precious cargo of passengers in the cabin. Yet stormy weather was often unavoidable. The solution lay in the ability to fly somehow at altitudes over the top of most storms and rough air. Planes could not fly that high because the air was too thin for the engines at cruising speed and for cabin comfort without oxygen.

At its inaugural flight in 1938, the Boeing 307 Stratoliner became the first four-engine commercial airliner with a pressurized cabin. Based on the Boeing B-17 Flying Fortress bomber, the Stratoliner represented a first step toward the ability to fly above severe weather. Compressors forced air into the fuselage, creating pressure inside the airframe that exceeded ambient external pressure. As the airplane climbed from 8,000 to 14,000 feet, cabin air pressure remained at levels found at 8,000 feet. Above 14,000 feet, cabin air pressure could creep up to levels found naturally at 10,000 feet. Flying at the higher altitudes permitted the Boeing 307 to avoid most adverse weather and to operate more efficiently. Assuming that its engines produced the same power, the aircraft could fly 17 percent faster at 20,000 feet than at sea level because the thinner air decreased drag. TWA's Boeing 307 flew coast-to-coast in a scheduled 14 hours, including two stops—4 hours faster than scheduled DC-3s.[69]

Six years after flying a TWA DC-2 between swims in the Atlantic and Pacific oceans within a single day, Wayne Parrish experienced the wonders of air travel in a pressurized airliner. TWA invited Parrish aboard one of its Boeing 307 Stratoliners for a "rehearsal" flight several days before the type officially began transcontinental service in July 1940. Even though the Boeing cruised at nearly 20,000 feet, Parrish marveled that he experienced no inner ear discomfort, rejoicing at not having to continually work his jaw to relieve the pressure in his ears. And at journey's end he felt none of the usual fatigue accompanying air travel. The pressurized cabin had made all the difference.[70]

Stratoliner passengers received special certificates from TWA to commemorate their flights. Signed by TWA president Jack Frye, teach certificate stated that the named passenger had flown at 20,000 feet on the date of his or her flight and was "hereby awarded membership in the Stratoliner Club." The passenger was now a member "of a small group of distinguished air travelers who have participated in the historical development of the science of upper-altitude flight." Passengers proudly displayed these certificates as proof of their part in advancing an important innovation in aviation technology.

The pressurized Boeing 307 brought passenger comfort to a new level. Airsickness, all too common on flights in the 1920s and 1930s, was rare aboard the pressurized airliners because they cruised above most turbulent weather. Unpressurized airliners remained at lower altitudes, where "air pockets" could cause a sudden drop that induced passenger sickness. Cruising at nearly 20,000 feet, however, passengers aboard Boeing 307s used few airsickness cups—an economic saving for the airline and a welcome development for passengers. Only 10 Boeing 307s were in commercial service before U.S. entry into the Second World War at the end of 1941. The Army Air Force purchased the 307s and stripped them of their pressurization systems to save weight for trans-Atlantic flights during the war.[71]

Despite the challenges of the Great Depression, commercial aviation grew in the 1930s. In 1927 the nation's domestic airlines had carried fewer than 9,000 passengers. Two years later that number had risen to over 160,000. But then the number of annual passengers remained relatively constant for the next four years and even dropped in 1934, before rising rapidly in the second half of the decade to nearly 4 million by the time the United States entered the Second World War. Three-fourths of the growth occurred after the introduction of the DC-3 in 1936. The DC-3 reigned supreme as the United States girded for war once again, this time against Hitler's Germany and imperial Japan.[72]

Wartime Flying

CHAPTER **4**

The Second World War propelled America into the age of air travel. The war glutted the rail lines, leaving passengers with a keen desire for something better. It put thousands of uniformed men and women into the skies as pilots, aircrews, paratroopers, and military passengers, and it put money in the pockets of the middle class at home by creating high-paying jobs in factories. It accelerated technological advancement and led many more Americans to accept air travel as less of a novelty and more of a commonplace activity. American Airlines captain Hy Sheridan noted that air passengers before the war were a "special breed" with "the spirit that used to send people over strange seas in tiny ships or across the plains in covered wagons." He added, "They flew with us when they could have done better by railroad, and accepted hardships without complaint." But the postwar years witnessed a shift, as Sheridan pointed out: "Nearly everybody flies, or wants to, and our passenger lists are about as exclusive as those of the trains and busses." Even so, less than 10 percent of the American public had taken a flight in a commercial airliner. Given the high number of repeat flyers, perhaps as few as 5 percent of Americans had flown before the war.[1]

The war made first-time flyers of thousands of Americans. The military purchased not only DC-3s (as C-47 Skytrains) and Curtiss C-46 Commando twin-engine transports but also longer-range, four-engine Douglas DC-4s (as military C-54 Skymasters) and Lockheed Constellations (as military C-69s) to fly military personnel overseas. Without realizing their transformation, the young GIs aboard these planes became air-minded. Now acquainted with the benefits of air travel and its potential as a routine mode of long-distance transportation, they would become the airline passengers of the postwar era.

The Second World War produced two landing systems for aiding pilots landing in reduced visibility conditions. The ground-controlled approach (GCA) system, shown here with a Douglas C-47 (military version of the DC-3), and the instrument landing system (ILS) permitted aircraft to safely land in adverse weather. Thanks to advances in electronics during the war, air travel became more reliable because airlines canceled fewer flights due to weather. (From the *St. Louis Globe-Democrat* Archives of the St. Louis Mercantile Library at the University of Missouri–St. Louis)

An American Airlines advertisement reminds the nation that air transportation is vital, especially when ground transportation falters in the grip of winter's snow and ice. (From the author's collection)

Winter emphasizes the fact that *there is no substitute for air transportation in our war effort....*

AMERICAN AIRLINES *Inc*
ROUTE OF THE FLAGSHIPS
BUY WAR BONDS

Stateside, all means of transportation were unpleasantly crowded. In addition, travel by private car was limited during the war. Manufacturers ceased making passenger cars in favor of tanks, jeeps, and warplanes, and the federal government rationed gasoline and rubber because they were essential to the war effort. Together with the rationing, a nationwide speed limit of 35 miles per hour discouraged long-distance highway travel. So air travel became a preferred method of travel for anyone who could find a seat.[2]

When the United States entered the war, the military requisitioned 183 aircraft from commercial airlines to use directly in the war effort around the globe. The airlines faced the prospect of maintaining regular schedules with only 176 aircraft—less than half the number they had before the Pearl Harbor attack on December 7, 1941. Airlines answered with increased aircraft utilization rates. Nearly all their available planes were pressed into flying an average of 15 hours each day—about twice the peacetime rate. In 1943, domestic airlines carried 1.5 million more passengers than they had in 1939, using half the number of aircraft.[3]

The Priority System

To ensure that personnel essential to the war effort could fulfill their mission, a priority system was established, specifying a precise pecking order of air passengers. The categories of travelers were defined as follows:

Priority 1: White House personnel and others working directly for the president
Priority 2: military and civilian pilots assigned to ferry aircraft
Priority 3: military and other government personnel, as well as civilians, whose air travel had been deemed essential to the war effort
Priority 4: military cargo that the War Department had ordered moved by air

Air travelers without any priority ranking found themselves subjected to a set of circumstances with names destined to endure for decades to come. Those without a priority, and even some with Priority 3, ended up at the end of every line as "standby" passengers. If the airplane was filled with priority passengers, those on standby waited for the next flight, hoping that some priority passengers who had booked seats failed to materialize. The standbys could then take the seats of the "no-shows." Confirmed reservations were nonexistent because, at any time until the airplane left the ground, someone with a higher priority could "bump" lower-priority passengers from the flight. Bumping also happened at any intermediate stop during a flight. Many Priority 2s bumped Priority 3s. In fact, for at least the early years of the war, ferry pilots alone occupied up to 90 percent of all available airline seats. Those with high priority numbers became known as VIPs—very important persons.[4]

Entirely full flights became the norm rather than the exception. Before the war America's domestic airliner loads averaged 60 percent of capacity. In wartime that number jumped to 90 percent. Given this new reality, the airlines ceased selling tickets through travel agents and stopped advertising. Most promotional devices were suspended for the duration of the conflict. With so many nurses occupied in the war effort, airlines dropped the nursing requirement for hiring stewardesses. The new stewardesses, lacking training in nursing, brought a change in cabin service. They spent less time fussing over individual passengers, except small infants or the elderly—people who truly needed special attention. And as men signed up to serve in the military, women were often hired to take their place, filling about 40 percent of all airline jobs during the height of the conflict.[5]

Leisure travel by air was nonexistent during the war. Civilians who needed to travel because of illness or a death in the family found themselves at the mercy of the priority system, often unable to buy a seat on an airliner at any price. Even airline executives,

TWA hired its first female passenger agent in 1942, seen here checking a customer's luggage. Women filled many jobs during the war that had previously been viewed as strictly a male domain. (From the TWA Archives of the St. Louis Mercantile Library at the University of Missouri–St. Louis)

such as Eastern's Eddie Rickenbacker, and the First Lady of the United States, Eleanor Roosevelt, had to give up seats to those with high priority ratings.

Air Travel without a Priority

Those who flew long distances without a priority embarked on air-age odysseys. One such person was a newspaperman named Don Eddy, who published an article in *American Magazine* to describe his wartime journey from California to New York and back without a priority. Eddy's experiences provided a glimpse into the human side of air travel during the war.[6]

When his editor summoned Eddy to New York by the fastest means possible, Eddy called several airlines to make a reservation. The response of airline employees to his request included the possibility of a seat in 30 days, outright laughter, and an invitation to come to the airport as a standby. After only five hours at the airport as a standby, Eddy found himself on a flight south to Los Angeles. There he spent three hours standing in lines to give his name to three different airlines. In the wee hours of the morning, a female agent called his name for a seat on a plane to Phoenix, where, as well as at other stops along the line eastward, Eddy waited anxiously for the dreaded news that he had been bumped. But he made it all the way to Dallas before someone with a priority took his seat.

For eight hours Eddy occupied a bench in the Dallas airport while he drank warm sodas and ate cold sandwiches. He contemplated telling the female agent behind the counter a lie about his importance and the urgent nature of his trip in the hope that she would put him on the next plane. But after seeing a man claiming to be a medical doctor with an ill patient in Little Rock exposed as a veterinarian, Eddy kept silent. The airline put Eddy on a plane bound for New York that evening. Amazingly, no one bumped him at any of the intermediate stops. Eddy smugly congratulated himself for flying coast-to-coast without a priority in only 44 hours.

His business complete and with instructions to return to California right away, a self-assured Don Eddy arrived at the terminal, expecting to quickly secure a seat on a westbound plane. But none of the airlines had seats available. While other would-be air travelers booked tickets on trains and buses, he determined that he would leave New York only by air. He sat in the terminal for six days, going to a hotel each night to catch a nap before returning in the morning. Due to a wartime limit of how many consecutive nights a guest could occupy a room, the hotel desk notified Eddy that he had to get out after the sixth night. Making his rounds to the airline ticket counters on the seventh day, he received a glimmer of hope that a departing airliner might have a seat available. After a canceled flight and more long hours spent waiting nervously, he at last boarded a flight bound for Chicago.

The airport waiting room in the Windy City offered standing room only. A large contingent of tense, sleep-deprived people reclined at various angles across the seats. Eddy skipped the waiting room to canvass the ticket counters. After making the rounds, he stayed within eyesight of the agents so he would not miss out if an opportunity presented itself. Miraculously, one of the ticket agents found a seat for him on a waiting airliner. His luck held in Kansas City and Wichita, but he soon became well acquainted with another ticket counter after losing his seat in Amarillo. Exhausted, his frustration got the better of him as he erupted at the female agent after several airplanes arrived and departed without any available seats. Sixteen hours and many icy stares from airline employees later, the California-bound newspaperman boarded a plane. He immediately fell asleep for the first time in two days.

In Albuquerque, only a couple hours west of Amarillo, the stewardess awakened Eddy, ordering him to give up his seat. He protested. The pilot walked back to the cabin and explained that since the airplane carried U.S. mail, Eddy would be committing a federal offense if he obstructed its delivery by not surrendering his seat. Eddy immediately disembarked. He stayed in a local hotel and received a telephone call the next morning, informing him that there was space on the next flight to San Francisco. Without fanfare, Eddy arrived home with a new appreciation for the Herculean task the airlines performed during the war. He proved that it was theoretically possible to fly coast-to-coast without a priority, but his experience also demonstrated the frustrations of wartime travel.

He could have taken a train or a bus, yet those modes of transportation were also filled to capacity. More passengers rode the rails during the Second World War than before or since. Standing room only was common on many rail lines. Passengers endured discomforts while riding old dilapidated rail coaches that had been pressed into emergency service. Many Americans anxiously looked forward to the day when they could abandon intercity rail travel for seats on swift, comfortable airliners.[7]

That day was just around the corner. By the time peace approached in 1945, Americans had become air-minded, partly through necessity; the manufacturers had produced superb transport planes; and visionary airline leaders such as C. R. Smith of American and Juan Trippe of Pan American wished to make air travel more affordable.

Near the end of the war, American Airlines published this advertisement to thank its employees and passengers for enduring the inconveniences of wartime. The airlines collectively looked forward to peacetime, when normalized civilian air travel would return with the end of the priority system. (From the author's collection)

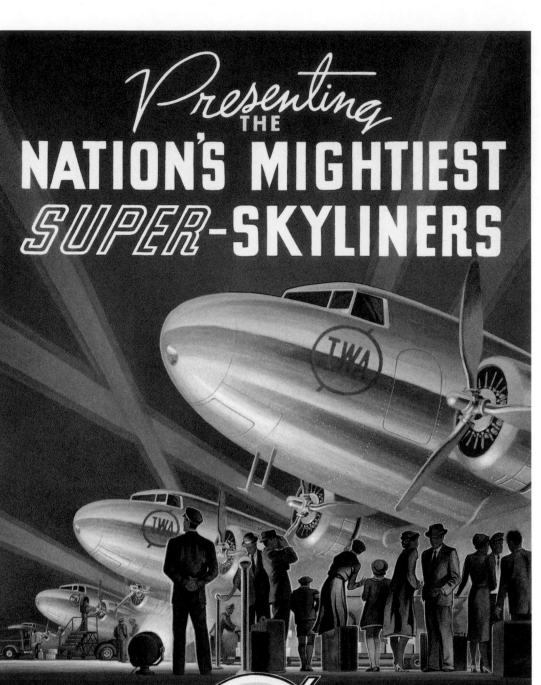

"Atomic Age Swashbuckling"

CHAPTER **5**

At the end of the Second World War, an aviation pioneer looked at passenger air travel in America and proclaimed that the future was not luxury but economy. American Airlines' president and chairman, C. R. Smith, outlined his vision for low-cost air travel in a 1945 article entitled "What We Need Is a Good Three-Cent Air Line."

C. R. Smith's Vision

A native Texan, Smith had become president of American in 1934, at age 35. Over the next several years, he brought order to American's patchwork of routes and standardized the airline's fleet around the Douglas DC-3. His proven leadership abilities attracted the attention of military leaders, who tapped Smith to help create a military air transport command when the United States entered the War in 1941. He rose to the rank of major general before returning to American Airlines after the end of hostilities. With a clear grasp of air transportation's past, and intimate familiarity with its state in 1945, Smith peered into the future and declared that the coming age belonged to lower-cost air travel. He foresaw the price of airline tickets at a level of 3 cents per mile. At that rate, a passenger would pay less than $80 to fly from New York to Los Angeles. Such a passenger would soon have many flying companions. The average domestic passenger airfare had already declined from a high of 12 cents per mile in 1929 to a low of just under 5 cents per mile in 1945. Smith wanted it even lower.[1]

While he conceded that 3 cents per mile was not possible in 1945 nor in the near future, he believed it was a goal the airlines should strive to achieve. He warned that the leaders of the industry were "in danger of becoming snobs, like the salesman at the plush end of Automobile Row with a sixteen-cylinder limousine in the window." While the limo salesman dealt with a select group of wealthy and elite clientele, he had no hope of reaching the levels of revenue that salesmen of inexpensive cars attained while selling vehicles to the masses. If the commercial airline industry hoped to turn profits, they had to fill a greater number of seats on new, larger aircraft. The leap from the 21-passenger DC-3 to the significantly increased capacity of the 56-seat DC-6 and other similar aircraft after the war meant that airlines had more seats to fill. Either the airlines could continue to cater only to those who could afford to pay high fares, such as those on expense accounts, or the lines could broaden their appeal to the middle class, who had limited resources.

Until the postwar era, businessmen and wealthy individuals who flew at least several times each year constituted the vast majority of airline patrons. A United Air Lines survey of a sampling of passengers traveling on its aircraft in the early 1930s revealed that corporate executives made up 60 percent of the line's passengers. Lesser corporate employees, including engineers and sales representatives, accounted for another 20 percent. If the airlines were to fill their new airliners and turn a profit, they needed to attract passengers other than those who were able and willing to pay a premium price.[2]

Smith called for nothing less than a sea change in the way that airlines conducted their business. He prescribed additional seating in existing postwar airliners. For instance, he pointed out that the DC-4, normally equipped to handle 40 passengers, could easily seat 58 and still give the passengers an acceptable level of comfort. While seats on the aisle would not afford much of a view outside, Smith questioned if such a view was worth the amount that passengers on such an airliner would save at the reduced fares. He declared: "To sell transportation at reasonable prices, we must use all the airplane's carrying capacity consistent with safety and comfort." Fitting more seats into existing airliner cabins meant reducing seat pitch, the measurement between identical points on two seats, usually the distance from the back of one seat to the back of the next. Forty-two inches was the typical seat pitch in the single-class airline cabins of the immediate postwar era. Placing the seats three to eight inches closer together permitted several additional rows of seats and thus more passengers. Higher passenger volumes would translate into higher levels of revenue than were formerly possible carrying only the affluent.[3]

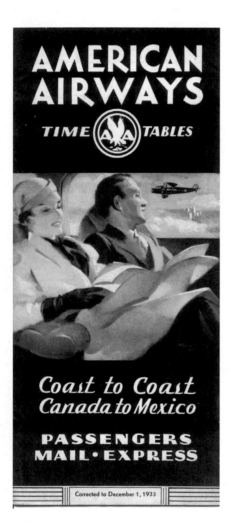

American Airways timetable cover from December 1933 depicts the typical well-heeled clientele attracted to early transcontinental air travel. Large-scale growth in passenger numbers would require airlines to seek passengers with more moderate income levels. (From the collection of Dr. Charles C. Quarles)

American Airlines

Airmail pilot Charles Lindbergh flew the first mail between Chicago and St. Louis on April 15, 1926, for the Robertson Aircraft Company. That would prove to be the most famous first flight of a company later to become part of American Airlines. Founded in 1929, the Aviation Corporation, or AVCO, brought together approximately 13 airlines with a complicated assortment of routes to create American Airways in 1930. Changing its name to American Airlines after the airmail crisis, the firm hired Cyrus Rowlett Smith as president in 1934. C. R. Smith's insistence prompted Douglas to create the legendary DC-3. Except for a brief period during the Second World War, Smith steered the airline as it matured, until his retirement in 1968.

In 1942 the airline created a subsidiary called Sky Chefs to prepare meals for its own passengers as well as for other airlines. By 1949 its fleet had become the first in the United States to be entirely equipped with pressurized passenger cabins. American began nonstop transcontinental service in 1953, flying the Douglas DC-7. Six years later the airline introduced the Boeing 707 jetliner in coast-to-coast service. In conjunction with IBM, American developed SABRE (Semi-Automated Business Research Environment) in the early 1960s for tracking reservations. Throughout the 1960s the airline added jetliners such as the Boeing 727 and the turboprop Lockheed L-188 Electra II. American was first to put the McDonnell Douglas DC-10 into scheduled service in 1971. In the 1980s the airline began adding the McDonnell Douglas MD-80 and the Boeing 757 to its fleet. These two types were the most numerous in American's fleet at the turn of the twenty-first century.

Under the leadership of Robert L. Crandall, American made many strides. In 1981, it introduced the first travel awards program. Called AAdvantage, it rewarded frequent flyers as a means of building brand loyalty. The following year, stockholders approved the creation of AMR Corporation, the holding company of American Airlines Inc. The airline announced the creation of American Eagle in 1984. The American Eagle system operated a feeder network of regional airlines supplementing American Airlines connections. In 1992 the airline commenced a premium three-class transcontinental service called American Flagship Service, a name dating back prior to the Second World War. Four years later American began offering ticketless travel. After successfully leading American into the age of deregulation, Robert Crandall retired in 1998.

Under the leadership of Donald J. Carty, American began adding Boeing 777 and 737-800 aircraft on the eve of the twenty-first century. The airline expanded again when it bought the assets of TWA in 2000. On September 11, 2001, teams of terrorists hijacked two of American's flights, ramming one plane into the North Tower of the World Trade Center in New York City and the other into the Pentagon. In spite of setbacks the airline suffered in the wake of September 11, American rebounded to expand international service. American inaugurated service to China in 2006. By 2007, it had become the largest airline in the world, as measured by passenger miles.

Seat Pitch

Seat pitch is commonly defined as the distance from any point on one seat to the exact same point on the seat in front of or behind it. While not synonymous with the amount of legroom available, seat pitch is a good indicator of the space available for seated passengers.

The first modern airliner, the Boeing 247, carried 10 passengers in seats with a 40-inch pitch in 1933. The Boeing's direct competitor, the Douglas DC-2, matched the Boeing in passenger seat pitch.

Douglas DC-3 airliner sported 21 passenger seats with 39-inch pitch. Lockheed Constellations had 42-inch seat pitch in the 1940s. Douglas announced in 1952 that passenger seats in its forthcoming DC-7 would have a typical 40-inch pitch. But airlines wished to crowd in more passengers aboard coach flights. American and TWA had both reduced seat pitch to 39 inches by the end of the decade.

Seat pitch continued to shrink for coach seating, especially after airline deregulation in the United States. In the mid-1970s, coach seats typically had a pitch between 34 and 36 inches. By the late 1980s, the typical coach-class seat pitch was 31 to 32 inches. The airlines' need for revenue from additional seats trumped legroom.

In the 1990s, TWA bucked the dominant trend, increasing legroom in coach class. The airline removed seats to accommodate an additional two to three inches of legroom for each coach seat and called it "Comfort Class." Popular with passengers, the extra legroom lasted fewer than two years, as TWA seat pitch shrank from 36 to 33 inches. American Airlines tried a similar feat in 2000 called "More Room in Coach." The airline removed more than 9,000 seats to allow for greater coach seat pitches. Economic realities after the terrorist attacks of September 11, 2001, prompted American to reinstall thousands of seats. Each coach seat could generate more than $130,000 in revenue for American annually—not an inconsequential consideration in an era of skyrocketing fuel prices and strong competition.

As of 2007, passengers continue to squeeze into economy-class seats with a 30- to 32-inch pitch. However, domestic first-class passengers enjoy the legroom afforded in seats with 38- to 40-inch pitch—a world apart from the conditions of economy class.

Sources: "Boeing's New Model 247 Transport," *Aviation* 32 (April 1933), 124; "Douglas Airliner for Transcontinental Service," *Aviation* 32 (October 1933), 331; "New DC-7 Details Revealed," *Aviation Week* 56 (June 16, 1952), 91; Solberg, *Conquest of the Skies*, 347; Betsey Wade, "Practical Traveler: Sizing Up Airline Seating," *New York Times* (November 6, 1994); Steve Huettel, "The Chair," *St. Petersburg Times* (July 21, 2003); David Grossman, "Getting a Good Airplane Seat," *USA Today* (November 3, 2006).

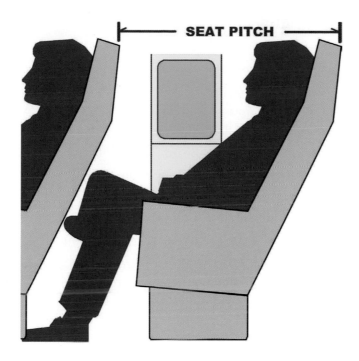

According to Smith, the airlines should examine every aspect of their operations, in the air and on the ground, looking for ways to cut costs. He questioned the long-standing practice of free in-flight meals. All passengers subsidized the cost of meals, whether they actually ate them or not. Even passengers on short flights without meal service paid a higher ticket price because of the airlines' meal service. Directly charging for meals or eliminating them altogether would lower airline costs and, in turn, allow for lower air fares.

After the Second World War, the U.S. airlines as a whole persuaded the Civil Aeronautics Board (CAB) to approve an across-the-board airfare increase of 10 percent, effective April 1947. However, instead of the decrease in fares that C. R. Smith had recommended, a second increase became effective eight months later. As a result, domestic air fares in 1948 averaged 5.75 cents per passenger mile. Rising ticket prices meant more unfilled airline seats, or, to put it another way, a lower "load factor" (available seats divided by the number of passengers). In 1945, domestic airlines had enjoyed a load factor of 88 percent. Just three years later, the load factor had dropped to less than 58 percent because of the end of wartime flying, the airlines' purchase of higher-capacity aircraft, and the escalation of fares.[4]

The Nonscheduled Airlines Emerge

Into this situation appeared a host of new, nonscheduled airlines, soon to be called simply "nonskeds." A Civil Aeronautics Authority (CAA) ruling in 1938 had permitted providers of nonscheduled air services to operate without a Certificate of Public Convenience and Necessity. By federal law, all scheduled airlines had to possess such certificates. To the CAA, reformed as the Civil Aeronautics Board two years later, nonscheduled services meant contract or charter operations, sometimes acting as air taxis. The members of the board did not foresee that it had created a loophole that veterans of the upcoming war would exploit.

A glut of used military transports and experienced pilots wishing to fly, coupled with middle-class Americans' desire to fly when it was within their budgets, resulted in scores of small air operators taking passengers on charter flights and at more regular intervals between major cities. Within only a few months after the cessation of hostilities in 1945, the number of aircraft in irregular operations dramatically increased. Less than a year after the war ended, a CAB survey revealed nearly 3,000 nonscheduled carriers, operating more than 100 twin-engine Lockheeds, nearly 340 DC-3/C-47s, 75 DC-4s, a baker's dozen of Curtiss C-46s, plus more than 5,000 other smaller aircraft types. Significantly, more than two-thirds of the total number of nonscheduled carriers in the immediate postwar era flew small aircraft as air taxis from fixed bases. The hundreds of remaining nonscheduled operators were about to create a new market for air travel.[5]

The nonscheduled airlines were just that—nonscheduled. Unlike the scheduled airlines, such as United or American, the nonskeds did not need CAB permission to fly wherever or whenever they wished. The scheduled airlines were required by the Civil Aeronautics Board to obtain a certificate from the board, to maintain regular air service on specific routes, and to charge only CAB-approved rates. Those rates were standard, and scheduled airlines did not compete in terms of ticket price. Before the Second World War, the few nonscheduled operators in the United States were relatively free from regulation. Except for the licensing of airplanes and pilots, they answered to no one commercially. However, after May 1946 the CAB added requirements for a new category of nonscheduled operators it termed Large Irregular Carriers (there were also a category of Small Irregular Carriers). These companies now had to ask the CAB for permission to fly large aircraft, such as the DC-3, and they were explicitly prohibited from operating routine or scheduled flights between any two city pairs. Effectively, this protected the existing airlines from low-fare competition.[6]

The air travel experience of these men, looking dapper in suits and hats as they deplaned from a TWA Constellation at LaGuardia Airport in 1945, was a far more refined experience than that of passengers flying one of the nonscheduled lines after the Second World War.

The primary allure for would-be nonscheduled operators was cargo. The Flying Tiger Line, soon to be one of the nation's dominant cargo airlines, started as a nonscheduled operation flying goods to various destinations in North America. But the true value of nonsked cargo operators was demonstrated during the Soviet blockade of West Berlin, from June 1948 to May 1949. Faced with the monumental task of supplying the physical needs of the city's three million residents for an extended time by air, the U.S. military contracted with nonsked operators to fly food, coal, and a multitude of other provisions into the city. Nonscheduled contractors again served as a vital military airlift link during the Korean War, when they delivered half of the commercial air tonnage required in the theater of combat.[7]

Most of the nonscheduled airlines lasted a few months at best. However, several lines turned a profit by catering to price-sensitive passengers whose pocketbook kept them from flying on the scheduled lines. Transporting the less affluent on transcontinental flights at rates far below those the scheduled lines offered, the Large Irregular Carriers brought air transportation to a broad segment of the American public. Wartime car travel prohibitions, unpleasant experiences aboard crammed trains pushed into emergency service, and a general rise in prosperity—these were factors that created an unfulfilled demand for swift, inexpensive, long-distance travel.

Stanley D. Weiss, an army pilot with wartime experience as an instructor and then as a pilot ferrying large aircraft over the Himalayas into southwest China, became one of the first to offer extensive air coach service in the United States. Most Americans understood that "coach" meant less than plush traveling conditions at a reduced price. While the major airlines charged over $140 plus tax for transcontinental passage, Weiss flew the first transcontinental air coach passengers from Los Angeles to New York on January 17, 1946, for about $100 each. Other companies, such as Viking Air Lines and Sky Coach, soon offered transcontinental tickets for $99. The nonscheduled lines could make such an offer because, although fuel and maintenance costs were no different from those of scheduled lines, crews flew for lower pay, and overhead costs were kept to an absolute minimum. Air coach service was completely no-frills. The lines provided onboard coffee and bread rolls to passengers, but typically not meals.[8]

Fred A. Miller, president of a nonscheduled line called Air America, expressed a common sentiment among nonsked operators when he publicly stated that nonscheduled lines aimed to keep their expenses low enough to offer coast-to-coast fares for less than $100 and not to depend on a dime of airmail pay to turn a profit. Miller declared that the scheduled airlines could maintain the "many and diverse embellishments of existing air-going parlor cars and sleepers" in the sky, while the nonscheduled lines would cater to people previously denied access to air travel because of price.[9]

Flying on a Nonsked

Respected aviation writer Paul Andrews decided to find out for himself what it was like to fly nonsked across the country in the fall of 1948. His "fly-witness" report, published in *Aviation Week* magazine, detailed his experience as a passenger aboard one of the "99ers"—that is, nonsked airlines offering transcontinental flights for less than $100 each way. Andrews randomly selected a nonsked from among the multitude that offered $99 fares coast-to-coast. He purchased a ticket over the telephone on Air America to fly from LaGuardia Airport in New York to Los Angeles and back. At the airport he and 49 other passengers boarded a Douglas DC-4 that had only Spartan accommodations. The airplane lacked overhead racks, magazines, reading lights, and coatracks. Passengers draped their coats over a pipe fixed to one side of the cabin. One "dour stewardess" served passengers warm water and cold coffee. The airline provided no in-flight meals. "Here was bus travel in the clouds," observed Andrews.[10]

Pondering his situation, Andrews realized why the nonsked line was making a good profit while a scheduled line flying the same route was not. A major airline operated a four-engine airliner equipped with luxury furnishings for approximately 50 people, yet typically carried only about 23 passengers. Each passenger paid $293 (excluding 15 percent tax) for a round-trip from Los Angeles to New York. In contrast, a nonsked airline usually filled every available seat on a four-engine airliner with a 50-passenger capacity. If each passenger paid $198 (excluding tax) for a round-trip transcontinental journey, then the nonscheduled line, with its low operating costs, would gross nearly $10,000. Meanwhile, the comparable scheduled line offering the luxury service would gross only $6,740. Here was a clear example of how the nonskeds were turning a profit when the scheduled airlines found themselves with empty seats and red ink. Even with relatively low passenger loads, the nonskeds could still make a profit.

After a 30-minute delay, Andrews's flight left Los Angeles and landed at Kansas City's Fairfax Airport nine hours later, just as the sun was peeking over the eastern horizon. The airport restaurant was not yet open for breakfast. Few passengers complained. Half a

Trans Atlantic Airways, founded by Edward W. Tabor, briefly offered the American public transcontinental flights for only $99, plus tax, in 1948. (From the collection of John T. Corpening)

One of the earliest successful nonscheduled airlines, Standard Air Lines offered low-fare transcontinental passenger service in the late 1940s. However, the line did not recover after one of its planes crashed in July 1949, killing 35 passengers. (From the collection of John T. Corpening)

dozen of them, including Andrews, followed the pilot's advice to take a taxi in search of an open café during the hour the plane took on fuel. On some portions of the trip, Air America served snacks on paper plates. The line's version of a "snack" was "sandwich, sweet-roll, apple juice, and coffee."

Disenchanted with the privations of nonsked flight, Andrews attempted to scalp his return ticket to someone for $50. A frequent Air America passenger in the LaGuardia terminal explained to Andrews that the plane that the airline had used for his flight was used only when nothing else was available. The passenger assured Andrews that the return trip would be better. Andrews took the man's advice and kept the ticket. He was thankful he had, because the airliner on his return trip featured mahogany veneer paneling on the interior walls, comfortable seats, reading lights, and overhead racks. And as 14 of the 50 seats remained unoccupied, the passengers did not feel like sardines in a can.

While flying back from New York, Andrews pondered the fact that the 36 passengers aboard his flight "were saving a week's pay while sacrificing nothing but cheesecake." He surveyed the demographics of his fellow passengers and discovered some interesting facts: "70% were flying for the first time on any commercial airline; 50% would have stayed home if their choice of transportation were limited to trains, buses, or scheduled airliners; 60% were women, generally unmarried and with modest incomes; 80% were traveling for pleasure or for purely personal reasons; 90% intended to patronize the sky-coach service in the future; 30% had switched from scheduled airlines because of the cost; 10% [told Andrews that they would] patronize regular airlines in the future, regardless of sky-coach economies." The results of this admittedly small-sample survey hinted at something that the scheduled lines did not wish to admit: the nonskeds had tapped a new market for air travel. The service and amenities of scheduled service were nice, but for someone on a budget, the nonskeds provided a low-fare alternative without sacrificing a great deal of speed.

Many critics disagreed that this was in fact a new air travel market, however. The major airlines, including American, TWA, and United, pointed out that the Large Irregular Carriers flew only between cities with great traffic potential, where they could "skim off the cream" of the traffic. In 1948 the nonscheduled airlines carried an estimated 10 percent of all air passengers between New York and California. In defense of their operations, the nonskeds emphasized that their passengers would not have flown on a regular airline at all, even if the nonskeds had not existed. A revealing survey taken during the summer of 1948 bore this out. Ninety-five percent of passengers flying on the nonsked Standard Air Lines had never before flown long-distance. When asked what other means of transportation they would have taken had air coach been unavailable, nearly 70 percent would have taken a bus, train, or automobile.

Only 20 percent would have purchased a ticket on a scheduled airline. About 10 percent would have stayed home if not for air coach.[11]

After reading about Paul Andrews's nonsked experience, another aviation writer and pilot, Blaine Stubblefield, took a nonsked flight from San Francisco to Washington, D.C. Stubblefield admitted that he chose a nonsked in 1948 "partly out of curiosity and mostly to save about 50 bucks." The $99 fare was less than the cost of a railroad ticket in a Pullman, and the nonsked airline delivered him to his destination at twice the speed of a train.[12]

He purchased his ticket from a ticket agency rather than from a specific nonsked line. Several ticket agencies emerged after the CAB issued the so-called 3 and 8 Rule in 1948. The CAB made this rule after the major airlines cried foul when the nonskeds began to act as if they were scheduled operators. Under this provision, irregular carriers could fly no more than three round-trips between some high-volume airports, and no more than eight round-trips each month between any two pairs of cities. In response, some nonskeds combined their operating certificates as Large Irregular Carriers into a pool, each taking turns flying their limited number of flights every month between key cities and thus legally providing the appearance of scheduled departures. A ticketing organization, such as North American Airlines agency, would sell the lines' seats to the public. The nonsked passenger bought a ticket from the agency and flew on any number of nonsked lines coordinating with the agency.[13]

As Blaine Stubblefield discovered, ticket agencies and the nonsked lines themselves offered less than stellar customer service. Stubblefield arrived at the Oakland Airport expecting a 5 P.M. departure, only to wait for some agency or airline employees finally to appear and begin checking in passengers. Around 11 P.M. that night Stubblefield and the other passengers boarded a modified DC-3. Although clean, it lacked reading lights, effective soundproofing, and air vents. Entering the lavatory, Stubblefield discovered he must place his foot against the door to keep it closed.

The airline served only pastries and coffee in flight, but passengers could get meals when the airplane stopped at airports along the way. Airports in the postwar era were notoriously crowded, with few amenities for the throngs of people passing through them. The number of domestic airline passengers in the United States doubled in 1946 over 1945, which itself had experienced a doubling of traffic over prewar years. Yet, in 1946, airports remained largely in their prewar condition. Airport authorities simply did not have the time or the budgets to respond to the rapid rise in air passenger traffic. At one airport, which Stubblefield chose not to identify to his readers, he and his fellow passengers stepped out their plane, looking for lunch. They found that their only option was "one of the incredible greasy spoons that characterize U.S. airports." Overlooking the restaurant's faults, the hungry passengers ate anyway.[14]

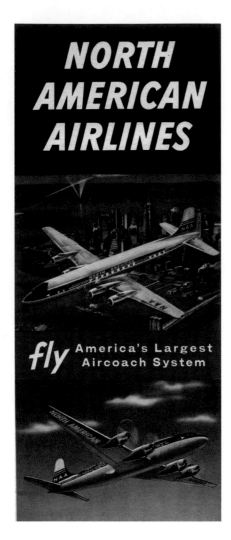

NORTH AMERICAN AIRLINES

fly America's Largest Aircoach System

A 1955 North American Airlines promotional brochure demonstrates the level of sophistication some nonscheduled lines achieved. North American Airlines briefly thrived as a nonscheduled airline in the early 1950s by bringing together eight nonscheduled operators to fly under its name. (From the collection of John T. Corpening)

Stubblefield and the others were hungry again as their airplane approached Pittsburgh. The passengers hoped that the pilot would stop there at least to get a bite to eat, but learning that weather conditions at the Washington airport were deteriorating, the pilot skipped the stop and sped up, hoping to make a landing at Washington before conditions worsened. Some sandwiches Stubblefield had kept stowed since leaving California "dulled the edge of general starvation."

In spite of passengers' rumbling stomachs, nonsked pilots and stewardesses usually promoted an atmosphere of frivolity in the cabin. Forerunners of Pacific Southwest Airlines' corporate culture of fun and humor, the nonsked crews on Stubblefield's transcontinental trip encouraged the passengers to join them in acting as if the flight were a Chaucer pilgrimage or a jolly holiday excursion. When Stubblefield and the other passengers had boarded the flight in Oakland, they were frustrated and angry at the crew because of the delay and the sparse accommodations. Yet as the DC-3 hopped from airport to airport, Stubblefield marveled that, apparently, everyone "began to have a good time." He summarized his experience: "The ride is not plush, but it's not pioneer stuff either. It costs less than Pullman, and it's twice as fast."[15]

Another passenger encountered the similar circumstances on a nonsked flight. Larry Jacobs, of Washington, D.C., wished to spend his vacation in California but thought that he lacked both the money and the time to make the trip. The nonsked airlines made his vacation possible. This nonsked flight was Jacobs's fourth transcontinental journey: the first time he hitchhiked, the second time he rode with some friends in a car, and the third time he flew on a major airline. He had enjoyed the airline flight, but not the high price tag that accompanied it. So for his fourth transcontinental trip Jacobs decided to fly on a 99er.

Jacobs flew from Washington to California in a Trans American Airways DC-3. A mirror image of Stubblefield's aircraft (both were ex-military planes), Jacobs's plane lacked overhead racks, reading lights, and air vents. The crew exuded the same spirit as the pilots and stewardesses that Stubblefield encountered. Jacobs noted: "The starched formality of the scheduled airlines was missing and in its place was the informality of a house party." Westbound over Oklahoma, the stewardess circulated a ballot among the passengers, asking each to vote for or against stopping in Albuquerque, New Mexico, for a meal. Several impassioned speeches later, the passengers desiring a meal carried the ballot and the pilot followed their directive.[16]

During rough air over the deserts of the southwestern states, Jacobs witnessed the stewardess become airsick, unable to perform her duties. A passenger voluntarily took over her tasks. Jacobs thought the situation unusual, but the copilot informed him of an occasion when a new stewardess first experienced a bumpy flight. She dropped to her knees and prayed for deliverance right there in the narrow aisle.

Jacobs called his journey "a sort of atomic-age swashbuckling." His return trip aboard Airline Transport Carriers took a most curious route, going from Los Angeles to Albuquerque and Kansas City, then backtracking southwest to Amarillo to pick up a crew member for the flight from Kansas City. The pilot enlisted a group of cowboys standing near the Amarillo airport runway to use their rope and a car to turn the propeller of an uncooperative engine on the DC-3. Together they got the engine started. Back in the air, the flight returned to Kansas City. Instead of heading for the next anticipated stop at Dayton, the pilot flew to Chicago because a family onboard wished to vacation there. Then it was on to Cleveland, and the advertised destinations of Washington and New York. However, over Pennsylvania a stewardess explained to the passengers that the flight would fly directly to New York City because so much time has been lost en route. Jacobs made arrangements to fly home to Washington, D.C., on Eastern Air Lines. Seated in the comfort of the Eastern airliner, Jacobs found himself missing the informality of the nonsked crew and passengers. The six other passengers on the Eastern flight did not speak to each other over the empty seats scattered throughout the cabin. Jacobs arrived home fondly recalling his nearly 24-hour adventure touring the continent in a packed, war-surplus DC-3.

The Nonsked's Strategy

Transcontinental air coach aboard the nonsked lines proved popular. During the 12 months before July 1, 1949, the leading eight irregular carriers that provided nonsked service between New York and Los Angeles flew a total of 1,722 flights. Two leading nonskeds, Standard Air Lines and Viking Airlines, accounted for nearly half of that total, averaging over two flights each day of the year for what was hardly "irregular" service.[17]

Citing the 3 and 8 Rule, the CAB revoked some of the nonsked lines' registrations for operating flights too frequently. To survive, Standard, Viking, and other nonscheduled lines banded together in the spring of 1949 to form the North American Aircoach System, offering transcontinental air coach service. Nonsked lines individually could not legally provide

Howard Hughes, shown here at the controls of a Lockheed Constellation in 1951, was instrumental in the development of the Constellation as one of the finest airliners of its time. This sleek aircraft featured a pressurized cabin that allowed it to fly over most inclement weather, thus providing a smoother ride for passengers.

frequent service between popular transcontinental destinations, but together they had a chance to get around the CAB's restrictions. Known as a "combine scheme," North American Aircoach System effectively combined several nonsked operations under the North American name and sold tickets through its own North American Agency. From the passengers' view, North American was a single airline, with frequent $79 service between the coasts. The combine allowed the lines to pool their resources, divide up the traffic, and thus appear to the public as providing a regular service on supposedly nonscheduled flights. North American soon spawned imitators. Columbia Aircoach System advertised $75 fares from New York to California, with a 10 percent discount on the return trip.[18]

A woman from New York, Georgia Macris, heard a Columbia Aircoach advertisement on the radio. After decided to visit relatives in Oakland, California, during an upcoming three-week vacation in the summer of 1950, she called the ticket agency a month in advance of her flight and the agent assured her that she would fly on a four-engine airliner. Macris paid $75 and looked forward to flying to California without breaking her budget.

On the eve of her departure, a friend made contact with Macris to say that she had just returned from California on a twin-engine Columbia Aircoach plane "she swore must have done duty with the Wright brothers" and that Macris should reconsider her trip. Looking for reassurance, Macris called Columbia to confirm her reservation and that she would be flying on a four-engine airliner. After a lengthy conversation with few forthright answers, Macris learned that if she had wanted to fly in a four-engine aircraft she should have paid $88 for her ticket. Upset, Macris explained that she made the reservation especially for a four-engine airplane a month ago. The agent eventually admitted that Macris had been scheduled for the next day's four-engine flight, but the flight was canceled. She was stuck flying in a twin-engine airplane at a time different from her reservation. Macris had already paid for her flight to California but was determined not to complete the transaction for her return to New York on Columbia Aircoach. Still upset, she promptly called TWA and reserved a return ticket from California, which she said cost her $126.[19]

The hot, humid air did not lift Macris's spirits as she waited in line at LaGuardia's air coach counter. The passengers steamed together, waiting to check in before making their way to an area beyond the airline gates, where a long line of nonsked planes arrived and departed. Two men shouted over the airport public address system to announce departing nonsked flights. Macris and about 26 passengers finally made their way to a waiting Curtiss C-46 Commando, operated by a nonsked called World Wide Airways. The passengers, about half of them young soldiers in military uniform and probably headed for combat in Korea, settled into their seats. The flight departed an hour and a half after the advertised departure time.

Like North American Airlines, Trans Continental Airlines combined several nonsked carriers under one name to offer coast-to-coast passenger service in the mid-1950s. (From the collection of John T. Corpening)

Macris found the aircraft cabin comfortable and the solitary stewardess pleasant. The flight hopped to Chicago and Kansas City before making a stop in Albuquerque for fuel before supposedly heading for Oakland. To the surprise of Macris and 13 other passengers, the flight terminated in Los Angeles at noon on Sunday, hundreds of miles from Oakland. The stewardess bid the passengers farewell and told them where to pick up their luggage at the World Wide counter. An airline employee apologized for any inconvenience and promised to arrange a flight to Oakland. He told the passengers to eat some lunch while he worked out the details. Macris could not help thinking of her friend waiting for her arrival in the Oakland airport since before 10 A.M. that morning, but she had no way of contacting him. Back at the World Wide counter, the passengers learned that their flight to Oakland would leave at 9 P.M.

At her wit's end, Macris dashed over to the Western Air Lines counter just as that line announced a flight leaving immediately for Oakland. Western had space for Macris if she boarded without delay. She raced back to World Wide for her baggage and returned, panting, in time to see the flight leave without her. World Wide put the displaced passengers on a 4 P.M. flight to Oakland. When Macris found her friend shortly after she arrived at 6 P.M., he was beside himself with frustration. He had met every flight from the East Coast since 10 that morning, asking questions but getting no answers from airline personnel. Macris promised her friend that she would never fly Columbia Aircoach System again.

But a few days later she reconsidered as she prepared to write a $126 check to TWA for her return flight. Flying home on Columbia would cost only $77.63. Was the difference in service worth 50 bucks? Macris decided to purchase the return portion of her ticket on Columbia and go shopping with the savings.

Macris approached the return flight expecting bad things to happen. And they did. The airline canceled her Friday-night flight without notice and put her on a Saturday-afternoon flight. But that flight experienced mechanical difficulty, resulting in a 3 A.M. Sunday departure in an Arrow Airways DC-3. At Oakland, Macris climbed aboard, later noting in a magazine article that "a carpet with upturned edges would have been all right with me by that hour." Along the way to New York, the three-man aircrew took turns staffing the cockpit and serving the passengers, as the flight had no stewardess. Flying short hops across the country, not sure exactly where they would land next, they stopped for fuel at Prescott, Arizona; Tucumcari, New Mexico; Kansas City; and Chicago. Macris noted: "No one was trying to give us the impression (not that they could have) that this was a smoothly organized operation, and this time I don't think anyone cared." The crew explained to their passengers, "We don't make much money, but we have a lot of fun." Macris summed up the flight as "a big, friendly joke." She did not even mind landing at Newark instead of LaGuardia at 1:30 A.M. Monday morning.

Georgia Macris told *Aviation Week's* readers that she would "certainly" fly nonsked again if she had extra time but was short on money. However, she warned that "a non-scheduled plane is non-scheduled." As Macris discovered, the nonskeds canceled flights at will and flew when and where they wished, not necessarily when and where customers wished or expected.

Nonskeds Opened the Door

Despite the shortcoming of nonscheduled airlines, their prices were so low that they tapped a new market for air travel, a market that the regular airlines had thus far left untouched. Middle-class Americans—the housewives, the grandparents, the college students, and a host of others for whom air travel had been out of reach—now took to the skies. Their air travel experiences, as evidenced in written firsthand accounts, were vastly different from those of passengers on contemporary, scheduled airlines. The service on nonskeds was informal, the airplanes were war-weary veterans, and the routes circuitous, but the price made all the difference.

In the face of the nonsked lines' success, the scheduled lines could not ignore the mass appeal of discount fares. In the fall of 1948, *Aviation Week* magazine declared: "Air coach service is here, thanks to the pioneering nonscheduled carriers." The nonskeds had opened the door to "flying on the cheap," and the major airlines found they needed to respond.[20]

Economy and Elegance

6

After the Second World War, the major airlines purchased newer and larger four-engine aircraft. The Douglas DC-4 and then the pressurized Douglas DC-6 and DC-7, in addition to the elegant Lockheed Constellations, became the workhorses of the transcontinental routes in the later 1940s and the 1950s. These graceful ships in the sky offered unprecedented capacities, carrying, by the end of the decade, up to 100 transcontinental passengers with one or no intermediate stops.

United Air Lines introduced the DC-6 into coast-to-coast service on April 27, 1947. The 10-hour flight required only one stop en route. Relative to the Ford Tri-Motor, introduced almost two decades earlier in transcontinental service, the DC-6 could carry more than four times the number of passengers for 65 percent less cost to the airline, at speeds nearly three times as fast, across unrefueled distances eight times greater.[1]

Such larger, faster airliners required airlines to attract more passengers than ever before if they hoped to turn a profit. But even with 13 million domestic passengers flying in 1948, the airlines bled red ink, in large measure because of the high cost of purchasing new aircraft. In the bleak days of 1948, many critics pointed to the success of the nonscheduled lines as a lesson for the transcontinental airlines, which offered one class of service for the relatively few who could afford it. The editor of *Aviation Week* magazine, Robert H. Wood, editorialized that coach-class fares were essential for the expansion of the air travel market: "Commercial aviation can never hope to be a prosperous, mass transportation medium if it offers only deluxe service." Although several years elapsed before all the transcontinental airlines offered coach service, the major airlines eventually recognized that they needed to offer more than a single luxury service if they were to achieve desired levels of ridership.[2]

Most famous for her role in Howard Hughes's 1943 film, *The Outlaw*, actress Jane Russell boards a TWA DC-3 airliner in the 1940s. Such photos epitomize the glamour of air travel in the postwar era. Until 1935, however, Hollywood actresses and actors had signed contracts forbidding them from flying because studio executives believed air travel was unsafe. (From the TWA Archives of the St. Louis Mercantile Library at the University of Missouri–St. Louis)

A line of passengers in dresses and business suits boarding a TWA Constellation airliner in the late 1940s shows that travel by air was an event worthy of passengers' finest apparel. Note that the passengers are exposed to the weather as they walk to the airplane and climb stairs before entering the cabin. (From the TWA Archives of the St. Louis Mercantile Library at the University of Missouri–St. Louis)

Family-Fare Plans

Short of offering coach fares, the airlines implemented family-fare plans to bring more people aboard their planes. In an attempt to generate more traffic early in the week (a period with fewer seats filled than later in the week), American Airlines petitioned the Civil Aeronautics Board in the later 1940s for permission to implement the first family-fare plan. Under the plan's provisions, adults paying full price but could bring along their spouse and children under the age of 21 for half the normal fare. But the CAB reacted negatively. The board feared that instead of attracting more first-time riders, the plan would merely prompt those who paid full fare to alter their schedule so they could fly earlier in the week, thus generating little new traffic.[3]

The CAB's fears proved unfounded. The family-fare plan did boost sagging numbers of air passengers on the typically lean traffic period of Mondays through Wednesdays. During the first five months American Airlines offered the plan, from mid-September 1948 to February 1949, 11 percent of its passengers flew at half price, and American's traffic on Mondays through Wednesdays increased nearly 8 percent, resulting in consistent load factors seven days a week. Additionally, American proudly announced that more than 30 percent of its full-fare family plan travelers were taking their first ride in a commercial airliner, while a significant 40 percent of half-price family fare travelers were taking their first flight. In contrast, less than 15 percent of passengers on a typical airline flight in the late 1940s were first-timers.[4]

Over the course of an eight-month period in 1949, approximately 40,000 families flew under the provisions of the family-fare plan on United Air Lines. The plan worked so well that American, United, and other airlines petitioned the CAB for an extension of the promotional offer. By the fall of 1949, almost all domestic airlines had family-fare plans. But this was only a partial step in attracting more people to air travel. Airlines soon reacted to the nonskeds with an entirely separate class of ticket, a move that would revolutionize the air travel experience.[5]

Puerto Rico Discounts

Immediately after the Second World War, nonscheduled air operators discovered a significant market for their services by bringing tightly packed planeloads of people from Puerto Rico to New York. Desperate to escape the low-income labor and working conditions in the American territory in the Caribbean, large numbers of Puerto Ricans wished to come

Built in the mid-1930s, the Pan American International Air Terminal in Miami, Florida, featured a giant rotating globe that was ten feet in diameter. The Art Deco building has served as the City of Miami's City Hall since 1954.

to the United States. The high cost of ship passage to the mainland had prevented a large-scale migration before the war, and most Puerto Ricans could not afford the standard airfare aboard Pan American World Airways. The newly formed nonscheduled lines now provided an affordable means of escape. Juan Trippe, head of Pan American Airways, witnessed the Puerto Rican exodus to New York aboard the nonskeds and decided to act. Instead of letting the upstarts take all the low-fare business, Pan American established what it called tourist-class service between San Juan and New York City. The airline removed galleys from DC-4s and crammed 63 seats into a previously 40-seat airplane. Passengers received only one modest meal during the 12-hour flight. Paying $75 each, rather than the standard $133, more than one million Puerto Ricans flew tourist class aboard Pan American from San Juan to New York during the next few years. Trippe's discounted flights had set in motion nothing less than a mass migration.[6]

Coach-Class Fares

Before the war, the only major airline to experiment with low-fare flights was United Air Lines, which briefly flew aged Boeing 247s during off-peak hours, with limited success. On November 4, 1948, Capital Airlines became the first scheduled domestic airline to offer regular coach-class service. Leaving New York at 1 A.M., its all-coach nighttime DC-4 flights arrived in Chicago by dawn after a stop at Pittsburgh. The flight featured no meal service and only one stewardess. Capital's president, James H. "Slim" Carmichael, reasoned that such coach-class flights were good business because during the night they used otherwise idle aircraft. The first week of service witnessed a rush of customers willing to pay the $29.60 one-way fare. Rail coach for the same journey took nearly four times as long and cost $27.30, or $44.10 for Pullman service. Capital soon added more flights each way, with its airliners averaging 65 percent of capacity. Initially skeptical, other airlines were impressed. The CAB soon was soon deluged with requests from other airlines wishing to start coach service.[7]

Northwest Airlines was the first of the largest U.S. airlines to adopt coach-class fares. The CAB permitted Northwest to become the first scheduled airline to start transcontinental coach service on March 24, 1949, using Douglas DC-4s. The airline also operated special no-frills flights between Seattle and Anchorage with $70 one-way fares (regular fare was $120). Because the latter service was so popular, Northwest soon offered it four times a week.[8]

American and TWA also introduced coach fares along their respective transcontinental routes. To compete with Capital Airlines between New York and Chicago, the CAB permitted TWA to fly Boeing 307s equipped with 33 seats between the cities, starting May 31, 1949. In December 1949 both TWA and American commenced coach flights between New York and Los Angeles, charging only $110 per one-way ticket. Capacity loads aboard their coach flights prompted the airlines to replace their DC-4s with larger, pressurized airliners such as the DC-6 and the Lockheed Constellation. Belatedly, United offered coast-to-coast $110 coach fares in 1951 between San Francisco and New York.[9] Passenger traffic statistics at Oakland Municipal Airport gave proof of the rapid acceptance of coach-class air travel. In October 1949 more coach passengers (11,172) passed through its gates than passengers paying full fare (7,720).[10]

Airlines used planes equipped with more seats than their standard airliners to fly only coach passengers. These all-coach flights were successful, but they bypassed many communities generating insufficient traffic to justify both regular and coach flights stopping there. Giving in to popular pressure, TWA became the first airline to offer two-class airliner cabins in the United States. A curtain separated the smaller first-class section from the majority of passengers flying at a discount.[11]

In 1950, American Airlines offered "Blue Ribbon Coach" transcontinental flights, costing only $110 one way. (From the collection of Dr. Charles C. Quarles)

This 1956 American Airlines booklet contained a passenger ticket for coach air travel between Los Angeles and New York. (From the author's collection)

Coach passengers occupied an increasing percentage of seats aboard domestic airlines. Although only 11 percent of its passengers flew coach class in 1950, American Airlines carried more transcontinental passengers in coach than in first class as early as 1952.[12]

To demonstrate the advantages of coach-class air travel, *Aviation Week* magazine editor and low-fare advocate, Robert H. Wood, told his readers of a flight he took in 1954. He flew an American Airlines DC-6 from LaGuardia to Los Angeles International for the base fare of $99 one way; including taxes, his ticket cost $113.85. Wood noted that he spent less than $5 "for incidental expenses," such as a $1.25 box lunch purchased during a stop in Chicago. A first-class ticket, providing better accommodations and food, would have cost him $59.85 more.[13]

Even relative to transcontinental bus travel, coast-to-coast air coach was a bargain. To prove the point, TWA hired a firm in 1954 to send a person across the continent on a commercial bus trip. The traveler tracked every expense, including meals and hotel rooms. The transcontinental bus traveler spent more than $110—roughly equal to the price of air coach. Instead of spending uncomfortable and tiring days aboard a bus, travelers could cross the continent in mere hours for the same price.[14]

A 1951 advertisement for TWA employed the heartwarming scene of a father with his family at the airport. Even though the father had to travel on business, he could be home before the next day, thanks to the speed of air travel. (From the author's collection)

Scheduled Airline, Railroad, and Interstate Bus Service

From the nineteenth century until the mid-twentieth, railroads were the chief public carrier of intercity passengers in the United States. In 1916, railroads carried 98 percent of such passengers (approximately 1 billion). Facing increasing pressure from the private automobile, American railroads experienced a drop in passenger traffic during the 1920s. But even when railroads accumulated 34 billion passenger miles in 1929, airlines that year could boast of a mere 35 million passenger miles. And even the fledgling bus lines carried 15 percent of all commercial intercity passenger traffic in 1929. Ten years later, railroads were still king among commercial passenger carriers, with 23.7 billion passenger miles (70 percent of the total), buses came in a second with 9.5 billion passenger miles (28 percent), and air carriers were a distant third with 800 million passenger miles (2 percent).

During the Second World War, domestic passenger traffic aboard railroads spiked to nearly 98 billion passenger miles in 1944, only to drop off steeply after the war. Unlike the railroads, postwar bus traffic decreased only slightly from a peak of over 27 billion passenger miles in 1945 to a nadir of 19 billion passenger miles in 1960 before rebounding to a level between 22 and 28 billion passenger miles annually through the 1980s. Air travel also increased during the war, to over 4 billion passenger miles in 1945, despite the government's acquisition of commercial airliners for wartime service overseas. The airlines racked up over 7 billion passenger miles in 1946. Like the other modes of commercial passenger intercity transportation, the airlines experienced a dip in passenger traffic in the immediate postwar years. However, starting in 1949, domestic airlines in the United States amassed ever-increasing passenger-mile totals each year through the 1960s.

Interestingly, all three modes totaled roughly equal passenger mile records in the mid-1950s. With 26 billion passenger miles in 1951, passenger traffic aboard airlines eclipsed that on railroads for the first time. The airlines quickly became the dominant commercial mode of passenger transportation in the United States. Annual passenger-mile totals jumped from 30 billion in 1960 to 53 billion in 1965 and nearly doubled again within the next five years, to 110 billion. In the 1970s the total rose to 212 billion, and by 1990 the airlines were racking up 345 billion annual passenger miles, whereas Amtrak could claim only a relatively minuscule 6 billion. One hundred years after the Wright Brothers flew at Kitty Hawk, North Carolina, airlines in America boasted more than 500 billion annual passenger miles.

Sources: F. A. Smith, *Transportation in America*; Carter, *Historical Statistics of United States*; Stover, *Routledge Historical Atlas of the American Railroads*; U.S. Department of Transportation, Research and Innovative Technology Administration, Bureau of Transportation Statistics, *National Transportation Statistics*, table 1-37, http://www.bts.gov/publications/national_transportation_statistics/ (accessed April 12, 2007).

Coach service appealed primarily to people traveling for reasons other than business. For instance, an August 1956 survey of United Air Lines passengers traveling more than 1,000 miles revealed that 6 percent of those flying on business held coach-class tickets. Two-thirds of surveyed coach passengers were traveling for pleasure. Among first-class passengers, 38 percent were traveling for business reasons and 34 percent for pleasure. An additional 10 to 12 percent of both first-class and coach passengers were combining business and pleasure.[15]

Landscapes from Above

Renowned geographer and historian Bernard DeVoto wrote one of the best-known accounts of a coast-to-coast flight in his regular *Harper's Magazine* column. Entitled "Easy Chair," it described his experiences flying from Washington, D.C., to Los Angeles, via Denver, on a United Air Lines Douglas DC-6 in 1952. The airplane soared "above the weather," thousands of feet higher than the airplanes of a decade or two earlier, thanks to the development of cabin pressurization.[16]

DeVoto spent much of his time gazing out the window as his flight droned across the continent in "the smoothest and most relaxing travel." But if the passenger did not keep in touch with the passing geography far below, DeVoto insisted, boredom would result. Maps were essential tools for identifying rivers, mountain ranges, and cities along the route. In flight, DeVoto noted the Mississippi River and the perfect patches of Iowa farmland, one square mile each. He marveled at the flooding Missouri River, spreading its muddy water far beyond its banks. Over the sandhills of Nebraska, he sensed the pilot turning south toward Denver before the Rocky Mountains came into view. Flying with a map close at hand, DeVoto was participating in what one passenger of the era called "a superior sort of geographical solitaire, played out on a board of endlessly unexpected beauty and meaning."[17]

After a stop in Denver, DeVoto's flight took to the air once again. As the skies began to darken, DeVoto glanced about the cabin and noted how "looking out of the window brought a sense of peace and order to passengers": "They were physically removed from the busy world below, and that physical distance could put psychological distance between the passengers and their earthbound cares." Travelers could relax within the dimly lit cabin and watch the glimmer of passing lights far below.[18]

Outside his window DeVoto perceived the "faint silver ribbon that was unmistakably the Green River." Glistening snow blanketed southern Wyoming and northern Utah, and the lights of Salt Lake City and the other cities along the Wasatch illuminated the night sky, silhouetting the range's craggy outline as the plane approached

Sign of a good time to fly

When ground travel is slowed to a snail's pace or bogged down altogether, when the somber voice of winter is whispering, "Put off your trip"—don't listen. Because there's one clear road that never needs a snowplow. It's that wide, smooth path *above* surface storms and clouds where luxury TWA Skyliners fly—the high way thousands of passengers take daily right through the winter.

This year, try the swift, comfortable TWA way and

discover for yourself how relaxed and really easy winter travel can be. Settle down in a roomy Skyliner seat, enjoy warm, friendly TWA service. Yes, and marvel as you will at the amazing smoothness of five-mile-a-minute Skyliner flight.

Whether your goal is across the U.S. or across the Atlantic, remember this: it's a *pleasant* crossing by world-proved, winter-proved TWA. See your travel agent or call TWA for information and reservations.

A snow-obscured road sign somewhere in the Middle West juxtaposed with a TWA Constellation airliner aimed to convince people to fly rather than forgo travel because winter weather has earthbound transportation halted. (From the author's collection)

from the east. Beyond Salt Lake City, the dark spaces between small clusters of lights grew larger. As the airliner continued westward, DeVoto noticed the multicolored lights of Reno, Nevada, a city that he proclaimed to be "far more beautiful by night than it ever is by day." All cities, in DeVoto's opinion, appeared in greater splendor after dark than when daylight revealed their imperfections.

While the lights of cities regaled the airline passenger at night, another sight could strike a chord of fear. The sparks and flash of engine exhausts could light up the night sky. One writer compared the glow of exhaust from the engines of a DC-7 to fireworks on the Fourth of July. Even though she knew that it was "just the hot exhaust gases escaping," she still believed that it looked "like the burning of Rome." Flames shot from the turbocompound engines' short exhausts whenever the plane climbed or descended or the pilot reversed propellers after landing. After hearing reports that the flames frightened novice passengers, American Airlines instructed its stewardesses to forewarn passengers over the public address system that the flames they might see out the windows were part of normal operations.[19]

Nonstop Coast-to-Coast

The turbocompound was the ultimate in piston-engine development before the introduction of the turbojet and the propjet. Exhaust gases from a piston engine spun a turbine, which in turn powered a supercharger that forced the fuel-air mixture at sea-level pressure into the cylinders to give the engine greater power at higher altitudes. The overall arrangement was more efficient than the piston engine alone and provided aircraft with increased range. The turbocompound engines on the Douglas DC-7 and the Lockheed Super Constellation allowed the airliners to go coast-to-coast nonstop in about 8 hours. TWA became the first airline to offers nonstop transcontinental air service aboard its 60-seat Lockheed Super Constellations on October 19, 1953. The next month, American Airlines introduced nonstop transcontinental flights on its 58-passenger DC-7s. Pushed by the powerful winds of the high-altitude eastbound jet stream, an American DC-7 flew from Los Angeles to New York in 1955 6 hours and 10 minutes, over a route scheduled to take about 8 hours. First observed during the Second World War, the narrow river of strong horizontal winds blowing west to east across the northern Pacific Ocean and North America at high altitudes became known as the jet stream. Aircraft traveling eastbound and capable of high-altitude flight could take advantage of these winds, which sometimes exceeded 250 miles per hour. Westbound flights, which typically took more than 8 hours to arrive in California, usually faced the jet stream, so they avoided it whenever possible.[20]

The culmination of transcontinental speed by a piston-engine airliner, United Air Lines DC-7 Mainliners could cross the continent in under 8 hours. (From the collection of Dr. Charles C. Quarles)

Soon after the Lockheed Super Constellation made nonstop coast-to-coast crossings possible in 1953, the famed red-eye overnight flights between Los Angeles and New York enabled Angelenos and New Yorkers to swap cities without losing precious daylight. The flight took more than 8 hours, and passengers emerged sleep-starved with bloodshot eyes—hence the term "red-eye." Nevertheless, the service proved popular, especially with entertainers, and inspired John Sebastian, of the 1960s group Lovin' Spoonful, to pen a song titled "Red-Eye Express."[21]

Coping with Noise

The cacophony of engines and propellers could be disconcerting—particularly for first-flighters and those who were hypersensitive to every sound aboard an airliner. Writer Louisa Comstock described herself as one of a "race of travelers known as Listeners": "The minute we step into any plane we become miserably, chronically alert to every whisper of the engines, doggedly expecting the worst at the slightest change of sound or rhythm. And we suspect our name is Legion." In an attempt to overcome her fears associated with in-flight sounds, the author spoke with a United Air Lines captain, who explained the sources of the sounds heard throughout the flight. In turn, Comstock shared that information an article to calm the fears of her fellow "Listeners."[22]

According to the pilot, the engines and propellers made different sounds throughout the flight, based on the throttle settings and pitch of the propellers. During takeoff the engines made the most noise. The throttles were wide open, the propellers biting fine slices of air at a high rate of revolutions per minute. After attaining cruise altitude, when the pilot reduced throttle and changed the propeller to a coarser pitch, the cabin became quieter. But during the flight the pilot might need to climb over weather or buck a headwind, necessitating more power—and increasing the noise level inside the cabin. And aerodynamic noise along the fuselage surface penetrated the cabin from takeoff to landing.

Anticipating the worst and alert to every sound, passengers were often startled if the pilot slowed the engines to "desludge" the superchargers, for the superchargers had to be periodically cleaned to maintain their efficiency. The sudden quietness of the engines could lead passengers to believe momentarily that the airplane had lost power and was headed down, but the engines soon belched back to life, the apparent crisis over.

The sounds of landing could also distress passengers. The moaning and clanking of moving flaps and landing gear were not the only sounds to frighten them. Comstock observed that "one of the greatest of all safety procedures can scare you out of your wits—the sudden, plane-shaking roar of the propellers when the pilot reverses them at high power, just after the plane has reached the ground," bringing the plane to a rapid stop.

Advances in In-Flight Service

While the loud noises and vibrations of flight were an unpleasant aspect of air travel in the 1950s, in-flight service typically proved to be a more enjoyable part of the journey. In contrast to the deprivation and inconvenience aboard the nonscheduled lines the late 1940s and 1950s, the scheduled airlines plied passengers with luxury. American offered a service called the Captain's Flagship aboard its DC-6s in the 1950s, complete with elegant meals placed before the passenger on satin tablecloths. Passengers loved it. Called the Mercury, American's transcontinental service featured a similar level of service. Passengers walked on a red carpet to their waiting Douglas DC-7 aircraft. Once inside, they took a seat they had preselected. Assigned seating was a new feature for the major airlines. In the early 1950s, TWA also had a similar practice that allowed ticketed passengers to specify, at check-in, which seats they preferred on the flight. Mercury passengers enjoyed drinks before and after meals while seated in chairs that one industry observer declared "the most comfortable yet." Sculpted out of foam rubber, the seat cushions were comfortable for long flights and had contour backs and headrests.[23]

Hoping to differentiate its coach-class service from the uncomfortably crowded planes and no-frills service others offered, American Airlines named its coach service the Royal Coachman. The airline hired actor Eddie Nugent to appear in television advertisements and at inaugural flights of the service. Royal Coachman passengers dined

Royal Coachman service aboard American Airlines DC-7s offered some frills during nonstop flights at discount prices. (From the collection of Dr. Charles C. Quarles)

on meals featuring stuffed celery rings, Hungarian beef goulash, poppy-seed noodles, lima beans and corn, tossed green salad, and a dinner roll. Served with the ubiquitous coffee, tea, or milk, desserts such as apple strudel completed the meals.[24]

The advent of large four-engine planes after the Second World War meant changes in meal service. The airplanes flew faster, 300 to 400 miles per hour, abbreviating mealtimes aloft. They also carried more people, requiring additional stewardesses to serve meals in a reasonable amount of time. Airlines moved more phases of meal preparation to facilities on the ground. Preheated and precooled meals took less time to prepare in flight. Installation of new, larger galleys also facilitated faster service.[25]

During the war, other improvements in airborne meal service arrived after James Kerby Dobbs got into the business. A restaurant owner from the South, Dobbs had helped an airsick stewardess aboard a 1941 flight over Texas. Noting that the in-flight food was unappetizing even to hungry passengers, Dobbs saw a business opportunity. He believed he could develop a food service company to provide airline passengers with hot, tasty meals.[26]

He succeeded. After purchasing an airport restaurant in his hometown of Memphis, Dobbs soon earned a reputation for supplying some of the best packaged meals for airlines available anywhere in the United States. "Meals by Hull-Dobbs" soon produced food at 21 airports and held contracts with 16 domestic airlines, including TWA, Eastern, National, Delta, and Continental. Hull-Dobbs kitchens solved the problem of egg preparation for airborne consumption. Completely cooked eggs continued to harden if kept at high temperature until a stewardess was ready to serve them. Hull-Dobbs discovered that the secret to serving eggs aloft was as simple as undercooking them in the kitchen and then allowing them to continue cooking in heated containers aboard the airliner.[27]

Another innovator, Jim Marriott, founded the Marriott Corporation to serve airlines' in-flight catering needs. The company thrived in the postwar era before becoming part of Cater Air and eventually LSG Sky Chefs—one of the largest airline caterers, with a history dating back to American Airlines' creation of Sky Chefs in the 1940s.[28]

Some airlines continued to use their own kitchens for food preparation. TWA's Kansas City facility prepared more than 70 percent of the airline's meals, while caterers supplied the rest. The centralized system worked because of the rapid freezing of each dish component separately before distribution to six TWA kitchens in other parts of the nation. Highly trained chefs and nutritionists formulated the menus, cooked the food, then froze it, packed it, and sent it out to the other kitchens for reconstitution and assembly before being placed aboard airliners. By the late 1940s the Kansas City kitchen produced nearly four tons of meals each week. TWA claimed that the seemingly elaborate system was more efficient than others and saved money because it could eliminate waste due to delayed flights, buy quantities of goods in season, and hire highly trained cooks only for its single kitchen.[29]

As airline food service increased in quality, so did the cost to the airline. Western Airlines, one of the first to offer in-flight meals, petitioned the Civil Aeronautics Board in 1948 for permission to stop serving complimentary meals on its flights. While considering a 10 percent fare hike in August 1948, the CAB had cited a study of the 16 major domestic airlines showing they could have saved nearly $11 million in 1947 if they had not served in-flight meals. Western's president, Terrell C. Drinkwater, pointed out that his airline had spent $339,733 for meal service during the first 10 months of 1948, the equivalent of more than 5 percent of gross passenger revenues.[30]

Subsequently, Western offered meals only aboard its longer flights. Thus, fewer than 50 percent of its customers had the opportunity to consume meals, and a quarter of those who were offered meals refused them. While roughly a third of its total passengers ate in-flight meals, all Western passengers paid for the service through their ticket price. Drinkwater concluded that the cost to the customer and the airline was not worth the return. "When Western introduced meals aloft in 1928, one of the desired results was lots of publicity," he observed. "But now we have reached the point in air transportation where we must decide whether the main tent or the sideshows are going to support the circus. No other transportation system gives away 'free' meals, and why should we?" Allowing Western to cease serving in-flight meals, the CAB also permitted the airline to drop its fares by 5 percent over a six-month trial period in 1949.[31]

Drinkwater's idea of eliminating complimentary meals to save the customer money was ahead of its time. Some passengers avoided Western during the six-month trial period. United had protested the loudest against Western's proposal, charging that it would be forced to follow Western's lead and reduce the price of its nonmeal flights by 5 percent. But, instead, United gained large numbers of passengers who shunned Western during the trial period.[32]

Air travelers liked the idea of in-flight meals, but frequent flyers quickly tired of airline food. Bernard DeVoto opined: "The airlines will hear no complaint from me if they go back to the box lunch they used to serve, and served well. They ran an excellent lunch counter in those days; they run a poor restaurant now. I have seldom had even a mediocre meal at it; most are definitely bad. Chair-bound for hours, I would trade the counterfeit banquet for a sandwich and a cocktail." By the 1960s, in-flight food decreased in importance for a majority of passengers because of the advent of the jetliners. The transcontinental trip that once required days and multiple stops could now be made in one giant leap spanning a mere six hours or less. Therefore opportunities for meals were reduced to one or two. Passengers could quite possibly eat before leaving one coast and wait until arriving at the other before partaking once more.[33]

American Airlines pioneered coast-to-coast jet service on January 25, 1959. Its new Boeing 707 jetliners ushered in a new era of speed and comfort for transcontinental passengers who could enjoy cocktails in the stratosphere during the four-and-one-half-hour flight. (From the author's collection)

Across the continent in 4½ hours on American's Jet Flagships

seats in the spacious cabin give you more privacy. You can see more because there is more window area. Ingenious innovations in lighting and air conditioning are yours to enjoy. Deluxe Mercury and economical Royal Coachman services will be offered in separate cabin sections on every flight.

A whole new world of flight. From a velvet smooth take-off, your 707 Jet Flagship will lift you promptly to radar-guided skyways, at tranquil cruising altitudes, far above or around the weather. Vibration is gone and engine noise incredibly reduced. At your destination, your baggage delivery will be speeded by another new convenience—American's luggage expediter system.

American Airlines invites you to be among the first to share the limitless opportunities of jet travel—the real pleasure of jet flight.

The Boeing 707 Jet Flagship is the most tested airplane ever to enter airline service

The prototype of the 707 made its initial flight in July, 1954. It has been flown continuously ever since, undergoing four years of the most thorough testing ever given any commercial airliner.

AMERICAN AIRLINES
First with Jets across the U.S.A.

Offering Alcohol on Flights

Until 1949, domestic airlines in the United States did not serve alcohol. Passengers were even prohibited from bringing aboard their own private supply of liquid comfort. European airlines took a more liberal view. From their earliest beginnings, European airlines dispensed alcohol to passengers. Great Britain's Imperial Airways served a selection of port, whiskey, sherry, gin, brandy, and lager, each available for a given price. Yet in the United States a Commerce Department rule against the transportation of intoxicating liquor or drunk passengers aboard commercial airplanes—a product of the Prohibition era—coupled with the fear that critics would decry the mixing of flying and alcohol, prompted U.S. airlines to steer clear of liquor. Pan American was an exception. Competing with European airlines on trans-Atlantic routes, Juan Trippe's airline served liquor and complimentary wine on some flights in the 1940s.[34]

Intoxicated passengers could be a danger to themselves as well as to the entire flight and had sometimes been troublesome. Before a flight to San Francisco in the late 1920s, Boeing Air Transport pilot Al De Gormo's single passenger, a businessman from Salt Lake City, boarded the Boeing 40 with his own supply of whiskey. De Gormo allowed it, betting that the man would get drunk and pass out during the bumpy flight. Over the Nevada desert, engrossed in the cockpit as he flew by instruments, De Gormo noticed that the airplane seemed out of balance. To his utter surprise and alarm, he looked out at the wing, where the inebriated passenger, holding onto a wing strut, grinned and waved at him. The pilot yelled at the man until he retreated into the small passenger compartment. A stern rebuff at an emergency field seemingly convinced the repentant passenger not to leave the cabin again during flight. However, back in the air minutes later, the passenger once again gave wing walking a try. The repeated shouts from De Gormo, as well as the chilly Sierra Mountain air, finally persuaded the man to crawl back inside the plane.[35]

As a safety measure, airlines could prevent passengers from boarding if they were obviously drunk. For example, seated in a corner at the Newark Airport while waiting for an American Airlines transcontinental flight in 1938, a young mother with an infant looked up as an intoxicated man tripped over her feet. He apologized with an exaggerated bow and then tottered away. The man held a ticket for the flight, but an airline ticket agent kept him under careful supervision to determine if his inebriated condition would endanger the flight. The agent had full authority to cancel the man's ticket.[36]

That same year, Olympic swimmer Eleanor Holm became intoxicated from liquor that she brought aboard an American Airlines flight. Arriving in Tucson, Holm emerged from the plane stark naked. Before departing, airline employees tied her to a tree so she would not wander off before coming out of her drunken stupor.[37]

Airline captain Hy Sheridan wrote of an intoxicated passenger aboard an American Airlines flight in the postwar era. Although the airlines had a strict policy of allowing no alcoholic beverages in flight, neither served nor brought aboard by passengers, a man on a long-distant flight entered the cabin apparently sober but soon displayed signs of intoxication. The stewardess failed to discover his secret, exclaiming to Captain Sheridan, "He's getting drunk without drinking!" Intrigued, Sheridan walked through the cabin, carefully observing the man. The passenger gave Sheridan "a soggy, self-satisfied smile" over the top of his newspaper—he was clearly drunk.

Watching from the galley at the rear of the plane, Sheridan noticed that he never turned the pages of his newspaper. When he presumably read to the bottom of the page, his head would dip and then rise as if starting at the top of the page. After some time Sheridan realized what was not immediately evident. Walking to the man's seat, Sheridan confirmed that the man was not reading the newspaper—that was only a cover for him to drop his head low enough to suck on two straws poking from a bottle of whiskey in his coat pocket. The man did not object when Sheridan confiscated the bottle. Asked why he had done it, the passenger replied, "Great big company says little man can't get drunk on airliner. But I did. Now I'm going to sleep."[38]

Some passengers believed that alcohol and airline travel were a good combination. Consuming alcohol could help nervous passengers remove themselves psychologically from the air travel experience. After they had imbibed liquor, their anxieties and discomforts melted into the background. Offering such liquid comfort in flight might prove a valuable lure for the airlines.

Airlines periodically surveyed customers regarding their opinion of serving alcohol onboard. While the general opinion of 1930s passengers favored strict prohibition of liquor on the airlines, a United Air Lines survey conducted during the war revealed a surprise. Of the 19,000 respondents, nearly 70 percent favored cocktails served before in-flight meals.[39]

Coinciding with the start of nonstop transcontinental flights in the mid-1950s, American and TWA quietly began to serve alcoholic beverages. Limited to two drinks per flight, passengers had to pay for the privilege. They responded positively to the service, and soon United gave in to the competition. During United's men-only Executive flights between Chicago and New York, passengers could sip cocktails priced at $3 each.[40]

Western Airlines soon joined the liquor service bandwagon in 1954 with its famed "champagne flights" along the West Coast. TWA already served champagne on coast-to-coast flights, but only on request. European airlines, such as SAS, had a lengthy history of champagne service. To compete with United on West Coast routes, Western's leadership created an innovative experience that passengers relished. Complimentary champagne arrived with a steak dinner, complete with a salad and a roll. Women received fresh orchids and free perfume, while men gladly accepted free cigars. The champagne flights contributed approximately 20 percent of Western's increased traffic in 1955. As one Western executive explained, "They liked champagne for three reasons: They thought it was stronger than it really [was], they considered it mildly wicked, and it relaxed them." Another airline official noted that "for many people, a flight in an airplane very definitely [was] a special occasion," to which champagne added "a nice touch." Evidently, most passengers accepted the complimentary bubbly. Western estimated that 93 percent of its champagne flight passengers drank at least one glass.[41]

Yet along with alcohol service came new problems. In 1955 the Airline Stewardess Association, as well as pilot unions, asked the airlines to end all in-flight liquor service. The employees cited unruly passengers who had too much to drink as the primary reason for their petitions. Drunken passengers had taken swings at pilots in the cockpit, stewardesses had to deal with inebriated passengers who acted up in flight, and some stewardesses had been cut when champagne bottles occasionally exploded. Disruptive passenger behavior added to the attendants' responsibilities and could endanger the safety of the flight. For example, a drunken Hollywood producer once took off his shoe and attempted to knock out a window because he felt too warm. If he had been successful, the explosive decompression of the pressurized cabin would have been catastrophic. Commenting on the issue of liquor and the airlines, one editorialist emphatically stated: "At airports and on planes, liquor has no more rightful place than in automobile traffic." Clearly, not everyone was thrilled with in-flight alcohol service.[42]

Beverages

Scotch

Martini

Manhattan

Bourbon

Vodka Martini

Canadian

Dubonnet

Beer

Tomato Juice

Ginger Ale

Salted Nuts Will Accompany
The Beverage Service

AMERICAN AIRLINES

T-351

American Airlines offered its jet-setting passengers in the early 1960s a variety of alcoholic beverages listed within this menu. Passengers could select from a range of drinks including martinis and Manhattans, as well as scotch, beer, Dubonnet, and bourbon. (From the author's collection)

The Civil Aeronautics Board contacted the president of the Air Transport Association (ATA) in the fall of 1955, warning him that the airlines serving alcohol needed to take "corrective steps" if they wished to continue the service. Seizing the initiative, the ATA suggested that airlines adopt a common code regulating in-flight liquor service. Recommended items for the code included not permitting clearly intoxicated people to board flights and not serving drinks on flights of less than two hours' duration. These were merely tentative suggestions for airlines to police themselves, but the airlines flatly rejected the proposed code, declaring the issue to be the responsibility of each air carrier, not the industry as a whole.[43]

Next, Congress threatened action. In 1956 a House committee set forth a bill requiring prohibition of all in-flight alcohol service on domestic flights. Under pressure, six U.S. airlines voluntarily agreed to limit in-flight alcohol consumption. American, Northwest, National, Eastern, TWA, and United Air Lines would refuse to give individual passengers more than two 1.6-ounce containers of hard liquor per trip. The airlines noted, however, that they would not restrict beer and wine service. A pilots' union representative argued that this action did not go far enough, because altitude increased alcohol's effect on the body. According to the union representative, two in-flight drinks at altitude had the same effect as four consumed on the ground.[44]

After being accosted by a drunken passenger on a domestic flight, Speaker of the House Sam Rayburn pushed for a bill forbidding alcohol service on airliners, only to see it die in the Senate. The following year, Senators Strom Thurmond and Richard L. Neuberger drafted legislation demanding no alcohol service aboard domestic or international flights. Countering the charge that alcohol endangered the nation's airlines, the CAB revealed that in not a single case among nearly 2,000 recent complaints of drunks on airliners had the inebriated passenger endangered the flight.[45]

In January 1960, Elwood Quesada, the administrator of the Federal Aviation Agency, gave in to requests from pilots and flight attendants who wanted a reduction of liquor consumption on commercial flights. Quesada ruled that no commercial air passengers could drink alcohol except that which crew members served. Going a step further, Quesada ordered flight crews not to serve alcohol to anyone appearing intoxicated.[46]

In 1966, American, TWA, and United began to charge for alcoholic beverages served to coach-class passengers aboard coast-to-coast flights. Drinks were still complimentary in first class. This practice has continued into the twenty-first century.[47]

Commuter Tickets

Just as alcohol became more accepted in the 1950s, so did the purchase of airline tickets on credit. In the early days of commercial air travel, flying was primarily a cash-and-carry proposition—people paid the entire fare before an airline issued tickets. Then, in the early 1930s, American Airlines began to offer scrip books. An individual or a company spent $425 for a booklet worth $500 in air travel. Frequent air travelers wishing to impress clients or colleagues flashed scrip books as a status symbol. These soon gave way to identification cards linking the bearer with a prepaid account containing a deposit of at least $425. Frequent air travelers liked the convenience of the card and the automatic 15 percent off standard fares. But cardholders still prepaid for all tickets. This changed in 1936, when the airline industry inaugurated the Universal Air Travel Plan (UATP) to facilitate corporate travel payment. Air passengers could use an Air Travel Card, one of the first credit cards, to buy tickets on any participating airline and receive a bill later. Besides the convenience of deferred payment, a 15 percent discount on tickets charged to the card made the plan even more attractive to frequent air travelers. Resuming after a suspension during the war, the UATP rapidly expanded, with nearly 600,000 cardholders by 1953. In the 1960s the CAB ruled that the airlines participating in the plan could no longer require a $425 deposit. At the same time, large credit card companies such as American Express and Diners Club persuaded American Airlines and Delta Airlines, among others, to accept their cards. The concept of "fly now, pay later" created a surge in middle-class passengers.[48]

Flight Insurance

Another change following the war was that flight insurance became a more routine part of air travel. Most air passengers in the early decades of air travel were well-to-do and carried significant amounts of life insurance. However, believing that air travel carried with it an inordinate level of risk, insurance underwriters placed restrictions on policies for people who frequently flew on commercial airlines. In 1930, for every 100 million passenger miles on domestic airline flights, 28.2 passengers died in airline accidents. Even in 1936, when the rate had dropped to 10 passenger deaths, less than 4 percent of the leading U.S. life insurance companies issued policies without limits on domestic air travel. Safety gains in the 1930s reduced the corresponding accidental death rate to 1.2 by the end of the decade. Recognizing air travel's significant safety gains, at least 65 percent of life insurance underwriters placed no air travel restrictions on new policies issued immediately after the war, and another 22 percent offered policies if anticipated air travel did not exceed approximately 50,000 miles annually. Amazingly, only two decades had elapsed between the time when airlines began carrying a significant number of passengers and when most life insurance companies accepted that air travel was no more dangerous than rail travel. This change epitomizes the great strides made in the 1930s with the development of the modern airliner and safety measures in the air and on the ground.[49]

In 1929, insurance companies offered the first supplemental flight insurance to airline passengers in the United States. Train travel policies cost $0.25 for 24 hours of coverage. Because an aircraft could cover the same distance as a train in approximately four hours, insurers set rates at $0.25 for four hours of coverage. In the spring of 1930, Travelers Insurance Company of Hartford, Connecticut, offered insurance on a per-flight basis to passengers on Boeing (soon to be United Air Lines). The cost was $2 for $5,000 coverage, and the policy expired 24 hours after purchase.[50]

The amount of coverage rose rapidly as air traveler fatality rates dropped to below a single death per 100 million passenger miles in the early 1950s. Air passengers aboard scheduled lines could purchase $50,000 of air-trip accident insurance for $2.50 in 1952. Two years later the benefit increased to $65,000.[51]

Nearly 5 million of the 34 million Americans who flew on commercial airlines in 1955 purchased supplemental air trip insurance. The process of buying air trip insurance was easy, as underwriters placed policy-vending machines near ticket counters in airports. Any passenger could insert one to 10 quarters and out popped a policy to sign that provided coverage from $6,250 to more than $60,000. First appearing in New York City's terminal after the war, the machines freed airline ticket agents from the time-consuming task of filling out customer insurance forms. The increasing safety of air travel meant that underwriters could raise coverage levels and still make healthy profits. For example, the three primary companies offering air trip insurance paid out $376,000 in 1954 but grossed $2.5 million in premiums. Insurers discovered that women purchased fewer policies than men, and coach passengers purchased more than first-class passengers did.[52]

Supplemental insurance did not relieve airlines of their liability to passengers. But one distinct advantage of supplemental insurance was that claims were paid promptly for a set amount, unlike settlements with an airline after an incident left a passenger maimed or killed. Airlines carried liability insurance, in their capacity as common carriers, to provide for injured passengers or for the families of passengers who died in air accidents.[53]

Women, Too

Traditionally reluctant to fly because of safety issues, women generally avoided air travel for a variety of reasons. *Ladies' Home Journal* conducted a survey in 1947 regarding women's attitudes toward air travel. Approximately 70 percent of the 2,000 women polled had never flown on a commercial air carrier. The comparatively high cost of air travel, coupled with inferior facilities at airports and the need for a car after arriving at the airport, kept them away from the airlines. Despite their reasons for not setting foot in an airliner, the survey found that more than 70 percent of women who had not yet flown on a commercial airline intended to do so sometime in the future. Why were these women interested in air travel? The survey revealed that they were attracted to the advantages of "speed, cleanliness, courtesy, and ease of traveling with small children."[54]

The advent of coach-class fares on the transcontinental airlines attracted middle-class women in record numbers. After making periodic checks of the gender ratio on their coast-to-coast flights leaving Los Angeles in 1950, TWA and American Airlines discovered that half of their passengers were female. Coach-class fares lured women aboard because most of them traveled for pleasure, not business, and thus paid for their ticket out of their own pockets. Nevertheless, the airlines still did not perceive an immediate or significant shift of ridership from the nonscheduled lines to the new coach class on the major airlines. Perhaps women's economic status played the determining role, because a transcontinental coach ticket on a scheduled airline cost up to $50 more than a comparable ticket on a nonsked.[55]

Airline marketing to women was not new. Several airlines in the 1930s had hired women to conduct publicity campaigns targeting the American female—even Amelia Earhart had helped publicize TAT. Thanks to such campaigns, Eastern and United boast a 25 to 30 percent increase in female ridership over a three-year span in the mid-1930s.[56]

In 1950, TWA launched a new sort of advertising campaign aimed at women. The airline hired five female travel advisers and gave each of them the fictitious name Mary Gordon. The Mary Gordons crisscrossed the nation, speaking to women at social gatherings and in private homes. According to *Business Week*, "Mary Gordons [told] women what to wear, where to go, how to pack, what to see and do." TWA believed that education was the key to filling airline seats with women in the 1950s. As TWA press relations director Ed Boughton explained in 1954, "Women are no longer tied down to their homes. They have the money to fly, and they want to go places and see and do things." With growing affluence and the advent of coach class, vacationing women became a growing phenomenon aboard airlines such as TWA. Partly because of the Mary Gordon campaign, the airline learned that housewives made up the "largest occupational group flying vacation trips."[57]

Hoping to attract more women travelers, TWA's Mary Gordon campaign produced pamphlets suggesting gender-specific wardrobe items to pack for a trip on the airline. (From the author's collection)

A professional-looking stewardess gazes from the cover of an American Airlines welcome booklet dating from 1952. The 50-page publication contained a wealth of information about every aspect of the air journey. It even had a glossary of terms common to air transport. Upon boarding, passengers received a packet of information, including a welcome booklet, a system map, postcards, and a comment form to fill out and send to American Airlines president C. R. Smith at the airline's expense. (From the author's collection)

Women were taking to the skies, and they seemed to enjoy the experience. In the 1940s and 1950s, large airlines such as American and Eastern provided cards in flight to passengers, asking them to write down complaints or compliments. Nearly a third of the compliments airlines received directly focused on stewardesses, and a large percentage of cards praising stewardesses came from female passengers. These compliments reflected the genuine friendliness most women felt toward the female flight attendants.[58]

However, not all women took kindly to stewardesses. An American Airlines pilot explained: "There is a species of female who seems to regard it as a point of honor to lord it over the stewardess. It is the sort of thing which makes our girls wonder if they aren't just aerial waitresses after all, and if they couldn't do better at Jerry's Diner." The pilot observed that some female passengers seemed to expect royal treatment from a personal lady-in-waiting. Luckily for the airlines, such passenger expectations were not the norm.[59]

When they flew, women rarely traveled alone. Perhaps accompanying a husband on a business trip or going with the entire family on a holiday, they usually had other family members in company. After the introduction of coach-class service, women and children flew mostly in the coach section, not first class. Therefore, first class was primarily the domain of affluent males. Recognizing this fact, American Airlines targeted a promotional brochure at the unmarried female passenger looking for a potential mate: "If you are interested in meeting a man en route, consider flying first class — at least one way. Since most businessmen, and very few women, travel this way, you'll find it easier to see, and be seen." A first-class ticket gave businessmen a place to meet other businessmen without the distractions of many women and children, while some matrimonially minded women may have bought a first-class ticket to take advantage of the lack of competition.[60]

Men Only

While most airlines concentrated on increasing the number of women among their passengers, United Air Lines started a men-only service in 1953 called the New York Executive. The daily afternoon flight between New York and Chicago catered to men who enjoyed smoking cigars and pipes (prohibited on other commercial flights) in a relaxed atmosphere. A printed list of house rules advised passengers to relax, kick off their shoes, slip off their suit coats and ties, take out their pipes and complimentary cigars, and enjoy the ride in an environment free of female passengers. United stewardesses served alcohol and steak dinners, complete with baked potatoes and vegetables. In addition to Chicago and New York newspapers courtesy of the airline, United also provided in-flight closing stock market quotations. The Executive service proved so popular that four years after commencing the service, United added a second daily Executive flight.[61]

At least one woman tried to board an Executive flight. In January 1958, Mrs. Edythe Rein wished to fly on the Executive ostensibly "for business purposes." Rein was the senior vice president of a New York firm supplying shows to television. She was also an active champion of women's rights. United turned her away from the flight because of her gender. Even an appeal to the Civil Aeronautics Board could not gain Rein a seat on the flight. While the CAB disapproved of "undue, unjust, or unreasonable discrimination," the board ruled that the Executive's men-only status was permissible because other flights, just as good, were available.[62]

The flight's appeal endured until the late 1960s, when ridership slipped to a dismal 40 percent of capacity. Judging from the abundance of empty seats on later Executive flights, men of the late 1960s preferred to travel in the company of women rather than in the atmosphere of an exclusive men's club. The last Executive flight left Newark on a Wednesday evening in January 1970. Some of the passengers on the final flight expressed sadness that an era was coming to an end. One 49-year-old executive from Illinois replied to a reporter's question: "You want to know the real reason why we're here? It's not because of no women. It's because there are no squalling kids. We get enough of that at home." On the other hand, the National Organization for Women declared a victory, asserting that United gave up the flights because NOW had picketed United's headquarters in protest the previous year, as well as filing complaints with the CAB. Officially, United ended the Executive flights because they were no longer profitable.[63]

Racial Discrimination

While airlines in the United States diligently sought to increase the numbers of female passengers, African Americans were not as welcome. The practice of racially segregating air passengers was different from the practice on other modes of transportation. By the turn of the twentieth century, every southern state had enacted legislation, known as Jim Crow laws, that specifically prohibited the mingling of blacks and whites aboard trains. Streetcars, taxis, and buses soon came under similar laws. Yet no Jim Crow laws officially segregated passengers in the air. Even to the most ardent segregationist "there was doubtless something slightly incongruous about requiring a Jim Crow compartment on a transcontinental plane, or one that did not touch the ground between New York and Miami." Few African Americans took to the skies aboard commercial airlines, however. The cost of flying was prohibitive for most of them, and those who could afford to fly found that racism existed not only on the ground but also in the air. Some airlines found excuses not to sell tickets to customers who were identified as African American. If successful in purchasing tickets, African Americans often discovered several empty seats separating them from the rest of the passengers.[64]

Major league baseball star Willie Mays and his wife, Margherite Wendell Chapman, posed in front of a TWA Lockheed 1649A Starliner on January 3, 1958, before flying from New York to San Francisco, where they would make their new home. Both the New York Giants, Willie Mays's team, and the Brooklyn Dodgers moved to California in 1958—making them the first major league teams to locate west of St. Louis. Air travel made it possible for teams such as the Los Angeles Dodgers and the San Francisco Giants to compete against the rest of the league without spending excessive amounts of time traveling on the ground. Even though Mays and his wife did not encounter racism in the air, they did experience it while attempting to purchases a new home in California. (From the TWA Archives of the St. Louis Mercantile Library at the University of Missouri–St. Louis)

One example of racial segregation aboard an airliner occurred during the Second World War. An official of the African American USO (United Service Organizations) took his assigned seat in the front of the cabin, far removed from the rest of the people on a Delta Airlines flight. When he asked a member of the flight crew why he had been seated away from the other passengers, the crew member replied that he had been assigned his seat so as to prevent his embarrassment at the behavior of the other passengers. The USO official immediately perceived he had been seated alone because of his skin color.[65]

Another example happened in February 1946. The man who was to become the first African American major league baseball player endured racism at the hands of American Airlines. Jackie Robinson and his bride of two weeks, Rachel, bought tickets on the airline from Los Angeles to Daytona Beach, where the athlete was to complete spring training. Their eastward journey was uneventful until, without explanation, the airline bumped them from the flight in New Orleans. Robinson's appeals to reboard the aircraft fell on deaf ears. The last airplane of the day departed without Robinson and his wife. Desiring something to eat, the Robinsons were denied access to the airport coffee shop. Fortunately, before they had left Los Angeles, Jackie's mother had prepared chicken dinners for them to take on the flight. She was from the South and knew about the prejudice that her son and daughter-in-law would encounter. Thankful for her foresight, the Robinsons sat on a sagging bed in a dilapidated New Orleans hotel room eating cold chicken dinners. The next day the Robinsons successfully boarded an American flight only to be told, without a plausible explanation during a stop in Pensacola, that they must find another means of transportation to Daytona Beach. The couple endured a humiliating ride in the back of a segregated bus to their destination.[66]

Federal law prohibited racial discrimination on the airlines. The Civil Aeronautics Act of 1938 included a nondiscrimination clause similar to one found in the 1935 Motor Carrier Act and originating in the Interstate Commerce Act of 1887. The clause stated: "No air carrier or foreign air carrier shall . . . subject any particular person, port, locality, or description of traffic in air transportation to any unjust discrimination or any undue or unreasonable prejudice or disadvantage in any respect whatsoever." A 1956 federal lawsuit invoked this nondiscrimination clause. Jazz singer Ella Fitzgerald and two of her touring companions claimed that Pan American World Airways had discriminated against them on the basis of race. Fitzgerald and the others had purchased first-class tickets between San Francisco and Australia, but Pan American bumped Fitzgerald's group from first class to coach for the Honolulu-to-Australia portion of the flight. The civil suit demanded $270,000 in damages under the Civil Aeronautics Act's nondiscrimination clause. The parties settled out of court for $7,500.[67]

Even though airlines did not officially discriminate between passengers on the basis of race, some airports did. Following the precedent of rail and bus depots, many airports in the segregated South enforced the use of separate facilities for whites and African Americans. Black air passengers waited to board flights in rooms separate from whites, were prohibited from eating at many airport restaurants, and had to use separate washroom facilities.

Private lawsuits and federal pressure effectively spurred the desegregation of many southern airports by the late 1950s. For a few years immediately after the Second World War, Washington National Airport racially segregated passengers until the Civil Aeronautics administrator decreed an end to the practice at the federally controlled facility in 1948. Eight years later the Civil Aeronautics Administration forbade the use of federal funds to construct portions of airports where racial segregation would be imposed. Even at a time when most rail stations and bus depots remained segregated, a 1959 study of passenger transportation facilities in some of the South's most significant cities concluded that a large number of airline terminals were "desegregated or rapidly being desegregated." Emboldened by a 1960 Supreme Court ruling that air terminal operators and concessionaires were subject to federal standards, the U.S. Justice Department sued and won a case in federal court against the city of Montgomery, Alabama, in 1961. After desegregating the Montgomery airport, the Justice Department surveyed more than 160 commercial airports in the South, revealing that various forms of segregation existed at airports in 7 of the 14 states studied. Letters from the department to officials at airports still practicing segregation resulted in all but three airports voluntarily desegregating. Legal action against New Orleans prompted the city to racially integrate its airport in 1962. Shreveport and Birmingham refused to desegregate their airports until federal courts ruled against them in Justice Department lawsuits. By the mid-1960s, all airports in the United States were officially desegregated.[68]

Changes in the Cockpit

The 1950s and 1960s also witnessed a change in how the public regarded airline pilots. Much of this change was due to the huge influx of veteran military pilots following the Second World War. No longer were the airline pilots a small fraternity in the sky. In the 1920s, airline pilots had close to celebrity status. Even by 1935, airlines in the United States employed fewer than 1,000 pilots and copilots. Fifteen years later they listed nearly 6,000 on their employment rosters.[69]

Beyond sheer numbers, the public regard of airline pilots changed with the publication of literature critical of them. Books such as George Johnson's *The Abominable Airlines*, published in 1964, spoke of airline pilots as "tarnished knights." The respect that had

In the 1950s, Hertz Drive-Ur-Self System offered the Hertz Plane-Auto Travel Plan. Hertz invited airline passengers to fly and then rent a car for ground transportation at their destination. (From the author's collection)

accompanied the title of "airline pilot" waned. Critics in the postwar era noted that as air travel became routine, pilots lost some of their luster. Cockpit doors had effectively removed pilots from passengers' view, increasing the physical and psychological divide between cockpit and cabin. Pilots also became the subjects of increasing federal scrutiny after evidence of widespread misconduct became public. Photos appeared of pilots in the cockpit reading books for pleasure, sleeping, and even groping stewardesses who sat on their laps. Air passengers began wondering if pilots were actually worthy of their admiration and trust.[70]

Johnson summarized the status of the 1960s airline pilot: "People no longer look at him in awe. They question his integrity and his ability, which in his secret heart he knows is slipping. His confidence is declining, too, as the machine gets bigger. . . . He is, in short, human like you and me." And being human, with the care of hundreds of lives in his hands each day while he zoomed through the skies, meant that only one small misstep lay between a job well done and a large loss of life.[71]

Accidents such as a midair collision over the Grand Canyon on June 30, 1956, pointed out the limitations of pilots' abilities to fly ever-faster aircraft in increasingly crowded skies. On a sunny day over northern Arizona, a TWA Super Constellation and a United DC-7 collided at 21,000 feet. Everyone aboard the planes perished, including their nearly 130 passengers. Apparently the pilots of both planes had been busy in their cockpits and did not see each other's approaching aircraft in time to avoid the collision. Airline pilots in the 1950s flew "contact" when the skies were clear, relying on their eyes and reflexes to keep from running into other aircraft. Radar-equipped ground controllers monitored the airspace around large airports, but when flying cross-country, pilots were not on any controller's radar screen. Pilots were trained to stay in lanes 10 miles wide and to follow no closer than 10 minutes behind traffic ahead of them. They kept in radio contact with ground control operators who assigned them particular altitudes. But with the number of planes in the sky steadily growing, and no radar to monitor the exact location of each plane, a collision was inevitable. The Grand Canyon disaster accelerated the passage of the Federal Aviation Act of 1958, which created the Federal Aviation Agency, tasked with ensuring the safety of air passengers and thereby gaining and keeping public confidence in commercial aviation.[72]

While pilots lost some of their freedom of movement in the skies over America, they also lost the sense of rapport with their passengers. Pilot-passenger interaction changed as a direct result of the large number of passengers aboard each flight. By the late 1940s and early 1950s, Super Constellations and DC-6s were routinely transporting nearly 100 passengers at a time. During flight, the postwar airline pilot was reduced to a disembodied voice over the public address system, a new addition to the airline travel experience.

UP-TO-THE-MINUTE FLIGHT INFORMATION ★ Suggest you check your position on route map in the seat pocket.

Date _8-8-39_ Enroute from _GLENDALE_ to _NEWARK_

Our position at _3:44_ A.M./P.M. (_EASTERN_ standard time) over _BRISTOL, VA._ (A RADIO CHECK POINT). This information was given by radiotelephone to our ground radio station at _BRISTOL_. Our next position report will be given to _BRISTOL_ at approximately _4:31_ A.M./P.M. over _ROANOKE, VA._ (A RADIO CHECK POINT). Our air speed is _172_ MPH. Ground speed _188_ MPH. Temperature outside _58_° Altitude above sea level _9000_ ft. Above ground _5000_ ft. We will arrive _WASHINGTON_ at approximately _5:38_ A.M./P.M. Flight Conditions there are _ABOVE OUR STANDARDS_ Ground Temperature _88_ °F.

REMARKS: _____

Your stewardess Miss _HEDMAN_ is eager to answer any questions. Please pass this slip to the passenger back of you. Your Stewardess will be glad to provide you with a copy of this report if requested.

AMERICAN AIRLINES Inc. CAPTAIN _HUNTER_ FIRST OFFICER _ASHLEY_

(OVER)

Before the widespread installation of public address systems in airliners after the Second World War, pilots scribbled notes to curious passengers informing them of the flight's status. By the late 1930s, airlines had created forms for this purpose. The flight information form seen here was used during an American Airlines transcontinental flight in August 1939. Passengers reading the completed form would know where they were along the airway, how fast the airliner was traveling and at what altitude, an estimated time of arrival at their destination, the outside and ground temperatures, and the names of the members of the flight crew. The stewardess's title was listed as "Miss" on the form because no stewardess was permitted to wed and keep her job in 1939. (From the author's collection)

TWA had installed some of the first commercial radio receivers for passengers aboard some of its DC-3s just prior to the Second World War. Passengers could enjoy music during the flight, and pilots needed only toggle a switch to cut in and speak over the system. In the late 1940s, American Airlines installed public-address systems in all its DC-6 airliners. Located throughout the cabins, the scratchy-sounding speakers came to life even before takeoff, when the stewardess announced the flight plan, gave current weather conditions and the weather prediction for the route, and provided information about the forthcoming meal service. In flight, the captain's voice came over the system, identifying points of interest on the ground below and giving the airliner's current speed and altitude, as well as the flight's estimated arrival time. Of course the voice over the public address system also expressed the airline's distinct pleasure at having each passenger aboard the flight. Even before the jet age, seasoned air travelers complained about the frequent, static-filled intercom messages from the flight deck. The contact was strictly one-way and impersonal. One writer compared the flight crews' excessively cheery welcome speeches over the public address system to an ever-present toothache.[73]

The changing image of airline pilots became fodder for comedians of the 1950s. Shelley Berman, in a sketch included on his Grammy Award–winning album *Inside Shelley Berman*, asked his audience to envision an airline pilot. After a long pause, Berman described what the audience had in mind—the stereotypical airline pilot straight out of the Lindbergh mold with "a crooked smile, but straight teeth." The pilot was someone who looked danger in the eye without blinking, yet always had the passengers' safety as his first priority. Once the audience was fully engaged in Berman's visualization exercise, he told them that they had heard a click over the public address system, meaning the pilot was about to speak. At this point, Berman impersonated the voice of an airline pilot—a distracted, aloof, perhaps even incompetent pilot who could hardly recall his flight's destination.[74]

The sketch made the point that although the flying public had a romanticized vision of how an airline pilot was supposed to look and behave, that image did not always match reality. America was ready for a new set of heroes—the first astronauts. By the 1950s and 1960s, the frontiers of outer space had fired the imaginations of a new generation of Americans.

A *Saturday Evening Post* cover published in 1952 captured this change well. The painting depicted a perturbed young mother boarding an airliner with her grade-school-age son. The boy sported a toy space suit—his glass helmet gleaming. His mother held his hand as she escorted him up the stairs, away from a bewildered-looking young pilot standing with a clipboard. Obvious to the viewer, an incident had just occurred. A note found inside the cover explained: "Little Johnny Tomorrow has just walked past young Mr. Today, making the latter look aged and out of date." The cover reminded the Post staff of a similar incident: "An airliner captain asked a little passenger if this was his first time up. 'Fourteenth,' said the lad. 'Can't ever get up higher'n five, ten thousand feet in these old planes, though. How's the United States ever going to build a space platform if you fellas can't make altitude?'" The captain, the epitome of modernism, opened his mouth in disbelief and crept away to rev up his creaky old engines. The pilot had been eclipsed. Technological progress marched on, leaving him, once the very symbol of the future, at the controls of an airliner soon to become a museum piece.[75]

The 1950s dreams of space travel turned into 1960s reality. Astronauts now held the title of the fastest people alive. Rocketing into outer space, just as John Glenn or Alan Shepard had, held youth's attention in the same way that piloting aircraft had only decades previous. The 1960s equivalents of the 1920s aviation heroes, astronauts captured the public's imagination and adulation. Airline pilots, however, were now viewed as only a step removed from Greyhound bus drivers.[76]

As the 1950s drew to a close, domestic airlines looked back over an era of great change, particularly in relation to the number of passengers they carried. In 1950 the airlines could boast that more than 17 million passengers had flown on their aircraft. By 1960 that figure had risen to more than 56 million passengers—almost a quadruple increase. By 1957 the commercial airlines of the United States were completing more revenue passenger miles (the number of revenue-paying passengers multiplied by the distance traveled) than were the railroads. In that same year, North American Airlines became the last of the larger passenger-carrying nonskeds of the 1950s to cease operations because of pressure from federal regulators. The scheduled airlines breathed a sigh of relief when the lawyers for North American Airlines conceded defeat after the U.S. Supreme Court upheld the Civil Aeronautics Board's ruling against the nonscheduled airline. Even though the nonskeds no longer appeared to threaten the profitability of the scheduled airlines, the advent of air coach travel had fundamentally changed the industry. In 1961, domestic airlines flew more coach than first-class passenger miles, only 13 years after the airlines first reacted to the nonscheduled lines with a service appealing to a greater number of people.[77]

In the 1950s the nation's airlines passed through adolescence before finally maturing on the wings of jetliners that completely revolutionized passenger comfort and the speed of travel. As *Business Week* predicted in 1952. air travel was soon to become "about as glamorous as a trolley ride down Main Street."[78]

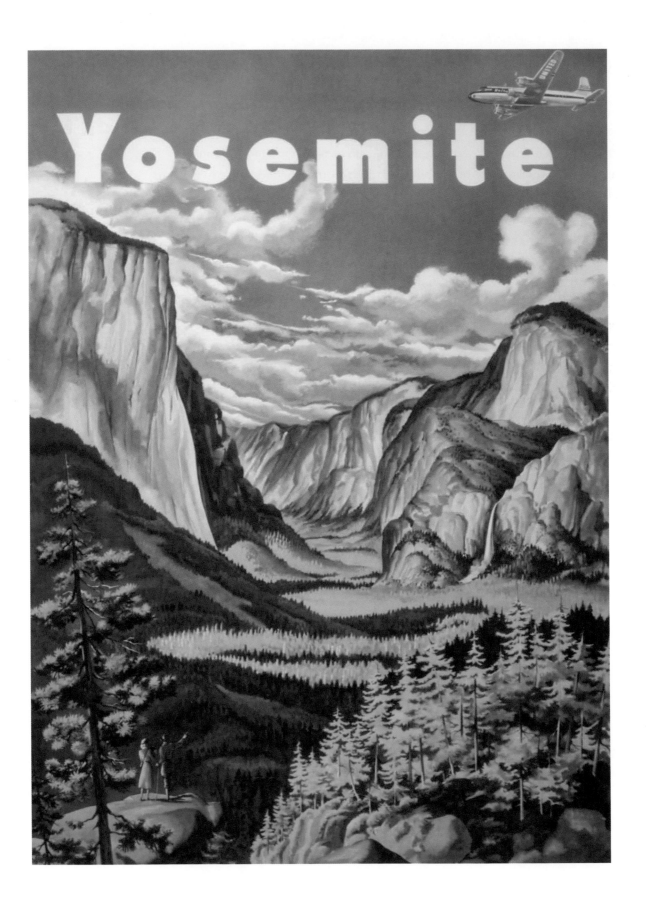

Leaving on a Jet Plane

From the wood-and-canvas mail planes of the early 1920s to the majestic Lockheed Constellations and Douglas airliners of the 1950s, all had piston engines and propellers. Piston engines provided power with controlled explosions that were caused by an electrical spark igniting a highly flammable mixture of fuel and air. These explosions moved pistons, rods, and crankshafts to spin a propeller that forced air to the rear and thus moved the aircraft forward.

During the Second World War, propeller-driven piston-engined aircraft reached the limits of performance. For instance, the famed Merlin engine powered the North American P-51 Mustang fighter to top speeds of more than 450 miles per hour. At these velocities the airplane's propeller tips approached the speed of sound, inducing drag instead of propelling the aircraft.[1]

The answer to overcoming this limitation lay in a concept at once novel yet ancient. According to Newton's third law of motion, for every action there is an equal and opposite reaction. Steam engines of centuries past had called upon this natural phenomenon to produce mechanical motion. The turbine was a rotary engine consisting of vanes that were moved by the force of water or steam about a shaft. Charles Parsons, from England, invented the steam turbine in the late nineteenth century and applied it to ship propulsion. The first modern battleship, HMS Dreadnought, sailed at 21 knots, thanks to Parson's steam turbine. The next development was the gas turbine, moved by heated air rather than steam. To operate most efficiently, the air was first compressed, then mixed with a fuel and ignited to produce the stream of high-pressure gas to move the turbine. If connected to the compressor, the spinning turbine could spin the compressor and keep running as long as sufficient fuel was injected. The gas turbine seemed to hold great promise for spinning a shaft to power other applications. But it proved inefficient and impractical.[2]

The idea gained new life with the invention of the supercharger, a device that introduced precompressed air into a piston engine. The greater quantity of air that a piston engine ingested increased its power without expanding its cylinder size. Superchargers attached to its engines permitted the Boeing 307 to maintain a pressurized cabin with greater air pressure inside than outside the aircraft. Superchargers also enabled piston engines to operate at higher altitudes, where the thin air would otherwise degrade performance. The venerable Boeing B-17 Flying Fortress and the amazing Boeing B-29 Superfortress rained death and destruction on the Axis powers during World War II from altitudes of more than 30,000 feet, thanks to superchargers attached to their piston engines.

Postwar transcontinental airliners, such as the Lockheed L-1049 Super Constellation and the Douglas DC-7, employed superchargers to wring maximum power from four massive 18-cylinder piston engines. The engines required copious numbers of spark plugs (two for each cylinder, or 144 per airliner) and frequent overhauls. All too often these complicated assemblages failed during flight. American Airlines stockpiled engines for its DC-7s in Denver, even though it was not a scheduled stop, because transcontinental flights made emergency landings there so often in need of an engine replacement. In the 1950s, TWA sometimes experienced 10 engine failures per day on its large airliners. Piston engines were stretched to their technological limit, and the airlines needed a new source of propulsion.[3]

The Turbojet Engine

That new source of power was the turbojet engine. It applied the gas turbine to move air for thrust rather than simply to turn a shaft. At a most basic level, a turbojet is a tube containing a series of fans compressing air, which is then mixed with fuel and combusted, and the hot exhaust ejected from the back of the tube propels the aircraft forward. Before leaving the tube, however, the exhaust powers a turbine connected to the fans at the front of the engine to sustain constant ignition. The shaft connecting the turbine with the compressor blades is essentially the only moving part of the turbojet engine.[4]

Royal Air Force officer Frank Whittle was, in the late 1920s, the first to conceive of a basic turbojet engine as he pondered ways to propel aircraft past 500 miles per hour. High-ranking RAF officials and British engine manufacturers spurned Whittle's ideas. Nevertheless, he ran his first jet engine in April 1937, and although disappointed with the engine's performance, he began to receive some government aid the following year. As he struggled for support and recognition, a German engineering student, Hans von Ohain, independently invented his own turbojet engine, with the support of the German aircraft

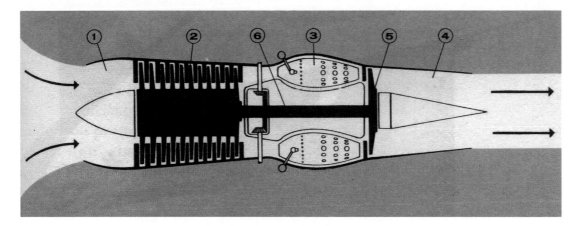

As depicted in a 1959 American Airlines welcome packet, a turbojet engine takes in air at the front (1); a series of compressor fans (2) squeezes the air before it is mixed with fuel in the combustion chambers (3); ignition of the fuel-air mixture produces a stream of hot air, propelling the engine forward, out the back of the engine (4) after passing through a turbine (5), connected via shaft (6) to the compressor fans, which draw in more air; and the process repeats. (From the author's collection)

company Heinkel. Credited with coinventing the turbojet engine, von Ohain saw his engine power the first turbojet-propelled aircraft, the Heinkel He 178, when it flew in August 1939.

Both British and German air forces deployed jet aircraft during the war—the Gloster Meteor and the Messerschmitt Me 262, respectively. The first American jet, the Bell P-59A, used turbojet engines copied from Whittle's design. A more promising jet fighter from Lockheed, the P-80 Shooting Star, entered military service near the end of the war. Jet-powered fighter aircraft demonstrated better rates of climb, faster speeds, and higher operational altitudes than their piston-engine predecessors. However, development of commercial jetliners lagged behind military applications for the turbojet engine. Commercial aircraft manufacturers had to wait until the military developed better turbojets before going ahead with jetliner designs. Additionally, engineers predicted high airline operating costs because jetliners would gulp copious amounts of fuel relative to that required by piston engines. The consequent high fares necessary to cover high fuel costs would prevent all but the most affluent from purchasing tickets for jet travel. And because of the required high initial development costs, few industry leaders were willing to gamble millions of dollars on a new innovation.[5]

Such caution did not prevent the British from forging ahead. In an attempt to overcome the time lost during the war, when all airliner production ceased, the British saw the jet airliner as a means of shortcutting the approach to technical superiority over the well-established American Douglases, Lockheeds, and Boeings. In 1949 the aircraft builder, de Havilland, rolled out the first turbojet airliner, the DH 106. Named the Comet, the sleek four-engine craft looked as if it were going fast even while parked on the ground. It flew at nearly 500 miles per hour over distances of almost 2,000 miles. Although it carried only 36 passengers, an analysis of its operating costs showed that the higher fuel consumption

This JUMO 004 turbojet engine arrived in the United States after the Second World War for analysis. Before the war's end, Germany had produced over 5,000 copies of this engine, which powered the world's first operational combat jet fighter, the Messerschmitt Me 262. (Courtesy of NASA)

costs were offset by the cheaper fuel (kerosene, not gasoline) and enormous economies in maintenance. The Comet earned profits for British Overseas Airways Corporation from the first scheduled flight in 1952. Comet passengers enjoyed a quiet, relatively vibration-free ride in the fully pressurized cabin as the jet plane cruised at more than 35,000 feet, where the jet engines were most efficient and turbulent weather almost nonexistent. Twenty-eight first-class passengers sat in reclining seats, four-abreast. Eight more sat in a forward compartment around two tables, sipping cocktails and conversing in normal tones.[6]

But several catastrophic accidents cast a shadow over the Comet. Even though the airliner had been subjected to stringent tests before going into service, in the span of two years several of the revolutionary new jets plummeted from the sky without obvious explanation. All Comets were grounded in early 1954 until investigators determined that metal fatigue, resulting from repeated pressurization cycles, induced small stress cracks in the aluminum skin at the corners of the rectangular window frames. When a crack split open in flight, the explosive decompression of the fuselage sucked everyone and everything out of the cabin in about two seconds as the airplane broke into pieces. Subsequent versions of the de Havilland Comet compiled a good safety record in coming decades, but not before American competitors came forward with better designs of their own. The jet revolution in commercial air transportation was just around the corner.[7]

America's First Jetliners

As investigators in Britain were learning about the deadly flaw of the Comet, Boeing Aircraft Company rolled out prototype jet aircraft dubbed the Boeing 367-80, or Dash Eighty. Within the company, the airliner version of the airplane became known as the 707. This version was really the seven hundredth Boeing design, but the firm's public relations department convinced corporate brass that they should use the higher number. Subsequent Boeing commercial jetliners deliberately carried forward the number, as the Boeing 727, 737, and so on. A version of the 707 for United Air Lines was originally labeled the 717 but was renamed the 720 because United's Pat Patterson objected. The 717 name resurfaced as the Boeing designation for the McDonald Douglas MD-95 after the two companies merged in 1997.[8]

Boeing had considerable experience designing large, jet-powered aircraft, notably the B-47 and B-52 jet bombers. Building on its expertise, Boeing had decided to launch a new program, which culminated in the 707. The new airplane had four turbojet engines individually attached in pods to underwing pylons, two below each of the swept wings. This position was in contrast with the Comet's engines, which were streamlined into the wings, necessitating special wing construction. The podded engines were much easier to maintain and, in the event of an engine fire, the distance between them prevented the spread of damage to the other engines. The Boeing 707's fuselage stretched 144 feet in length, the entire aircraft weighed over 100 tons, and it cruised at 600 miles per hour at 25,000 feet.[9]

The company invested $16 million, a quarter of the firm's net worth, into building the 707. From the start, Boeing hoped to sell a version to the U.S. Air Force as a jet-powered air-to-air refueling tanker and cargo aircraft, as well as selling it to the airlines. A lack of orders for the new jetliner would imperil the company's very existence. Boeing's decision to develop a jetliner went against company history. In the early 1930s it had designed the 247, only to see the Douglas DC-2 and then DC-3 take over the airliner market. The Boeing 307 had been a technical marvel, but Boeing sold only 10 copies. Military contracts had sustained the company. Now Boeing bet its future on yet another commercial design even though two other American manufacturers, Douglas and Lockheed, reigned supreme in that area. Lockheed decided to stay with propeller-driven aircraft, building the Lockheed Electra turboprop, but Douglas could not ignore the challenge of the Boeing 707. A year after Boeing revealed the 707 prototype in 1954, Douglas announced it would build a similar jetliner, the DC-8, as a successor to its DC-7. Pan American Airlines ordered 25 copies in 1955 before Douglas even built a prototype. Then United canceled its 707 order in favor of the DC-8 because the latter's fuselage was 15 inches wider, allowing for six-abreast seating rather than five. In response, Boeing quickly announced that it would widen the 707 fuselage by 16 inches, and airlines once again lined up to buy the 707. Boeing's gamble paid off. To the untrained eye, the DC-8 and the 707 appeared almost identical. Both had the same engine layout and carried over 120 passengers in mixed classes.[10]

The introduction of the Boeing 707 and the competing Douglas DC-8 jetliners revolutionized air travel in America. Before production ceased, Boeing sold nearly one thousand 707s of all models, and Douglas sold 556 DC-8s. Modern marvels, they cruised at one mile per six seconds and could fly more than 2,500 miles nonstop. The gain in speed over piston-engine predecessors was astounding. At the end of the First World War in 1918, the few commercial aircraft in existence had a top speed of 90 miles per hour. In the 1950s the Douglas DC-7 cruised at 360 miles per hour. The first American jetliners, the Boeing 707 and the Douglas DC-8, cruised at 600 and 580 miles per hour, respectively—a gain in speed over their predecessors almost equal to the gains achieved in the previous 35 years.[11]

After transcontinental jet service began, the airlines noticed an influx of people wanting to fly. "Almost miraculously, passengers began turning up at ticket counters in droves," reported *Business Week*. By the mid-1960s, the industry recognized that it was in a golden age as annual passenger numbers steadily climbed. Nearly 56 million U.S. passengers flew in 1959, when domestic airlines introduced jet service. By 1965 that number had risen to more than 92 million, and it topped 153 million in 1970. In the span of a decade, the

An American Airlines Boeing 707 became the first commercial passenger jet airliner in transcontinental service between New York City and Los Angeles on January 25, 1959. (From the author's collection)

For only $1, American Airlines passengers in 1959 could purchase model kits of the Boeing 707 by mail. (From the author's collection)

number of passengers the nation's airlines carried tripled. Flying became so commonplace that magazine articles dedicated to personal accounts of transcontinental air travel all but disappeared. The combination of fares affordable to a much wider stratum of income level and the unsurpassed speed of the jet airliners finally transformed air travel from a novelty to a mode of transportation that anyone in need of fast long-distance travel took for granted. One airline president stated in 1964 that those in the airline industry "used to be too enthralled with the helmet-and-goggle era." He noted that "in effect, we used to stand around and cheer for 15 minutes every time an airplane took off." By the early 1970s at least half of all Americans had taken one or more airline trips. In the jet age, airlines at last had a commodity so popular that it became a part of everyday American life.[12]

Until the arrival of the jet age, the myth of comfort aboard transcontinental airliners was just that—a myth. While passengers published accounts extolling the virtues of air travel, cabin conditions were primitive. The deafening roar of engines and propellers, as well as the bumpy ride only a few thousand feet over the earth, constantly reminded passengers they were not in the lap of luxury. Over the years of airline development, the airlines and airframe manufacturers had made great strides in reducing the unpleasantness of the experience. Creatively decorating, soundproofing, heating, cooling, and eventually pressurizing airliner cabins lessened the negative stimuli for passengers. Additionally, airlines devised a wide range of activities to distract passengers—complimentary magazines, brochures, and maps; in-flight information and radio programs; and attractive young women to serve them food and drink. The jetliner rounded off all these improvements and brought true comfort to flying. One passenger on a 1960 transcontinental jet flight stated that he loathed long-distance flights on propeller-driven aircraft; with the advent of jet travel, gone were the days of "long, boring, vibrating, droning air trip[s]." Now he could experience the "true relaxation" and "less boredom" that jet travel afforded.[13]

A passenger's first flight in a jet was a memorable event. In a 1960 article, aviation writer Lou Davis recounted his first time. By the time he took TWA transcontinental in a 707 early in 1960, more than a million people had experienced jet travel. Yet, as Davis explained, a significant number of the people on his flight demonstrated great excitement at the opportunity to fly in a jetliner. Those who had taken previous Boeing 707 flights willingly recounted their experience to the newcomers seated about them. Once the screaming jet took to the skies, "first-jet-flight anxiety drifted away." according to Davis. "Passengers relaxed as if to say, 'Why didn't someone tell us it was like this!'"[14]

Nevertheless, those early jet flights were not always so serene. C. S. Forester, well-known writer and creator of the fictional character Horatio Hornblower, flew from New York to San Francisco on a hot summer's day in 1959 aboard a Boeing 707. Much to passengers' dismay, the airplane's air conditioning system failed before the jet took off from

New York, but the airline ordered it to leave anyway. The cabin temperature hovered at more than 100 degrees for the duration of the five-hour flight to California. The pilot attempted to cheer the sweltering passengers over the public address system by informing them that the outside temperature was below zero, but the trip tested passengers' physical endurance. Stripped down to little else besides underwear, they drank all the water, soda pop, and tonic water aboard. Upon landing, the cool, moist air of San Francisco never smelled so sweet to a group of travelers.[15]

The View from a Jetliner

The view from a jetliner was breathtaking to the uninitiated because they were flying higher than ever before. In an airliner, the passengers' view was directly related to the plane's elevation from the earth's surface. At 2,000 feet above the ground, the horizon appeared at about 50 miles in the distance. At 10,000 feet altitude, the horizon was 150 miles away from the observer. Passengers aboard jets cruising at 30,000 feet could, on a clear day, see a horizon more than 200 miles away.[16]

Just as the horizon stretched farther into the distance as airline passengers flew at greater and greater heights, passengers' possible view of the earth's surface also increased. Assuming an unobstructed view at 10,000 feet altitude, an area of land nearly 50,000 square miles in size (approximately the entire state of New York) was visible. At 30,000 feet, passengers could conceivably view an area of more than 142,000 square miles (slightly smaller than the state of Montana). On the other hand, jet passengers were so distant from the ground that the view from the window was seldom as entertaining as that from an earlier airliner cruising tens of thousands of feet lower. One notable exception to this was crossing mountain ranges in the American West.[17]

In 1960 conservationist Harry C. James took his first jet flight, from Los Angeles to New York, and expected to see little of interest from the narrow window beside his seat. Beforehand, James's friends who had flown on commercial jets warned him that jet travel was boring—"You can't see a thing at 30,000 feet." James boarded the plane armed with a book and some magazines to keep him occupied during the expected idle hours ahead. However, he found the view spellbinding. Soon after climbing from Los Angeles, the jet passed over the mountains, "and the desert seemed to stretch illimitably in all directions."[18]

James gazed down at the slow-moving scene played out below. He noted: "At 30,000 feet the works of man fade into insignificance, even a major highway is but a pencil mark across the landscape, and only the great geological features of the land are of any

Passengers boarding some of the first transcontinental jet flights received welcome packets extolling the virtues of jet travel. (From the author's collection)

Area of the Earth's Surface Visible from Various Altitudes

For many passengers, one of the fascinating aspects of flying has been the view of the terrain scrolling below them. A simple mathematical formula enables passengers to calculate the approximate total land area visible at any given altitude. The visible surface area in square miles is 4.8 multiplied by the elevation of the aircraft above sea level, measured in feet. For example, airline passengers in the 1920s through Second World War looked down from the windows of their lofty perches from altitudes of about 5,000 to 10,000 feet elevation. At 5,000 feet, passengers theoretically could view an area the size of West Virginia, which is 24,000 square miles. At 10,000 feet above sea level, passengers could have viewed a panorama of 48,000 square miles—the size of North Carolina.

After the widespread adoption of cabin pressurization in the late 1940s and 1950s, the cruising elevations increased to 20,000 and even 30,000 feet. At those altitudes, passengers could view an area the size of Oregon (96,000 square miles) up to the land area of Montana (144,000 square miles). Many flights in the jet age cruised at 40,000 feet, affording passengers a theoretical view of 192,000 square miles, the combined area of Oregon and Wyoming.

Source: Wood, *Science from Your Airplane Window*, 119–24.

moment." A view from such an altitude had great appeal to him because the flight path crossed over wilderness areas in the southwestern United States where he had trekked, camped, learned about geology, and visited historic locations, such as the ruins of a Mormon settlement in southern Utah. James's previous appreciation of the Southwest reinforced his views of everything that he witnessed from the airliner. As a conservationist and a geologist, he better understood the relationships between the natural features on the ground than could a passenger with no such personal interest in the environment.

For Harry James, the lofty perspective provided a better understanding of the world that he had only known from the ground level. As he put it, "Only at great altitudes does our Southwest fall into perspective." Far above the deserts he perceived in one sweeping view how their features fitted together in a tapestry of intricate connections.

James's observations prompted memories that spanned the previous 40 years. As the landscape—the large, natural features on the land—was intimately familiar to him, he found the view personally fulfilling. Not surprisingly, he concluded his account with the airliner passing over the Rocky Mountains of Colorado. The vast plains of the Midwest appeared monotonous to him, so he turned to his book and magazines for the remaining hours of the flight to New York.

Over time, the novelty of seeing America from the air wore thin. Airlines relegated route maps to the back of their in-flight magazines for the few who cared to consult them—probably only to discover if the airline served a particular city or not.

Culminating with the jetliners of the late-1950s, transcontinental airline passengers experienced an ever-decreasing view of the world beyond their airplane. The size and number of windows per passenger evolved from no windows at all in an open cockpit biplane to small sealed portholes along the side of a jetliner. Pioneer airmail passengers who flew in the open cockpits had a 360-degree field of view. Two passengers squeezed into a Boeing 40A compartment were restricted to one sliding window on either side. The relatively roomy Boeing 80A had large windows next to 12 of the 18 passenger seats, offering a "relatively unobstructed" view of the sky and landscape to window-seat passengers. Yet those in middle seats had to look past their neighbors to catch a glimpse through the window.[19]

As advances in aviation technology resulted in airliners carrying increasing numbers of passengers, the ratio of windows per passenger did not keep pace. Each of the 14 passengers in a DC-2 had a window seat. But the large airliners of the post–Second World War era, such as the DC-4, had four-abreast seating, meaning only half of the passengers on a full flight had a window seat. This fact, coupled with shrinking window size, clearly changed the nature of the air travel experience for large numbers of passengers. Pressurized aircraft had smaller windows to withstand the forces of pressurization better than large windows. Jet-age passengers aboard a six-abreast Boeing 707 merely caught glimpses out narrow windows. Two seats removed from the nearest windows, aisle-seat passengers in a jet with such seating arrangements were effectively cut off from a view of the world beyond the jetliner. The 707 was the first airliner with sliding plastic window shades integrated into the aircraft. allowing passengers to block all light from coming through windows—and further limiting access to the view outside for passengers who did not have a window seat.

Onboard Entertainment

Recognizing passengers' relative isolation from the outside environment, airlines wished to introduce more onboard diversions. Movies provided a new means of in-flight entertainment designed to keep passengers' minds distracted from the flight. On an experimental basis, Transcontinental Air Transport equipped its planes with movie projectors and screens in 1929. One writer commented: "When the window shades are lowered air passengers may enjoy a cinema 3,000 ft. above ground. Films include everything from movie comedies to films promoting TAT services." Credit for showing the first in-flight motion picture went to Imperial Airways of Great Britain nearly five years before TAT tried out movie projectors in its planes. In general, the flights were too noisy and unstable to show movies. More than 30 years would elapse before in-flight motion pictures became standard on America's airliners.[20]

TWA became the first to offer in-flight movies on a regular basis aboard flights in the summer of 1961. Transcontinental passengers in first class watched Lana Turner and Efrem Zimbalist, Jr., starring in *By Love Possessed*, as the film flickered into aviation history. An overhead-mounted projector displayed the moving images on a giant screen located in the front of the first-class section. A firm called Inflight Motion Pictures invested more than $20,000 of its own money to install a movie projection system in each TWA jet. The company then charged the airline $150 per movie showing. The service proved highly popular, increasing the passenger loads. David Flexer, founder of Inflight Motion Pictures, asserted that a majority of airline passengers would gladly pay to see movies during flight. Whiling away the hours of a long flight himself, David Flexer became convinced that motion pictures would be a wonderful means of reducing in-flight boredom. He mused that "air travel is both the most advanced form of transportation and the most boring." He spent the next four years overcoming the obstacles of installing a projector system into the cramped confines of a jetliner cabin. His system used cumbersome 16-millimeter reels, each 25 inches across.[21]

TWA's innovation prompted its transcontinental competitor, United, to install Inflight Motion Picture systems in its planes also. An initial two-year deal cost the airline $7 million. American Airlines opted for a Sony closed-circuit television system. Passengers enjoyed passing the hours watching movies but bemoaned the selection of films that many of them had already seen in theaters.[22]

Movies in flight...another TWA first

First-run movies are now being shown on SuperJets. The choicest films from Hollywood and Europe are featured on selected daily flights between New York and California...projected on a special wide screen in the First Class section. Featherweight headsets bring the sound only to those who wish to see the movie. Others are not disturbed. Starting next month, movies will be shown on most TWA overseas flights. This is the latest innovation to make your flight seem even faster and more enjoyable aboard *TWA SuperJets*.

Fly TWA SuperJets across the United States and to leading cities in Europe and Asia

This advertisement from 1961 proclaims TWA as the first airline offering in-flight movies. Movies helped passengers pass the time by psychologically removing them from the flight experience into an onscreen world of imagination. (From the author's collection)

We built an airline for professional travellers.

American can't forget a request for diapers or a dinner of baby food.

We own the world's biggest business computer, just for remembering.

It remembers a businessman's order for chili instead of the regular main course. It remembers salt-free diets and kosher meals, too.

Of course we didn't build this computer for babies. We built it for professional travellers—businessmen who buy up to fifty plane tickets a year.

We go all out for customers like them.

In fact, we baby them.

Just as we do all our passen-gers, whether they're on their first flight or their hundred-and-first.

On American Airlines, everyone gets the full professional treatment.

That's the American Way.

American Airlines

Some passengers who did not wish to watch movies in flight complained that they were a captive and sometime unwilling audience, even though the films' audio tracks were delivered via headsets. First-class passengers received complimentary headsets, and coach-class passengers could purchase them for a nominal fee. Airlines also offered headsets for enjoying music in flight by plugging them into jacks located near passengers' seats.[23]

Checked Baggage and Jet-Age Airports

Just as it had led the way with in-flight movies, TWA became the first U.S. airline to possess an all-jet airliner fleet. Its last Constellation flight was on April 6, 1967 from New York to St. Louis. Only two years before, domestic airlines were able to revise their baggage policy because the bellies of jetliners had more cargo space than that in the old propeller-driven planes. From the beginning, airlines had weighed each passenger's luggage before flight, making sure that it did not exceed a total of 40—or sometimes 30—pounds. Understandably, the limit often elicited passenger complaints, especially from passengers traveling great distances and planning to stay for a long time. Additional weight had to be paid for as "excess baggage." But now the carriers allowed each passenger to check two or three pieces of luggage for no additional charge, as long as they each weighed no more than 70 pounds.[24]

The larger jetliners could accommodate more passenger baggage, but their size necessitated larger airports. Chicago's O'Hare International Airport emerged as the world's busiest airport in the mid-1950s but had to be located many miles from downtown. The Dallas/Fort Worth International Airport, sited on farmland 15 miles from both of the Texas cities in the 1970s, grew to become a premier center of air travel in the nation's heartland. A virtual city unto itself, it is bigger than Manhattan Island. Helicopter taxi service between a city's downtown and its airport appeared to be a viable, speedy alternative to ground transportation and was put into service in Los Angeles, Chicago, San Francisco, and New York City to reduce commuting times to nearby airports. But helicopters were expensive, had limited capacity, were unprofitable, and ultimately too accident-prone to be sustainable.[25]

Appearing in 1968, this advertisement points out that American Airlines caters to all air travelers, from business professionals to small children. The text makes reference to American possessing "the world's biggest business computer." Developed jointly between American and IBM, the Semi-Automated Business Research Environment, or SABRE, enabled American to computerize its reservations system and gain an advantage over the competition. (From the author's collection)

The creation of modern interstate highways held forth the hope of shorter driving times for passengers going to and from large airports. Under the authority of the Interstate Highway Act of 1956, the United States built more than 40,000 miles of divided highways between, around, and through the nation's cities. Yet traffic congestion frequently slowed travel to airports. Even in 1960, reporter Lou Davis drove from his home on Long Island to Idlewild Airport (later renamed the John F. Kennedy International Airport) on a new freeway already clogged with bumper-to-bumper traffic. "It's the jet age," Davis declared, "and the day of turtle-pace travel on super crowded highways."[26]

Once inside the airport terminal, passengers were in an artificial environment, far removed from the outside world. Climate-controlled ticketing and waiting areas led to gates and then to telescoping passenger-loading bridges. United Air Lines was the first to develop, in 1954, an enclosed walkway extending from the terminal to the door of waiting aircraft to ease passenger boarding. But such devices were not yet common in 1960 when Lou Davis and his fellow TWA passengers were exposed to the weather as they trekked from the terminal to a mobile stairway situated next to the aircraft. The long metal box eventually became a ubiquitous part of travel in the jet age. Passengers were in a climate-controlled environment from the moment they entered a terminal for departure until they left the terminal at their final destination.[27]

The Stewardess as Popular Culture Icon

In the pressurized comfort of jetliner cabins, stewardesses and stewards (more commonly called flight attendants after the mid-1960s) performed the same basic functions as Ellen Church and the first United Air Lines stewardesses had in 1930. But in the jet age, the professional image of stewardesses evolved into that of a sexualized icon in the skies. Abandoning the demure attire stewardesses had traditionally worn, Braniff Airways led the way in the 1960s, hiring Italian fashion designer Emilio Pucci to create eye-catching outfits for stewardesses. One of Pucci's more unusual designs featured a bubble helmet, before the widespread use of jetways, to keep the wearer's head dry when walking between the aircraft and the terminal.

In 1965, Braniff purposefully emphasized the stewardesses' sexuality with a ritual called the air strip. Over the course of a flight, a stewardess removed outer layers of clothing until she was dressed only in her skirt and blouse. Airline marketing campaigns of the early 1970s gave full reign to the sexual revolution. The most notorious example came from National Airlines. Its "Fly Me" advertising campaign featuring winsome females on television saying such lines as "I'm Debbie! Fly me!"[28]

The two most recognized intrastate carriers of the era, PSA and Southwest Airlines, made overt sexuality a cornerstone of their marketing. PSA advertised that its passengers preferred aisle seats so that they could get a better view of the sexy stewardesses wearing miniskirts. Raquel Welch look-alikes in hot pants and go-go boots on Southwest epitomized the airline's corporate image as the "love" airline.

The stewardess became an even greater popular culture icon with the 1961 introduction of a Barbie doll dressed as an American Airlines flight attendant, complete with a blue skirt and jacket, a white blouse, and a zippered flight bag. Only two years after the very first Barbie doll hit the toy market, the stewardess Barbie introduced young children to the romance of air travel. Subsequent dolls featured uniforms from United, Pan American, and Braniff. Mattel expanded the theme in 1964, when it marketed Barbie's boyfriend, Ken, dressed as an airline employee. In 1973, Barbie's Friend Ship appeared, a toy model designed to resemble a United airliner, complete with a serving galley and removable airline seats. In testimony to Barbie's significance in aviation popular culture, the National Air and Space Museum featured a 1995 exhibit of Barbie dolls dressed in a wide array of uniforms ranging from stewardess to Air Force pilot and astronaut.[29]

Hollywood's Take on the Jet Age

The first Hollywood movie showcasing airline travel, *Three Guys Named Mike*, was released in 1951 and starred Jane Wyman as a plucky American Airlines stewardess who became the object of affection of three men, all named Mike. Directed by Charles Walters, the lighthearted film chronicled a stewardess's training and provided a glimpse into the not-so-glamorous world of airline employment. Reflecting emerging feminist movement, the attitudes of male airline employees evolved over the course of the film—from looking down on Wyman's character as a klutzy "babe" to respecting her for her hard work and determination. Wyman's character even succeeded where men had failed, when she created a successful advertising plan for the airline despite having to overcome male prejudice. Interestingly, a young writer named Sidney Sheldon wrote the screenplay. As one of the most successful novelists of the twentieth century, Sheldon would eventually sell more than 300 million books worldwide, besides creating successful television shows such as *I Dream of Jeannie* and *Hart to Hart*.[30]

Three years after the release of *Three Guys Named Mike*, John Wayne starred with an impressive cast in the granddaddy of airline disaster movies entitled *The High and the Mighty*. Based on Ernest K. Gann's book of the same name, the film set the genre standard for decades to come. A generation of young people watched spellbound as John Wayne defied the odds in successfully bringing a crippled airliner in to land at San Francisco after

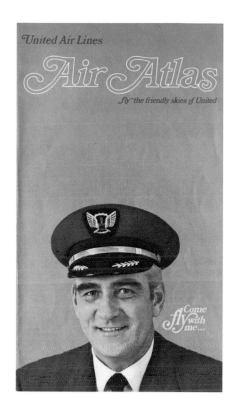

Paired with the slogan "Come fly with me," the pilot smiling from this United Air Lines map cover is the quintessential image of the confident, trustworthy, and safety-conscious pilot that the airlines fostered. Kicked off in 1965, United's "Fly the Friendly Skies" advertising campaign became the longest-running in airline history. (From the author's collection)

experiencing in-flight problems en route from Honolulu. The theme song, which won an Academy Award, was so closely associated with John Wayne that it was played at his funeral.

The airline disaster genre peaked in the 1970s with the *Airport* series. The initial film, based on an Arthur Hailey novel, featured a bombed Boeing 707 with a gaping hole in its side attempting to return for landing at Chicago. *Airport* and its three sequel movies all followed the common theme of heroic people coming to the rescue of crippled jetliners. A spoof titled *Airplane!* arrived in theaters in 1980, entertaining audiences with one sight gag after another. It poked fun at the unreality of airline disaster movies and created a cult following in the process. As commercial air travel became an experience most Americans shared, the subject was ripe for parody on the silver screen.

New Words

As air travel became commonplace, new terms inevitably entered the language to describe phenomena unique to flying. For example, after the introduction of jetliners into transcontinental service, a category of wealthy, socialite passengers acquired the label "jet set." One of the earliest references to the jet set described them as "men and women in a hurry, who seek to get as much fun out of their nights as they can pay for or get somebody else to pay for" and who "seek so much and attain so little they are usually bored." They were "the jet-propelled epitome of men who made money by hard work and left it to a third generation which is engaged in hard play." The name endured into the twenty-first century, as did anther term coined after jetliners became common in the 1960s—"jet lag."[31]

After a long flight crossing several time zones, passengers often experienced physiological distress. The cause of such symptoms lay in the natural internal clock of the human body. Called circadian rhythms, these biological cycles often corresponded to cues from the surrounding environment. The body set its own functioning to align with the regular pattern of daylight and darkness, as well as the rise and fall of temperatures. After moving quickly a great distance east or west, the body had to adjust its natural functions, such as sleep, blood pressure, and excretion, to match the new set of environmental cues. Symptoms during the time of adjustment, such as fatigue and irritability, became known as "jet lag."

Airlines could do little to help passengers cope with jet lag. Besides offering meal service corresponding to a mealtime at the destination, the airlines had scant control over passengers' adjustment to a sudden time change. At the dawn of the jet age, one Boeing spokesman bluntly stated, "The long distance traveler must ignore his stomach—or the sun. Or he can go by slow boat." After extensive study, experts in the 1960s determined that passengers needed several days before their bodies' internal rhythms became synchronized with the new environment.

Jet-Age Food

Although jetliners had shortened flight times, airlines still were still serving full meals. In fact, the lines competed on the basis of food service, sometimes resulting in elaborate menus. One such menu from a 1960 TWA transcontinental flight offered lettuce salad, broiled sirloin strip steak, stuffed baked potato, and string beans with mushrooms, accompanied by a dinner roll and assorted French pastries. Transcontinental jetliner passengers experienced the height of in-flight cuisine in the 1960s and 1970s, culminating, in first class, with flight attendants carving slices of hot roast beef right before passengers' eyes.

Starting with the Boeing 707, airline passengers encountered fold-down trays built into seat backs for storage. This innovation provided a convenient and sturdy surface for food, drinks, and other items during flight, and the trays could be quickly stowed out of the way when not in use.

Passengers enjoy an in-flight meal seated at a round table, covered with a white cloth, aboard a TWA Lockheed L-1011 TriStar jetliner in the 1970s. This scene soon succumbed to the installation of additional seats to earn the airline more revenue. (From the TWA Archives of the St. Louis Mercantile Library at the University of Missouri–St. Louis)

After the 1990 federal ban on smoking during domestic flights, airline safety cards reminded passengers to refrain from lighting up during any phase of the flight or in the lavatory. (From the author's collection)

Restrictions on Smoking

As food service became more extravagant during the jet age, cigarette smoking declined in popularity. By the 1950s, physicians warned airline passengers of the drawbacks of smoking in flight. Smoking produced concentrations of carbon monoxide in the smoker's bloodstream, preventing the cardiovascular system from delivering sufficient levels of oxygen at higher altitudes. In 1954, research showed that, even at lower altitudes, smokers experienced more oxygen deficiencies than did nonsmokers. Those who did not smoke or at least did not smoke for a period of time before flying felt less fatigued when subjected to altitudes over 8,000 feet. Additionally, smoking reduced the smoker's ability to view bright objects in a low-light environment. Even a single cigarette could affect one's night vision. Researchers concluded: "Obviously the average airline passenger might find his flight more comfortable if he avoids excessive smoking."[32]

American sensibilities toward smoking were changing, and so was nonsmokers' tolerance of cigarette smoke in airliner cabins. A drive to ban smoking, in at least certain portions of airliner cabins, gained momentum when consumer advocate Ralph Nader filed a petition with the Transportation Department as well as the Civil Aeronautics Board in 1969, demanding a complete ban of smoking on commercial flights because of the fire danger and the health risk to nonsmoking passengers.[33]

In 1969 Senator Mark Hatfield of Oregon and Representative Andrew Jacobs of Indiana introduced bills in their respective legislative houses calling for strict smoking and nonsmoking sections aboard U.S. airliners. Antismoking activists lobbied in support of the bills. Action on Smoking and Health led the way. This group had previously claimed a victory when the Federal Communications Commission (FCC) began to enforce a rule requiring cigarette packages to bear labels warning of the health dangers from cigarettes.[34]

Even so, many airline passengers in the early 1970s expressed indifference on the issue of in-flight smoking. Pan American asked all passengers boarding its new Boeing 747s whether they preferred to sit in a nonsmoking area. The overwhelming majority did not mind if they sat where others were smoking or not. In fact, an average of only six passengers per flight requested seating in the nonsmoking section.[35]

Change was on the horizon. Airlines began to segregate cabins into smoking and nonsmoking sections in 1971, and United Air Lines was among the first to do so. In 1973 the Civil Aeronautics Board proposed forcing all scheduled airlines to give domestic passengers a choice in seating according to smoking preference.[36]

Only five years later, when the CAB considered banning all pipe and cigar smoking aboard domestic airliners, the *New Republic* declared American smokers to be "our new official pariahs." The periodical pointed out that smokers were already "segregated at the back of the plane, where they can cough and wheeze and die slowly among their own kind."[37]

Airlines received an increased number of smoke-related passenger complaints in the 1970s and 1980s. Americans were becoming more sensitive to the issue of smoking and its detrimental effects on health. As one flight attendant stated in 1980, "It seems as if suddenly almost everyone is allergic to smoke, has a heart or lung condition, or just gave up smoking." In addition, smoking became more of an issue for air travelers because of the introduction of new-generation airliners. These jets, including the Boeing 737, recirculated a portion of the air back into the cabin. Whereas older jets, such as the Boeing 707, exchanged cabin air every three minutes, new-generation airliners replaced the air in the passenger cabin once every seven to nine minutes, reintroducing up to 50 percent of the same air back into the cabin. Recirculating cabin air meant more fuel efficiency for the airlines. By the 1990s, recirculating air was saving U.S. airlines an average of $60,000 per airliner per year. However, for the passengers, the efficiency measure meant that cigarette smoke stayed in the cabin longer, increasing eye, nose, and throat irritation.[38]

The American Medical Association and the National Academy of Sciences, among others, spearheaded an effort in the 1980s that led to a federal ban on smoking on all domestic flights. After the success of a law banning smoking on domestic flights lasting less than two hours, a national law prohibiting smoking on all domestic flights of less than six hours' duration went into effect in the spring of 1990. Ten years later the federal government decreed that all flights to and from the United States be smoke-free.[39]

Airline Security

Even more significant than the prohibition of in-flight smoking was the need for an increase in airline security. Before the jet age, the term "airline security" had little meaning. Fences rarely surrounded runways except to keep livestock from wandering into the path of landing planes. Airports welcomed the public to mill about, watching airplanes and passengers come and go. Passengers boarded flights without passing through any security measures such as metal detectors or baggage screening, secure in their belief that their safety would more likely be imperiled by mechanical failure or pilot error rather than by a criminal act.

One such criminal act did occur on November 1, 1955. A 23-year old man named John Gilbert Graham watched his mother board a United Air Lines flight at Denver's Stapleton Airport bound for Portland, Oregon. In his mother's luggage, Graham had placed 25 sticks of dynamite, set to detonate soon after the Douglas DC-6B departed. The midair explosion and fiery crash killed all 44 people aboard. Graham planned to collect the $37,500 life insurance policy that he had purchased in his mother's name at the airport, but the document was void without her signature. The State of Colorado executed an unrepentant Graham in 1957. Fortunately, horrific crimes involving airliners were rare events. Preventing the diversion, not the destruction, of aircraft would lead to the first passenger security measures at airports.[40]

On May 1, 1961, a Cuban identifying himself as "Elpirata Cofrisi" used a pistol and a knife to force the pilot of a National Airlines flight to divert to Havana, Cuba. Taking his name from an eighteenth-century Caribbean pirate, Cofrisi was the first air passenger in history to skyjack a commercial flight departing from a U.S. airport. Leaving the mentally unstable Cofrisi in Havana, the flight safely returned to U.S. airspace and landed in Key West, Florida.

At least 150 other skyjackers would follow in Cofrisi's footsteps. Over the coming decade, the majority of the skyjackers were homesick Cuban refugees, often in trouble with the law in the United States or mentally unstable. A travel ban between the United States and Fidel Castro's Cuba denied them opportunity to travel back legally to Cuba, and skyjacking meant fast transportation home. After news of a few skyjackers' successes, many others attempted the same feat.[41]

The American public demanded that the government take action to stop the skyjackings. Months after the initial incident, federal authorities reacted with passage of Public Law 87-197. For the first time in history the federal government could prosecute in criminal court any passengers who skyjacked an aircraft, interfered with members of the flight crew, or

An airline passenger walks between two slender poles connected via a power cord—one of the first metal detectors installed in an airport for passenger screening. Metal detectors were tangible evidence that the air travel experience had entered an age of terrorism. (From the *St. Louis Globe-Democrat* Archives of the St. Louis Mercantile Library at the University of Missouri–St. Louis)

brought weapons aboard an airliner. The law's passage and rapid enforcement stemmed the tide of skyjackings until suddenly 12 commercial flights were diverted to Cuba in 1968. The year 1969 witnessed the greatest number, with 33 of 40 attempts successful. Skyjacking almost became routine. When skyjacked, U.S. airline flight crews did not resist. The Federal Aviation Administration's primary concern was to protect passengers and crews of skyjacked airliners. The FAA established a communication link among air traffic control centers between Miami and Havana so that skyjacked airliners could be easily transferred. Landing charts to Havana's José Martí Airport became standard issue for U.S. commercial pilots.[42]

Additionally, the FAA established a Task Force on Deterrence of Air Piracy on February 17, 1969, to coordinate with airlines to create an anti-skyjacking system. U.S. marshals and customs agents soon appeared at major airports to seek out and stop potential skyjackers. Airlines voluntarily checked passenger lists against the criteria of a typical hijacker personality profile and secretly indicated such on the ticket of any suspicious passenger. Posters went up inside airport terminals warning potential skyjackers of the severe consequences of boarding an airplane with a weapon and diverting the flight with force. The posters also carried a message for all passengers: they and their baggage could be subject to search before boarding. Practices varied among airports, but typically passengers walked though a metal detector that alerted security if they carried metal objects such as knives or pistols. Some passengers who triggered a metal detector underwent identification checks, possibly a body frisk, and a hand search of any carry-on items. These voluntary measures became mandatory in 1972, when the FAA demanded that airlines or contractors working for airlines should ensure that all passengers undergo a three-stage screening process: hijacker profile, search of carry-on items, and metal detector screening. The occurrence of skyjacking in the United States declined dramatically, in spite of further highly publicized skyjackings, One such event occurred on November 14, 1971, when a man calling himself D. B. Cooper hijacked a Northwest Airlines jet flying from Portland, Oregon, to Seattle. After receiving a requested $200,000 in cash, Cooper ordered the flight back into the air. He jumped from the rear of the jetliner with the money and a parachute somewhere over the Cascade Mountains, never to be seen again.[43]

From the 1970s through the 1990s, the problem of skyjacking centered primarily on international flights, particularly between the United States and the Middle East as well as Asia. Airport security measures became a permanent feature of the air travel experience. Passengers traded convenience for security, standing in lines to walk through metal detectors and allowing complete strangers to x-ray and rifle their personal belongings.

The Road to Deregulation

Besides security issues, another trend gaining traction in the jet age and culminating in 1978 was airline deregulation. Federal economic regulation of the airline industry began with the passage of the Civil Aeronautics Act of 1938. The law created a regulatory body, known after 1940 as the Civil Aeronautics Board, to supervise, promote, and develop a safe, efficient, and cost-effective airline industry in the United States. It governed almost every aspect of the airlines' existence. The CAB awarded routes to airlines, restricted entry of new airlines into the industry (allowing only one new major airline with a full certificate during the next 40 years), established subsidy levels for lines operating less profitable routes, governed mergers and acquisitions, set fares for air passengers and cargo across the nation, and administered the smallest details of service quality. "True competition among the airlines," one airline observer noted, "has been reduced to a measure of warmth in the smile of a stewardess."[44]

Such regulation effectively prohibited airlines from engaging in ruinous competition and provided stability. The system had its faults, but, under regulation, the United States witnessed the creation of an air system that was the envy of the world. The number of air passengers steadily increased, airlines invested in ever-larger and faster airliners, and the industry remained relatively stable. But airlines still struggled to earn a profit. Upon his retirement in 1968, American Airlines' legendary head, C. R. Smith, looked over the airline business as a whole and expressed his belief that no one could make money in the industry as it existed.[45]

The situation was about to get worse. Boeing developed the 747 Jumbo Jet during the late 1960s. The Boeing 747 was a true giant, five stories tall, capable of carrying 350 to 500 passengers with 10-abreast seating and twin aisles within its massive 20-foot-wide cabin. Within the cabin, Boeing placed the first closable overhead stowage bins on a commercial airliner. This innovation allowed passengers to place more than coats and hats above their seats and not fear that their carry-on luggage might become a hazard should the flight encounter turbulence. The expansive cabin sported eight lavatories in the coach section, permitting airlines for the first time to specify some lavatories for women only. Although Pan American and the Boeing Company originally envisioned the 747 with two cabins stacked one on top of the other, the Boeing design team wisely chose a single-cabin layout so that the aircraft would be both a good passenger aircraft and a good freighter. The team placed the 747 flight deck above the cabin so that, with the addition of a hinged nose, a 747 freighter could accommodate cargo containers loaded from the front. A fairing behind the cockpit gave the 747 its famous hump. Some airlines creatively transformed the space

The Boeing 747, the first Jumbo Jet, set the standard as the largest passenger aircraft for the next three decades. Placing the cockpit above the main deck allowed Boeing designers to equip the cargo version of the aircraft with a hinged nose door that permitted loading straight into the airplane. (From the *St. Louis Globe-Democrat* Archives of the St. Louis Mercantile Library at the University of Missouri–St. Louis)

under that hump into a cocktail lounge. During what became known as the lounge war, American Airlines installed an electric piano accompanied by Frank Sinatra, Jr., in a 747 lounge for a flight from Los Angeles to New York in August 1971.[46]

Boeing's concern about designing the 747 as an effective aircraft for either carrying passengers or hauling freight sprang from the anticipated debut of the supersonic transport (SST). The aviation industry in the 1960s assumed that SSTs, flying at more than twice the speed of sound, would quickly relegate large subsonic airliners to hauling cargo. Many experts believed that the Anglo-French Concorde and the Boeing 2707, the company's flagship program funded by the federal government, would make subsonic jets obsolete. Among other airlines, TWA placed provisional orders for both the Concorde and the Boeing 2707 before technological, economic, political, and environmental considerations led the U.S. government to deny the SST program further funding. The Soviet Union's SST, the Tupolev Tu-144, grabbed the honor of being the world's first SST to fly, taking to the sky on December 31, 1968. Extremely expensive to operate, the Tu-144 spent less than three years in commercial service. The Concorde's maiden flight on March 2, 1969, earned it the title of the second SST to fly. Routinely cruising at 1,320 miles per hour nearly 10 miles above the earth, the awe-inspiring Concorde entered trans-Atlantic service in 1976 after Pan Am, TWA, American, United, and other U.S. airlines had cancelled their orders primarily because of the unacceptably high operating costs, mainly the unacceptably high cost of satisfying the aircraft's enormous appetite for fuel.[47]

Just when airlines began to introduce the Boeing 747 Jumbo Jet and the wide-bodied Lockheed L-1011 and McDonnell Douglas DC-10 into their fleets in the early 1970s, the entire national economy nose-dived, and an oil crisis sent fuel prices skyrocketing. Within two years, the price of jet fuel surged from 25 cents to more than $1 per gallon. Passenger growth did not keep pace with the creation of airline seats. Huge airplanes crisscrossed the nation, but they were often almost empty. Airlines lost money. The CAB's solution was higher fares, resulting in slower growth in passenger boardings. The number of people flying in 1975 was less than in 1974. Prevented from competing on fares, airlines competed with lavish amenities, such as a piano lounge atop a winding staircase in 747s, posh food service, and free hard liquor available even to coach passengers. Each new or altered amenity required CAB approval.[48]

In the midst of the economic crisis and the CAB's regulatory absurdities, airlines operating within the confines of one state, and thus not subject to CAB rule, succeeded. Pacific Southwest Airlines (PSA) in California and Southwest Airlines in Texas defied the odds,

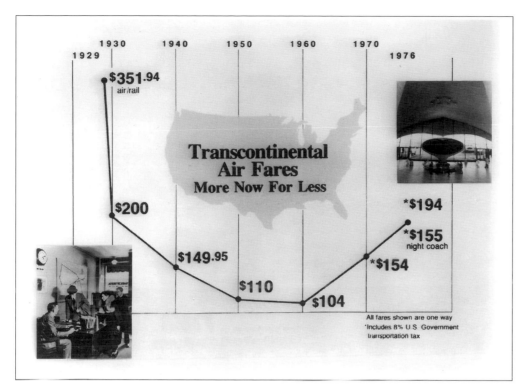

earning money by flying intrastate passengers at rates far below their interstate competition. A deregulatory movement gained momentum on Capitol Hill, and the Airline Deregulation Act was passed in 1978. Senators Edward Kennedy and Howard Cannon propelled the legislation toward passage in spite of opposition from airlines, unions, and safety advocates. These groups feared that, in an open market environment, unfettered competition and nonunion employees would compromise safety. The bill that President Carter signed into law in October 1978 set in motion sweeping changes by lifting economic regulations from the airline industry. Starting in 1981, airlines could enter the market and establish new routes without governmental approval. Beginning in 1982, the CAB could no longer regulate airfares. And the CAB itself was scheduled to disappear in 1984. Market forces, not a regulatory body, would now dictate the structure of the air transportation industry in the United States. A new and tumultuous era for airline passengers had dawned.[49]

The Era of Airline Deregulation and 9/11

Events moved quickly in the wake of airline deregulation. The transcontinental air passenger felt its influence almost immediately. A host of new airlines entered the market. In 1978 only 36 airlines using planes that seated 61 or more passengers operated in the United States. Six years later 123 such airlines vied for business across the nation. These upstarts, with names such as People Express and America West Airlines, competed with existing airlines on their most valuable routes and ignored the less profitable ones, particularly routes connecting smaller cities. The large airlines had to evolve strategies for survival in the deregulated environment.

Hub-and-Spoke Networks

One survival strategy the large airlines used was the widespread adoption of hub-and-spoke route networks. Under this system, an airline designated an airport as a hub, or central transfer point, from which routes radiated outward, like spokes on a wheel. Passengers at the airports at the ends of the spokes were flown to the hub in waves of flights called banks, which arrived at the hub within a short time of each other. Passengers then quickly interchanged to destinations at the ends of other spokes. The primary advantage of the hub-and-spoke network was that "by collecting passengers bound for all the spoke cities, [small] markets [could] be served more frequently, and usually more cheaply, than if all city-pair markets were served only by direct flights." A limited number of flights in a hub-and-spoke network could facilitate a much greater number of connections than could the same number of flights in point-to-point service.[1]

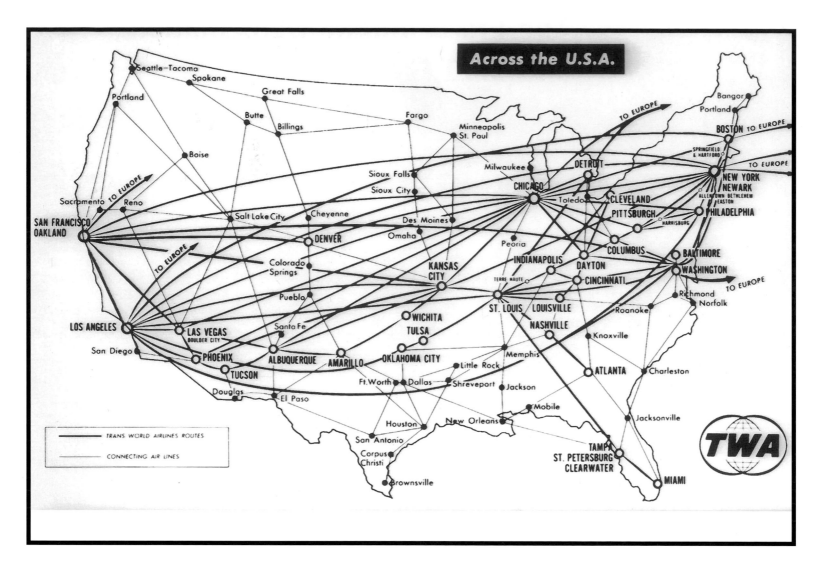

A TWA domestic system map on the eve of deregulation shows the
airline's reach to all quarters of the United States using a point-
to-point routing system. Most passengers flew directly from origin
to destination without changing planes en route. (From the TWA
Archives of the St. Louis Mercantile Library at the University of
Missouri–St. Louis)

The basic hub-and-spoke concept of route organization was not new in the late 1970s. From the time of the earliest airlines, some great centers of business and population, such as New York and Chicago, acted as hubs with routes radiating from them. Passengers on Delta Air Lines claimed that their flights were always via Atlanta. However, the idea of concentrating through-traffic at hubs was a more recent innovation. The first practical application of the concept was the idea of Lamar Muse. In 1967 this pioneer in modern air transport became president of financially troubled Universal Airlines. The company operated some passenger charter flights and held contracts with the military, yet found itself in financial trouble. Hoping to capture the air cargo business for domestic auto manufacturers, Muse developed a hubbing operation at Willow Run Airport, near Detroit, for shipping automobile parts. Every night, Universal handled almost 2.5 million pounds of cargo entirely through the single terminal at Willow Run. The hub-and-spoke experiment was a stunning success as Universal went from near financial ruin to a profit of $2.8 million within one year.[2]

Another air cargo operation based on a hub-and-spoke network began operations in 1973. Frederick W. Smith, only 29 years old at the time, founded Federal Express, using Memphis as the sorting hub for all cargo, specifically air express packages weighing less than 50 pounds each. Federal Express's Falcon business jets arrived during the night in Memphis, bringing packages from around the nation. Part-time workers quickly sorted the packages and loaded them back onto the jets bound for delivery before noon the next day. Smith and Muse had the freedom to use hub-and-spoke routing because their airplanes carried less than 7,500 pounds of cargo at one time, thereby exempting them from Civil Aeronautics Board regulation. Federal Express enjoyed phenomenal success as the small Falcons were soon joined by Boeing 727s and wide-bodied McDonnell Douglas and Airbus cargo jets.[3]

In spite of the CAB's restraint in awarding routes, by 1976 12 of the 15 largest domestic airlines had developed hubs, each with at least 50 daily departures by 1976. In that year, 52 percent of airline passengers boarding flights at Hartsfield-Jackson Atlanta International Airport were making connections to other destination cities. The figure climbed to 60 percent by 1980.[4]

The Airline Deregulation Act of 1978 opened the door for the hubbing of passenger traffic on a grand scale. By 1984 thirteen of the fifteen pre-deregulation airlines operated one or more hubs, each with more than 100 daily departures. Hub-and-spoke routing came to dominate airline operations. Each of the three largest airlines in the United States created two large hubs, with 200 or more daily departures apiece. An additional nine large airlines possessed one major hub, and many airlines also operated a number of secondary hubs with at least 100 daily departures.[5]

Airbus

Founded in 1970 as a consortium of European aircraft manufacturers, Airbus Industrie aspired to rival the dominance of American companies such as Boeing and McDonnell Douglas in the world aircraft market. In 1966, aviation firms from France, the United Kingdom, and Germany petitioned their respective governments for financial assistance to jointly develop the world's first wide-body twin-engine jetliner, dubbed the A300 the following year. After extensive negotiations and the British government's withdrawal from the consortium, Airbus Industrie emerged in late 1970 under an agreement that had a majority of the work on the A300 going to French and German firms and a minority to firms in the Netherlands, the United Kingdom, and Spain. The first airplane flew in 1972 and entered airline service two years later. The consortium struggled to compete with American firms, selling only 81 aircraft by 1979. A smaller-capacity twinjet, the A310— derived from the A300 and first flown in 1982—was one of the first commercial aircraft with a "glass cockpit" that replaced analog dials with electronic panel displays.

The development of the smaller A320 established Airbus as a vital competitor in the global aviation marketplace. Designed to compete against the Boeing 737, the A320 chalked up over 400 orders even before its first flight in 1987. The innovative A320 sported "fly-by-wire" controls that replaced the traditional wires and cables between the cockpit and control surfaces with an electronic system featuring a computer programmed to respond to a pilot's commands. In 1987, Airbus launched both the A330 twinjet and the A340 long-range, four-engine jetliner. The A330 flew in 1992, one year after its larger sibling's first flight and Airbus's first year of operating profit. Attempting to streamline its corporate structure, Airbus Industrie became Airbus SAS in 2000, with European Aeronautic Defence and Space Company (EADS) owning 80 percent, and BAE Systems the remaining 20 percent. In 2002, Airbus launched the four-engine, double deck, twin-aisle superjumbo designated the A380. First flown in 2005, it claimed the title of largest passenger airliner in the world, capable of carrying up to 853 passengers in one class. The company's next product, the A350, was launched in 2006 as a direct competitor to Boeing's 787. Today Airbus and Boeing stand alone as the two global giants of large commercial jetliner production.

Why the rush to establish large hubs? The answer was found in one word: competition. After deregulation in 1978, the big airlines suddenly found themselves vulnerable. A free-market environment invited the older lines, as well as the myriad upstarts, to take the pick of any route in America on which they thought they could make a profit. The large trunk carriers such as United, TWA, and American quickly answered the challenge with a strategy based on so-called fortress hubs, some of which had already been well established for many years. Choosing one or two strategically placed large airports as primary hubs, the lines transformed them into huge operating bases in control of the majority of traffic. Once it had claimed a fortress hub, an airline would spread a web of frequent daily flights from the hub to any city where the line's leadership believed a profit could be made.

A competing airline attempting to retain or garner any sizable share of the traffic at another line's fortress hub encountered a daunting task. The existing airline restricted new entrants by maintaining an array of connecting flights, often with surplus capacity or excessive frequency, in order to dominate the market. A new entrant would typically offer connections on other carriers because it did not have sufficient flights.[6]

The hub-and-spoke networks were not a panacea for the major airlines. Air traffic congestion at large hubs was the primary disadvantage. For a network to operate smoothly, banks of flights had to land within a narrow window of time so that passengers could connect with their continuing flights. Additionally, the air traffic control systems at large hubs had the responsibility to manage the waves of incoming and departing flights in short order while ensuring the safety of all within their care. If air traffic control system became overwhelmed, delays and possibly disaster could result. Therefore, airlines discovered they had to limit the number of departures from hubs according to the capabilities of the airports, regardless of market potential.

Another disadvantage for airlines using hub-and-spoke was the comparatively shorter flight distances. Before hubbing, what had once been a nonstop flight was now two flight segments connecting through a hub. For example, TWA passengers flying from Boston to Los Angeles in the 1980s and 1990s now had to connect through the airline's St. Louis hub, whereas the service had formerly been nonstop between the two cities. The need to change planes at the hub added one to two hours of travel time to the five hours that the nonstop flight had taken.[7]

However, despite the inconveniences of the hub-and-spoke network, deregulation contributed to declining airfares. The ink was barely dry on the 1978 Act when coast-to-coast fares plummeted to $99.99, a level reminiscent of the early 1950s introduction of coach class. Between 1977 and 1992, the average airfare in the United States, adjusted for inflation, declined by one-third.[8]

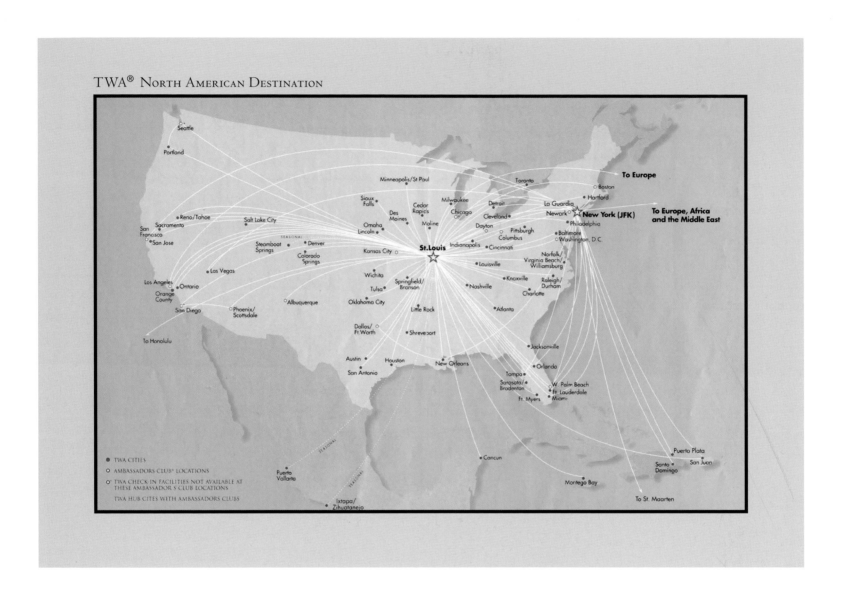

A TWA map of North American destinations dated 1998 graphically depicts the route changes made after the airline designated St. Louis as its primary domestic hub in 1982. For example, the flights that had been nonstop between Chicago and western cities, including Phoenix and San Francisco, in the 1970s were now connecting flights through the St. Louis hub. (From the author's collection)

Low-Fare Airlines

The growth of low-fare airlines played a key role in forcing airfares downward across the board. After deregulation, the quintessential low-fare carrier, Southwest Airlines, emerged from its home state of Texas to change the face of air travel. Led by the always cheerful Herb Kelleher, Southwest made air travel a truly democratic experience. Keeping costs to a minimum, it offered rock-bottom fares to passengers crowded into one-class, unassigned seating on its fleet of Boeing 737s. Aboard these buses in the sky, casually dressed flight attendants served limited snacks and beverages with a dash of humor. Albeit the flights were more comfortable and reliable, some aspects of the passenger experience aboard Southwest Airlines recalled the nonscheduled lines of the postwar era. The informality of the crew and the Spartan nature of accommodations on modern, low-fare lines was in some ways similar to what nonsked passengers endured in the 1940s and 1950s. But even Southwest's standards were havens of comfort relative to the austerity of the postwar nonskeds.[9]

Reporter Roy Furchgott wrote of his transcontinental flying experience aboard Southwest Airlines in 1999. He flew from Baltimore to Oakland with a half-hour stop in Kansas City and seven hours in the air. The airline, of course, served no meals but did offer three servings of snacks along the way. The "snack food banquet," according to Furchgott, started with a package of small graham crackers leading up to "a ham stick, sesame crackers, a cheese wedge, a NutriGrain Twist, nuts, raisins, and drinks." Seated next to Furchgott, a young engineer for Butler Manufacturing revealed that he had paid $356 for his ticket from Baltimore to Kansas City six days earlier. Other airlines had offered him similar flights for $850. "Five hundred dollars seemed like too much for a small food tray," he observed.[10]

In-flight food service underwent a dramatic change on most airlines after deregulation. American Airlines was among the first of the major airlines to begin removing perks when it decided in 1986 to eliminate olives from salads. That small measure was the start of paring back the multicourse meals in first class and even eliminating complimentary food service for coach passengers on many domestic flights. Two decades later, several airlines charged for in-flight meals. American, US Airways, United, and other airlines offered snacks and/or meals for $3 to $7 each to coach passengers on flights longer than three and a half hours. Other airlines, such as Continental, Delta, Frontier, Alaska, JetBlue, and Southwest, continued offering free snacks and nonalcoholic beverages.[11]

Roy Furchgott noted that the passengers on his 1999 Southwest flight acted congenially toward each other, starting with how they figured out their own seating arrangements upon boarding. In the absence of music or movies, passengers read books and magazines, worked on laptop computers, or visited with their neighbors. The Southwest flight crew kept the atmosphere of the flight positive even though, on this particular occasion, they did not tell many jokes or sing songs to amuse the passengers. Southwest kept its passengers happy by providing a consistent product at a low price. Little wonder that the airline could be called the "Wal-Mart of the skies."

In the deregulated environment, with its new set of rules, the domestic airlines lost a combined $12.7 billion between 1990 and 1993, causing several of the industry's most revered corporate names to pass into history. Pan American and Eastern Air Lines disappeared in 1991. The following year TWA, Continental, and America West Airlines were under Chapter 11 bankruptcy. TWA returned to bankruptcy once again before it was taken over by American Airlines in 2001. America West merged with US Airways four years later.[12]

Frequent Flyer Programs

In the cutthroat competition of the deregulated air travel market, airlines sought any and all means to attract and retain the loyalty of their passengers. In the late 1970s, American Airlines discovered that only 5 percent of its customers flew approximately 40 percent of its passenger seat miles. Taking a cue from S&H Green Stamps in the retail trade, American's Robert Crandall and Tom Plaskett created an airline loyalty program that allowed passengers to accumulate mileage toward free air travel. After flying a specified number of miles on American Airlines, passengers could redeem the miles for complimentary flights. Thus, in 1981, the frequent flyer program was born. Western and Southwest Airlines had introduced small-scale variations of the idea, but American, with its 25 million annual passengers, was the first to bring a frequent flyer program of such large extent to the industry. Within months of American's lead, all the major airlines had similar frequent flyer programs.[13]

Within the next quarter century, over 180 million people worldwide became frequent flyer members and took approximately 280 million free trips. Surprisingly, by the early twenty-first century, members earned a majority of frequent flier miles annually from activities other than flying. The primary way to earn miles became credit card purchases. Frequent flyer program members could spend accumulated miles to purchase magazine subscriptions, vacation packages, and electronics, to list only a few options. As one writer stated, "Frequent flyer miles have become a currency."[14]

A brochure from Southwest Airlines advertises the line's frequent flyer program called "Rapid Rewards." Instead of tracking miles flown, Southwest's program awarded a complimentary round-trip ticket to any Southwest destination after only eight completed round-trips. (From the author's collection)

The Impact of the Internet

Beginning in the 1990s, the Internet changed the nature of air travel. People seeking to purchase flight tickets had direct access to information previously available only through registered travel agents. Airlines themselves established websites to sell flights directly to the public, and other sites, such as Travelocity.com and Expedia.com, allowed comparison shopping among more than the few selected flights a travel agent would typically show. The Internet empowered the consumer and forced down prices even further through online discounting.[15]

Selling travel online allowed airlines to offer paperless ticketing and to couple it with the automation of other tasks. Passengers could check in at self-service kiosks in airport terminals, avoiding the long lines and overworked employees at check-in counters. Automation became so standard that airlines began charging a fee on tickets purchased over the phone rather than online.[16]

In stark contrast to the steak dinners set before passengers on other airlines, the packs of peanuts handed to Southwest's passengers became symbolic of the airline's thrift as it succeeded financially with low fares and few amenities. (From the author's collection)

Air Travel Frustrations

In the wake of deregulation, the number of domestic air passengers increased dramatically. Nearly 254 million passengers boarded domestic flights in 1978. That figure nearly doubled to 499 million by 1995. By the turn of the twenty-first century, more than 600 million souls crowded the nation's airliners and airports annually. Passengers wearied of long lines, cramped airliner cabins, canceled flights, and endless delays as the commercial air system struggled to keep up with the demand. The system was safe and affordable, yet the airline passenger's experience was anything but pleasant.[17]

Even before deregulation, popular magazines exposed the downsides of air travel. Articles with titles such as "The Two Worst Headaches in Air Travel" and "The Five Worst Hassles in Air Travel" shed light on flyers' frustrations.

For starters, airlines habitually sold more tickets per flight than there were available seats because a significant portion of ticket holders often failed to appear for boarding. Once an airliner pulled away from the terminal, any unfilled seats on the flight were as valuable as spoiled fruit. The inherent risk for airlines in overbooking, or "capacity management," was the chance that everyone who held a ticket for a flight would arrive to take the flight. The shortage of seats to accommodate all ticket holders would force the airline to bump the last passengers who obtained confirmed reservations. If the airline could not put the bumped passengers on a flight arriving at their destination within one to two hours of the original flight's scheduled arrival, they were entitled to monetary compensation. The number of airline passengers with confirmed reservations who were denied seats because airlines had oversold flights was estimated as high as 300,000 even in the mid-1960s.

In response, some passengers made it a practice before the widespread use of computers to book reservations on several competing airlines so that they could be certain of a seat on at least one. Airlines struck back with restrictions on discounted tickets, including no refunds or transfers without penalties. And instead of bumping passengers against their will, airlines implemented a new policy in 1978. They kept more customers happy by asking for volunteers willing to be bumped on overbooked flights. Some passengers even booked flights in the hope that the airline would call for volunteers to be bumped. In most instances the bumped passengers arrived at their destination an hour or two later than planned, but they received a free future flight and/or money from the airline.[18]

At the turn of the twenty-first century, airline passengers in the United States were fed up with the state of air travel. An April 2001 article in *Newsweek* magazine, "Why Flying Is Hell," succinctly stated the problems: "For many Americans, the hassles and exasperation at every stage of the trip have never seemed worse. Long lines at crowded airports. Grumpy airline workers. Delays at the gate. Fights for space in the overhead bins. More delays on the runway." The root causes included too many passengers flying through airports not built to accommodate the increased volume and an air traffic control system unable to handle all the flights in a timely fashion. Since a large percentage of flights in the nation connected through major hubs, even minor delays at Chicago's O'Hare, New York's JFK, or Atlanta's Hartsfield-Jackson rippled across the nation with a compounding effect. Passengers crowded into airport waiting areas and sat, sometimes for hours, trapped in aircraft anticipating clearance for takeoff. Once in the air, the situation was often not much better.

A reporter for the *Wall Street Journal* chronicled some of her experiences flying transcontinental in 2001. Flying from Newark to Los Angeles aboard a Boeing 737-800, Laura Landro waited for two hours to use one of the aircraft's three bathrooms. Airlines were using smaller aircraft instead of wide-body jetliners in transcontinental service as a cost-saving measure. But a full load of passengers on the smaller airplanes overwhelmed the lavatories, prompting at least one airline to eventually install an additional restroom in each of its Boeing 737-800s.

On another occasion, Landro flew business class on a Boeing 767 from New York JFK to San Francisco. Early in the flight the passenger in front of her fully reclined his seat and promptly went to sleep. Landro's dismay at having the man's head in her personal space was matched only by the loud-talking lawyer behind her. Ready for lunch, she lowered her tray table and discovered it was "caked with some previous passenger's meal remains." A flight attendant apologized for the mess and cleaned the tray with hand towels.[19]

Disabled Air Passengers

If the air travel experience was frequently unpleasant for the average passenger, it was even more so for passengers with disabilities. Individuals with physical disabilities rarely flew on commercial airlines before President Ronald Reagan signed the Air Carrier Access Act (ACAA) of 1986. According to the National Council on Disability, "Often, people with certain disabilities either chose not to fly or travel by air knowing they would probably face prejudice, hostility, disability stereotyping, as well as architectural and other physical barriers; sometimes they faced an outright denial of their right to travel."[20]

One of the first disabled airline passengers in United States history was Franklin Delano Roosevelt, then governor of New York. The day after learning that he had received the Democratic Party's nomination for president in 1932, Roosevelt flew from New York to Chicago on an American Airlines' Ford Tri-Motor with his family and staff members to address his party's convention. Airline personnel built a ramp so that he could be brought aboard the airplane in his wheelchair and seated next to the door. The flight energized Roosevelt's campaign, as he became the first presidential candidate to fly in an airliner. Except for Theodore Roosevelt, who took a brief flight in 1910 in an open biplane after he had left office, no president had flown at all before.[21]

Unlike FDR, other disabled Americans found airlines were not so accommodating. Disabled Americans who flew discovered repeatedly that wheelchairs were unavailable in airports, and airline personnel damaged wheelchairs belonging to passengers. Airlines frequently failed to provide assistance to the disabled or to provide accessible lavatories. Guide dogs often traveled in baggage compartments. Because safety and flight information in terminals and aboard aircraft was given verbally only, hearing-impaired passengers were left out. And navigating the expanse of a large terminal intimidated even the most determined disabled passenger.

After an extensive lobbying effort, Congress enacted the ACAA. The law forbade commercial airlines from discriminating against the nearly five million disabled Americans who needed access to air travel. A final rule from the Department of Transportation (DOT), outlining regulations for airlines to make accommodations for disabled passengers, would cost an estimated $400 million to several billion dollars. The rule called for, among other items, wheelchair-accessible lavatories in new, wide-body aircraft, onboard wheelchairs, and movable armrests on 50 percent of an aircraft's aisle seats. The rule also required airlines to modify ticketing, boarding, and seating practices to accommodate disabled passengers.[22]

Nevertheless, discrimination persisted. Ten years after the ACAA became law, the Paralyzed Veterans of America surveyed 500 air travelers with disabilities. All but 48 respondents had grievances about their access to air travel. Under the law, the Department of Transportation accepted formal complaints and had authority to fine airlines not complying with the ACAA. From mid-1990 until October 1997, the DOT received 1,728 disability-related complaints against airlines in the United States. Disabled individuals requiring wheelchairs filed nearly 60 percent of those complaints. Half of their complaints were against airlines that failed to provide them with wheelchairs or other necessary assistance in getting them to restrooms or to provide information appropriate to an individual's disability. Other common complaints were related to airlines losing or damaging assistive devices and refusing to board disabled passengers. The DOT fined several airlines for violating the ACAA, enforced compliance with the ACAA, and continued to investigate complaints from disabled passengers into the twenty-first century.[23]

September 11, 2001

Just when many air travelers believed that the inconveniences were nearly intolerable, terrorists used transcontinental jetliners to strike targets in New York City and Washington, D.C., on September 11, 2001. That morning, 247 passengers and crew expected to travel across the United States on four routine flights from the East Coast. They did not know that a team of 19 terrorists would use those airliners, symbols of the United States' technological power and might, as weapons of mass terror.[24]

Five terrorists boarded American Airlines Flight 11, leaving Boston for Los Angeles. They seized control of the airliner soon after takeoff, flew south to New York City, and crashed the fully loaded Boeing 767 into the North Tower of the World Trade Center. Five more terrorists took over United Airlines Flight 175 from Boston to Los Angeles and rammed it into the World Trade Center's South Tower. Less than two hours after the first tower shuddered with the impact of Flight 11, both towers collapsed to the ground.

As part of the coordinated attack, five terrorists seized American Airlines Flight 77, bound for Los Angeles from Washington's Dulles International Airport, and crashed it into the Pentagon. Four other terrorists boarded United Airlines Flight 93 at Newark International Airport, bound for San Francisco. Although they gained control of the airplane, passengers bravely confronted them, and the Boeing 757 crashed into the Pennsylvania countryside, short of the terrorists' intended target (the Capitol or the White House in Washington). The attacks that day cost the lives of nearly 3,300 Americans—the greatest loss of life on U.S. soil in a single day since the Civil War.[25]

Metal detectors and baggage screening devices similar to those in this photograph confronted air travelers in the 1980s and 1990s. The terrorist attacks of September 11, 2001, prompted many changes, such as the federalization of airport security employees and more thorough screening procedures. (From the *St. Louis Globe-Democrat* Archives of the St. Louis Mercantile Library at the University of Missouri–St. Louis)

This ubiquitous scene is replicated each day at every large airport in the United States. Before September 11, 2001, the general public was allowed to pass through security screening to gate areas of commercial airports. The Transportation Security Administration changed that, allowing only ticketed passengers to continue to the airline gates for departure. Passengers prove their status, presenting a boarding pass and photo identification to a TSA officer at the start of the security line. Notice the casual style of passengers' carry-on luggage and clothing, in contrast to the more formal styles in earlier decades of air travel. (From the author's collection)

Fearing additional attacks, federal authorities ordered air traffic controllers to ground all traffic in the nation's skies for 48 hours, before allowing a gradual return of airline operations. Air travel in the United States would never be the same. In the coming months and years, the federal government assumed more responsibility for passenger screening. The newly created Transportation Security Administration (TSA) placed federal employees at airport security checkpoints. Accustomed to meeting departing and arriving passengers at airline gates, nonticketed civilians discovered that they were no longer permitted to go through security into boarding areas of the airport. Seemingly at every turn, passengers had to prove their identity and underwent more intrusive levels of security screening than ever before. Security personnel instructed passengers to remove their jackets and shoes, waved electronic wands over their bodies, and even strip-searched some passengers. As one woman reported after taking a flight in early 2002, "In the space of only eight hours I was pulled out of line, patted down, wanded and, not to be coy, generally felt up at two major airports."[26]

Scissors, box cutters, fingernail files, and a long list of additional items were now subject to confiscation from carry-on baggage because they could be potential weapons. As the specific types of terroristic threats evolved, the TSA continued to revise the list of objects passengers could not carry aboard. After the discovery of a plot to blow up aircraft over the Atlantic Ocean using liquid explosives, the TSA temporarily prohibited passengers from carrying most liquids and gels aboard flights. The ban extended to quintessential travel items such as gel deodorant, toothpaste, hairspray, contact lens solution, and bottled beverages. Air travelers accommodated themselves to the new restrictions, but further inconveniences carried the potential to deter some passengers from air travel, put them on the nation's highways and rails, or even keep them at home. The threat of terror in the skies now overshadowed every part of the air travel experience.[27]

This United Airlines Boeing 777 symbolizes the advances made in transcontinental air travel over the span of 80 years. Filled with passengers of modest means who consider the journey routine, the jetliner has proved an efficient means of mass transportation unrivaled by ground modes for long-distance travel. Today's coast-to-coast air passengers take for granted the convenience, speed, and safety of jetliners such as the one depicted here. (Photography by Adrian Pingstone)

Conclusion

The attacks of September 11 prompted airline passengers to reflect upon the air travel experience. Gone were the days when stewardesses memorized each passenger's name, in-flight food arrived on china plates, passengers received formal certificates just for flying at altitudes over 20,000 feet, air travelers dressed in their finest clothes, airport security meant keeping livestock from roaming on runways, pilots strolled the cabin chatting with passengers, and complimentary meals and amenities were taken for granted. Yet even in the golden age of sleek Lockheed Constellations and Douglas DC-7s, air travelers put up with cabins filled with noise and vibration. Twenty-first-century passengers do not face the discomforts or high prices of decades past. In spite of coach passengers' gripes about cramped personal space, journeys in Boeing or Airbus jetliners are smoother than trips taken in most private cars.

Air travel, once feared, has become the safest mode of transportation. As of 2007, the U.S. safety record since September 2001 has been immaculate, while more than 40,000 people are killed on the nation's roads each year.

The transcontinental air travel experience certainly has room for improvement in the early twenty-first century, but within only 80 years it has evolved from a daring adventure for the select few into the nation's dominant commercial mode of transporting intercity passengers. By the year 1957, when the domestic airlines first recorded more passenger miles than the railroads, air travel had assumed a key role in the nation's economy and way of life because it overcame time and space, bringing people together as never before. Frequent flyers measured distance in hours; the actual miles between cities mattered little. Air transportation offered the shortest travel times over distances exceeding a few hundred miles.

Unprecedented speed was and is the single most important feature of the air travel experience. Air passengers, by and large, have boarded airliners not because they wanted to fly but rather because they wanted to reach their destinations in the shortest time possible. Pioneering transcontinental air passengers, such as Will Rogers and Marcia Davenport, were the latest in a series of intrepid travelers dating back to the amazing journey of Meriwether Lewis and William Clark. With each new technological advance, the pace accelerated. And although much of the glamour, the mystique, and the innocent excitement of air travel had been lost in the march toward lower fares and greater security, we should not lose sight of the positive aspects of flying across America.

Appendix

Airliner speeds increased rapidly until the dawn of the jet age. Early jets, such as the Boeing 707, cruised at approximately 600 miles per hour. Cruising speeds of 100 miles per hour had been the norm only 30 years earlier. The rapid increase of commercial aircraft cruising speeds gave way to an era of little change. Except for the supersonic Aerospatiale/BAC Concorde, no scheduled commercial airliners in the United States cruised above the speed of sound, because of economic, political, and environmental concerns.

Airliner Cruising Speeds and Passenger Capacities

Make and model of airliner	Year of first flight	Estimated cruising speed (mph)	Maximum passenger seats
Boeing 40A	1927	110	2
Fokker F-10	1927	120	12
Ford 5-AT-B Tri-Motor	1928	110	17
Boeing 80A	1928	120	18
Boeing 247	1933	160	10
Douglas DC-2	1934	170	14
Douglas DC-3	1935	180	21
Lockheed L-14	1937	250	12
Boeing 307 Stratoliner	1938	200	33
Douglas DC-4	1942	200	40
Lockheed L-049 Constellation	1943	300	54
Douglas DC-6	1946	310	56
Douglas DC-7	1953	360	99
Boeing 707	1957	600	181
Boeing 727	1963	600	131
Douglas DC-9	1965	560	90
Boeing 737	1967	570	119
Aerospatiale/BAC Concorde	1969	1,320	140
Boeing 747	1969	580	490
McDonnell Douglas DC-10	1970	550	345
Lockheed L-1011	1970	550	345
Airbus A300	1972	560	330
Boeing 767	1981	550	290
Boeing 757	1982	570	279
Airbus A320	1987	540	164
Boeing 777	1994	550	440
Airbus A380	2005	560	853
Boeing 787	2009	560	250

Sources: Boyne, *Beyond the Horizons*; R. E. G. Davies, *Airlines of the United States*; R. E. G. Davies, *Delta*; R. E. G. Davies, *TWA*; Gunston, *Illustrated Encyclopedia of Propeller Airliners*; Boeing Company, *Brief History of the Boeing Company*.

Notes

Introduction

1. See LeBow, Cal Rogers and the Vin Fiz; and Stein, *Flight of the Vin Fiz*.
2. Berg, *Lindbergh*, 112–77; Corn, *Winged Gospel*, 21–27.
3. Maury Klein, "The and the End of the Great West," *Invention and Technology* 11 (Winter 1995): 10.
4. Schwantes, *Long Day's Journey*, 97–100.
5. For the best account of the building of the first transcontinental railroad, consult Bain, *Empire Express*.
6. D. Brown, *Hear That Lonesome Whistle Blow*, 136–70.
7. The best bibliography of transcontinental car travel is Bliss, *Autos across America*. The first coast-to-coast journey by bus is recorded in Lewis R. Freeman, "From Chicago to Los Angeles on Common Carrier Lines." *Bus Transportation* 5 (June 1926): 295–98.
8. Davis, "Air Travel," 30, 92; R. E. G. Davies, *Fallacies and Fantasies*, 84; Solberg, *Conquest of the Skies*, 406.

Chapter 1: Flying with the Mail

1. Serling, Legend and Legacy, 9–10; Gunston, *Illustrated Encyclopedia of Propeller Airliners*, 46.
2. Warner, *Early History of Air Transportation*, 51; United Air Lines, *Corporate and Legal History*, 20; R. E. G. Davies, Airlines of the United States, 58–59; Serling, Legend and Legacy, 10.
3. Boyne, *De Havilland DH-4*, 31; Serling, Legend and Legacy, 11.
4. Leary, *Aerial Pioneers*, 10–29; Van der Linden, *Airlines and Air Mail*, 3–5.
5. Leary, Aerial Pioneers, 140–42.
6. Allen, *Airline Builders*, 51–69; R. E. G. Davies, *Airlines of the United States*, 31–79.
7. Cherington, *Airline Price Policy*, 140; H. L. Smith, *Airways*, 112.
8. R. E. G. Davies, *History of the World's Airlines*, 44–45: Serling, *The Only Way to Fly*, 39–40.
9. Serling, *The Only Way to Fly*, 40–41.
10. Ibid., 41–42; Solberg, *Conquest of the Skies*, 104.
11. *Chicago Herald and Examiner* (July 2–3, 1927).
12. Mead, "Journeying with the Boeing Air Mail," 990–93.
13. See Yagoda, *Will Rogers*.
14. W. Rogers, "Flying and Eating My Way East," 3.
15. Capt. Chas. W. Purcell, "Flying Not as Dangerous as Motoring," *Popular Aviation* 9 (November 1931): 13–14.
16. Solberg, *Conquest of the Skies*, 173.
17. Lane, "Flying with the Western Air Mails," 54.
18. Stearns, "All Aboard by Air," 35.
19. Serling, *The Only Way to Fly*, 36–37.
20. Lane, "Flying with the Western Air Mails," 54.
21. Ibid., 14; *Serling*, Eagle, 17.
22. W. Rogers, "Flying and Eating My Way East," 114.
23. Melissa Biggs Bradley, "Vegas: Where Anything—and Everyone—Goes," *Town and Country Travel* 3 (Summer 2005): 21.
24. W. Rogers, "Flying and Eating My Way East," 113; "The Boeing Mail Plane," *Aviation* 23 (July 4, 1927): 18.
25. Stearns, "Flying Across America," 82.
26. W. Rogers, "Flying and Eating My Way East," 113; Josephine Ripley Boyson, "Dining High," *Christian Science Monitor Weekly Magazine Section* (June 10, 1939): 4.
27. William E. Berchtold, "Food," *Aviation* 33 (November 1934): 355–56; Davenport, "Covered Wagon – 1932," 140; Mead, "Journeying with the Boeing Air Mail," 990–91.
28. W. Rogers, "Flying and Eating My Way East," 114.
29. R. E. G. Davies, *Airlines of the United States*, 61–62.
30. W. Rogers "Bucking a Head Wind," 6–7, 36.
31. Ibid., 36.
32. Leary, *Aerial Pioneers*, 206–207; Solberg, *Conquest of the Skies*, 120.
33. Henderson quoted in Komons, *Bonfires to Beacons*, 125.
34. Komons, *Bonfires to Beacons*, 125–45; Leary, *Aerial Pioneers*, 172–82, 197, 208.
35. "Aeronautical Beacon Lights," *Air Commerce Bulletin* 3 (February 1, 1932): 361.
36. "Lighting on the T.A.T.," *Airway Age* 10 (July 1929): 1045–47; "Aeronautical Beacon Lights," 362.
37. "Aeronautical Beacon Lights," 362; Komons, *Bonfires to Beacons*, 136.
38. "Aeronautical Beacon Lights," 362.
39. "America's Airways," *Air Commerce Bulletin* 1 (October 15, 1929): 1–2.
40. William M. Stair, "Air Lighthouses," *Flying* 29 (July 1941): 38–40.
41. "Aeronautical Beacon Lights," 363.
42. Stearns, "All Aboard by Air," 37.
43. W. Rogers, "Bucking a Head Wind," 36.

44. W. Rogers, "Flying and Eating My Way East," 113.

45. W. Rogers, "Bucking a Head Wind," 36.

46. Borkland, "We Take a Little Trip," 14.

Chapter 2: The Tri-Motor Era

1. Berg, *Lindbergh*, 188–90.

2. "The TAT Air Rail Service," *Railway Age* 87 (July 6, 1929): 14–15.

3. "All Aboard the Lindbergh Limited!" *Literary Digest* 100 (March 2, 1929): 54.

4. "TAT Air-Rail Service Started," *Aviation* 25 (September 8, 1928): 822.

5. "The TAT Airports," *Airway Age* 10 (July 1929): 1034.

6. For an excellent article on TAT, see George E. Hopkins, "TAT: Transcontinental Air Transport, Inc.," *American Heritage* 27 (December 1975): 22–28. See also "West to Have New Air-Rail Service," *Aviation* 25 (July 21, 1928): 265; and "The TAT Planes," *Airway Age* 10 (July 1929): 1025–27.

7. "Lindbergh Here Today," *Los Angeles Times* (July 6, 1929); "Gabel Returns from Flight to Pacific Coast," *Norristown Times-Herald* (July 3, 1929), TWA Papers, St. Louis Mercantile Library; Darling, "Across the Continent," 56.

8. Salmon, "I'll Take the High Road," 12.

9. "Train-Plane at West Goal," *Los Angeles Times* (July 10, 1929); Salmon, *I'll Take the High Road*, 18.

10. Darling, "Across the Continent," 53.

11. A. M. *Lindbergh, Hour of Gold, Hour of Lead*, 54–56.

12. Virginia Snow, "Meeting Women's Aircraft Demands," *Airway Age* 10 (November 1929): 1799, 1800; "TAT Planes," 1027, 1028; Holden, Fabulous Ford Tri-Motors, 97.

13. "TAT Planes," 1026–27; Darling, "Across the Continent in Forty-Eight Hours," 53.

14. "TAT Planes," 1027; Walter Prokosch, "Planning Transport Interiors," *Western Flying* 26 (May 1946): 50.

15. John Corpening, "First Steps," in McLaughlin, *Footsteps in the Sky*, 2–3; Serling, The Only Way to Fly, 72–73.

16. Hudson, Air Travel, 43; Solberg, *Conquest of the Skies*, 110–11; "TAT Planes," 1026, 1028.

17. McLaughlin, *Footsteps in the Sky*, 5; Darling, "Across the Continent in Forty-Eight Hours," 54–56.

18. Serling, *The Only Way to Fly*, 92.

19. Darling, "Across the Continent in Forty-Eight Hours," 55; Berchtold, "Food," 355.

20. Hopkins, "TAT," 26; "TAT Air Rail Service," 12.

21. "All Aboard the Lindbergh Limited!" 57; Berg, *Lindbergh*, 56; Darling, "Across the Continent in Forty-Eight Hours," 55.

22. Darling, "Across the Continent in Forty-Eight Hours," 56; Solberg, *Conquest of the Skies*, 114.

23. R. E. G. Davies, *Airlines of the United States*, 112–13, 591–92.

24. Allen, *Airline Builders*, 82–83; R. E. G. Davies, *Airlines of the United States*, 110–46.

25. Allen, *Airline Builders*, 84–89; Van der Linden, *Airlines and Air Mail*, 62–186.

26. Katherine A. Fisher, "Luncheon a Mile Up," *Good Housekeeping* 91 (July 1930): 84.

27. Ibid., 223.

28. *Aviation Industry*, 121.

29. Ibid.

30. Davenport, "Covered Wagon—1932," 33, 140; Solberg, *Conquest of the Skies*, 215.

31. Serling, *The Only Way to Fly*, 70.

32. Holden, *The Fabulous Ford Tri-Motors*, 96.

33. Stearns, "Flying across America," 81.

34. Davenport, "Covered Wagon—1932," 140.

35. Ibid., 143.

36. Gunston, *Illustrated Encyclopedia of Propeller Airliners*, 48.

37. Drake, "Pegasus Express," 668.

38. Harriet Fry Iden, as quoted in McLaughlin, *Footsteps in the Sky*, 17; Davenport, "Covered Wagon—1932," 143.

39. "Interiors of Cabin Airplanes," *Aero Digest* 14 (February 1929): 46; "The Boeing Model 80-A Transport," *Aero Digest* 14 (October 1929): 34.

40. Davenport, "Covered Wagon—1932," 143; Harriet Heffron Gleeson, "Pioneer in Aviation," in McLaughlin, *Footsteps in the Sky*, 20.

41. Davenport, "Covered Wagon—1932," 149.

42. Kerr, "Six Thousand Miles by Air," 75.

43. Elsa Schiaparelli, "Smartness Aloft," *Ladies' Home Journal* 46 (March 1930): 21, 69.

44. Kerr, "Six Thousand Miles by Air," 12.

45. F. J. Taylor, *High Horizons*, 116; Bowen, "Postman's Holiday," 17; Berchtold, "Food," 356.

46. Berchtold, "Food," 355.

47. Bowen, "Postman's Holiday," 17.

48. Davenport, "Covered Wagon – 1932," 149.

49. Bisgood, "Twelve Strangers in the Night," 181; F. J. Taylor, *High Horizons*, 116–17.

50. Bowen, "Postman's Holiday," 17.

51. "Smoking Permitted by Passengers," *Aviation* 31 (March 1932): 153.

52. From a report from Henry A. Burgess to Harris M. Hanshue in Serling, *The Only Way to Fly*, 90.

53. "Smoking Permitted by Passengers," 153.

54. Kerr," Six Thousand Miles by Air," 12; Harriet Fry Iden, quoted in McLaughlin, *Footsteps in the Sky*, 18.

55. F. Barrows Colton, "Aviation in Commerce and Defense," *National Geographic Magazine* 78 (December 1940): 711.

56. Bisgood, "Twelve Strangers in the Night," 180.

57. "Do Not Drop Cigarettes from Airplanes," *Aero Digest* 15 (June 1930): 94.

58. Peckham, *Sky Hostess*, 42.

59. McLaughlin, *Footsteps in the Sky*, 13.

60. Ibid.; Solberg, *Conquest of the Skies*, 212.

61. Judy Klemesrud, "Stewardess, 1930-Style," *New York Times* (May 15, 1970): 41; Drake, "Pegasus Express," 669.

62. W. B. Courtney, "High-Flying Ladies," *Collier's* 90 (August 20, 1932): 30; Drake, "Pegasus Express," 669.

63. Margaret Case Harriman, "Ring Bell for Hostess," *Woman's Home Companion* 64 (December 1937): 12.

64. Courtney, "High-Flying Ladies," 30.

65. Hudson and Pettifer, *Diamonds in the Sky*, 93; Harriman, "Ring Bell for Hostess," 12; Solberg, *Conquest of the Skies*, 215.

66. Bisgood, "Twelve Strangers in the Night," 182–83.

67. Quoted in Kenneth Hudson and Julian Pettifer, *Diamonds in the Sky*, 96.

68. Courtney, "High-Flying Ladies," 30.

69. Ibid., 29.

70. Bisgood, "Twelve Strangers in the Night," 180.

71. Gilbert Grosvenor, "Flying," *National Geographic* 63 (May 1933): 588.

72. Skinner, "Ground-Minded," 31–32.

73. *Aviation Industry*, 122.

74. Solberg, *Conquest of the Skies*, 109.

75. "Wives Travel Airlines Free," *Aero Digest* 32 (March 1938): 166.

76. Marjorie Shuler, "Their Home Is in the Troposphere," *Christian Science Monitor Weekly Magazine* Section (June 17, 1936): 5.

77. Wolfgang Langewiesche, "Eastward Bound," *Harper's Magazine* 197 (December 1948): 61.

78. James Warner Bellah, "Flying with Both Feet Off the Ground," *Saturday Evening Post* 201 (May 18, 1929): 37.

79. "Take an Air Trip," *Collier's* 89 (June 11, 1932): 50.

80. Drake, "Pegasus Express," 665. According to Greek mythology, Phaethon was the son of Helios, the god of the sun. Phaëthon learned of his father's identity later in life and, exuberant at the news, rashly asked his father's permission to drive the sun god's chariot across the sky. When Helios gave Phaëthon the reins of his mighty chariot, disaster resulted. Phaëthon was no match for the power of the chariot's immortal horses. Recklessly blazing across the sky and leaving destruction in its wake, Phaëthon's chariot even burned the ground when it came near the earth. Zeus, the ruler of the Greek gods, realized the danger of the situation and struck Phaëthon with lightning, killing him instantly.

81. See Lobeck, *Airways of America*.

82. Eleanor Roosevelt, "Flying Is Fun," *Collier's* 103 (April 22, 1939): 15, 88.

83. Porter, "Flying from Ocean to Ocean," 37.

84. Davenport, "Covered Wagon—1932," 33; Gray, "Diary of a Coast to Coast Flight," 185; Kerr," Six Thousand Miles by Air," 12.

85. Kerr," Six Thousand Miles by Air," 12.

86. Bowen, "Postman's Holiday," 17.

87. Davenport, "Covered Wagon—1932," 149.

88. Drake, "Pegasus Express," 665–66.

89. Gray, "Diary of a Coast to Coast Flight," 185.

90. Bisgood, "Twelve Strangers in the Night," 180.

91. Ibid., 182.

Chapter 3: The Modern Airliner

1. Wallace, Knute Rockne, 253–67; TWA telegram quote from TWA Papers, St. Louis Mercantile Library.

2. Lipsyte and Levine, *Idols of the Game*, 78–80; Wallace, Knute Rockne, 253–67; Robert J. Serling, "Clipped Wings: The Grounding of Airliners with Fatal Flaws." *Airliners* 15 (January–February 2002): 66.

3. Wallace, *Knute Rockne*, 255–58; Serling, "Clipped Wings," 66.

4. Komons, *Bonfires to Beacons*, 183–84; Serling, "Clipped Wings," 66; Serling, Howard Hughes' *Airline*, 23–25.

5. Komons, *Bonfires to Beacons*, 185–89; Holden, Legacy of the DC-3, 34–35.

6. "Why Not Parachutes?" *Outlook and Independent* 157 (April 15, 1931): 516.

7. Francis D. Walton, "Is It Safe to Fly?" *Nation* 131 (October 22, 1930): 438–39; R. E. Johnson, "How Safe Is Air Travel?" *Scientific American* 160 (May 1939): 279.

8. Stearns, "Troubled Airways," 364; U.S. Federal Aviation Agency, *FAA Statistical Handbook*, 1959 ed., 81.

9. Capt. Frank T. Courtney, "Flying versus Transportation," *Aviation* 30 (July 1931): 417.

10. Solberg, *Conquest of the Skies*, 149–50; Dierikx, Fokker, 140–45; Serling, "Clipped Wings," 66.

11. Pearcy, *Douglas Propliners*, 19–24. See also Biddle, *Barons of the Sky*.

12. Bowers, *Boeing Aircraft since 1916*, 182–186; Brooks, *Modern Airliner*, 75–78; Chant, *Boeing*, 39–42; Miller and Sawers, *Technical Development of Modern Aviation*, 66–69.

13. Heppenheimer, *Turbulent Skies*, 48–52.

14. Brooks, *Modern Airliner*, 67–90.

15. Holden, Legacy of the DC-3, 28–68; Francillon, McDonnell Douglas Aircraft, 1:149–55; quote from Allen, Airline Builders, 132.

16. Van der Linden, Airline and Air Mail, 260–91.

17. Komons, Bonfires to Beacons, 249–75.

18. Allen, Airline Builders, 90–94.

19. Parrish, "Spanning the Continent," 26–27.

20. Earl of Cottenham, *Mine Host, America*, 353.

21. Parrish, "Spanning the Continent," 26–27.

22. Reiss, "From Coast to Coast," 26–28, 109–10.

23. Solberg, *Conquest of the Skies*, 194–205. See also Whitnah, *Safer Skyways*. For a detailed analysis of the Cutting crash and what followed, consult Komons, *Cutting Air Crash*.

24. "Plane versus Train Travel," *Fortune* 13 (April 1936): 220–22; U.S. Department of Commerce, Bureau of the Census, *Historical Statistics*, 729, 769.

25. U.S. Federal Aviation Agency. *FAA Statistical Handbook*, 1959 ed., 114.

26. Solberg, *Conquest of the Skies*, 106; Leary, *Pilots' Directions*, 1–76.

27. R. E. Johnson, "How Safe Is Air Travel?" 279–81; Komons, *Bonfires to Beacons*, 147–63; Reiss, "From Coast to Coast," 110; Solberg, *Conquest of the Skies*, 132–37.

28. Komons, *Bonfires to Beacons*, 153, 157.

29. Wesley Stout, "How Much Speed Do You Want?" *Saturday Evening Post* 206 (October 28, 1933): 77; Roosevelt, "Flying Is Fun," 88.

30. U.S. Federal Aviation Agency, *FAA Statistical Handbook*, 1959 ed., 58; "Lines Slash Transcontinental Rates," *Western Flying* 12 (February 1932): 44; "Fares Generously Cut," *Aviation* 31 (February 1932): 85.

31. Drake, "Pegasus Express," 663.

32. E. Jay Doherty, "High Babes," *Flying* 28 (April 1941): 83, 84; Nina Phillips, "When Babies Fly," *Woman's Home Companion* 68 (June 1941): 10.

33. *Newsweek* 5 (January 26, 1935): 33.

34. Grosvenor, "Flying," 587.

35. "F.O.B., Anywhere," *Christian Science Monitor Weekly Magazine* Section (August 3, 1938): 5.

36. Doherty, "High Babes," 31.

37. "Half-Rate Fares for Youngsters," *Western Flying* 18 (August 1938): 26.

38. "Information for Mothers," *Today's Health* 28 (November 1950): 2, 10; "F.O.B., Anywhere," 5; N. Phillips, "When Babies Fly," 10.

39. "F.O.B., Anywhere," 5; Doherty, "High Babes," 83, 84.

40. N. Phillips, "When Babies Fly," 10; "Abortive Press Release," *Aviation Week* 49 (December 6, 1948): 52.

41. Serling, Eagle, 109; R. E. G. Davies, *Fallacies and Fantasies*, 87; U.S. Department of Commerce, Civil Aeronautics Administration, *CAA Statistical Handbook*, 36; Cherington, *Airline Price Policy*, 140.

42. Daniel L. Rust, "Nick Mamer and the First Quarter Century of Aviation in the Inland Northwest." *Journal of the West* 43 (Summer 2004): 71–77; *New York Times* (August 17, 1929); N. B. Mamer, "Texaco across the Sky," *Texaco Star* (1929): 32.

43. Mamer, "Texaco across the Sky," 3; Plehinger, *Marathon Flyers*, 151–52.

44. Roger Bilstein, "Air Travel and the Traveling Public," in Trimble, *From Airships to Airbus*, 91–95; Heppenheimer, *Brief History of Flight*, 158; Serling, *Howard Hughes' Airline*, 11–12; Solberg, *Conquest of the Skies*, 106–16.

45. Brooks, Modern Airliner, 67–90; Komons, *Bonfires to Beacons*, 211; R. K. Smith, *Seventy-Five Years of Inflight Refueling*, 10–11.

46. Boyne, *Beyond the Horizons*, 65–82; "When Slowed Down, Plane Flies 50 Miles Faster than Average Need," *Newsweek* 10 (November 15, 1937): 43; "Flaming Arrow," *Time* 31 (January 17, 1938): 43.

47. Gunston, *Illustrated Encyclopedia of Propeller Airliners*, 59–61; Serling, Eagle, 55–58, 108–109; Holden, *Legacy of the DC-3*, 95–127.

48. Holden, *Douglas DC-3*, 118–22; R. E. G. Davies, *TWA*, 38.

49. "Aerial Luxury for Women," *Nation's Business* 25 (August 1937): 46; Holden, *Legacy of the DC-3*, 114.

50. Reiss, "From Coast to Coast," 26.

51. Margaret Macphail, "I Wish and I Wonder," *Scribner's Magazine* 105 (January 1939): 38; Alexander Klemon, "American Passenger Air Transport—III," *Scientific American* 141 (December 1929): 517.

52. "Wages and Hours of Labor in Air Transportation, 1931," *Bulletin of the U.S. Bureau of Labor Statistics* (January 1933): 9; Drake, "Pegasus Express," 671; Pascal Cowan, "Patriarch," *Flying* 28 (January 1941): 43, 72–74.

53. Solberg, *Conquest of the Skies*, 175–77.

54. Gunston, *Illustrated Encyclopedia of Propeller Airliners*, 26–27, 42–43, 46, 106–107, 129; Bartlett, *Social Studies*, 29.

55. Hubbard et al., *Airports*, 146–50; Janet R. Daley Bednarek, "The Flying Machine in the Garden," *Technology and Culture* 46 (April 2005): 355.

56. Macphail, "I Wish and I Wonder," 38–39.

57. Serling, *Eagle*, 134–35.

58. F. Barrows Colton, "Our Air Age Speeds Ahead," *National Geographic* 93 (February 1948): 249.

59. Gunston, *Illustrated Encyclopedia of Propeller Airliners*, 42, 48, 81, 83; Parrish, "Spanning the Continent," 26–27.

60. Reiss, "From Coast to Coast," 27.

61. "Flashes from the Skyways of the World," *Aviation* 36 (April 1937): 27; Serling, Eagle, 148–49.

62. "AM 23-3: NK to GX," *Fortune* 29 (February 1939): 114.

63. Edna Backster Eastburn, "Meals in the Air," *Good Housekeeping* 105 (August 1937): 156; Boyson, "Dining High," 4.

64. Boyson, "Dining High," 4; Serling, *Eagle*, 147; F. J. Taylor, *High Horizons*, 118.

65. F. J. Taylor, *High Horizons*, 118–19.

66. T. Kent Morris, "What to Eat When You Fly," *Flying* 40 (March 1947): 31; "Dining Up," *New Yorker* 37 (July 22, 1961): 17; Marion Dartnell, "Kitchens in the Clouds," *Hygeia* (October 1938): 919; "Flying Tastes," *Business Week* (April 13, 1946): 98.

67. Colton, "Aviation in Commerce and Defense," 711; Dartnell, "Kitchens in the Clouds," 919; Eric Bramley, "Friday In-flight Meals: Fish or Meat?" *American Aviation* 15 (July 9, 1951): 42.

68. Serling, *Eagle*, 148.

69. Miller and Sawers, *Technical Development of Modern Aviation*, 138.

70. Wayne W. Parrish, "TWA Stratoliner Tops in Passenger Comfort, Cuts Flying Time to Coast," *American Aviation* 4 (July 15, 1940): 28.

71. R. E. G. Davies, *TWA*, 44–45.

72. U.S. Federal Aviation Agency, *FAA Statistical Handbook*, 1959 ed., 78.

Chapter 4: Wartime Flying

1. Hy Sheridan, "A Pilot Looks at the Passenger," *Saturday Evening Post* 220 (November 29, 1947): 50; Serling, *The Only Way to Fly*, 224–25; Serling, *When the Airlines Went to War*, 220.

2. Serling, *Eagle*, 180.

3. "The Airlines at War," *Western Flying* 22 (December 1942): 30–31, 86; Rose, *American Wartime Transportation*, 272–75.

4. Serling, *When the Airlines Went to War*, 220–24; Solberg, *Conquest of the Skies*, 274–75; Rose, *American Wartime Transportation*, 269–72.

5. Bruce Horton, "Wing Talk," *Collier's* 119 (May 31, 1947): 89.

6. Eddy, "Bumped Off," 32–33, 130–32.

7. G. H. Douglas, *All Aboard!* 382–86.

Chapter 5: "Atomic Age Swashbuckling"

1. C. R. Smith, "What We Need Is a Good Three-Cent Air Line," *Saturday Evening Post* 218 (October 20, 1945): 12; U.S. Federal Aviation Agency, *FAA Statistical Handbook*, 1959 ed., 81.

2. Grosvenor, "Flying," 587.

3. C. R. Smith, "What We Need," 13.

4. U.S. Federal Aviation Agency, *FAA Statistical Handbook*, 1959 ed., 81; Cherington, *Airline Price Policy*, 143; "Air Fare vs. Rail," *Business Week* (September 1, 1945): 46; Harold A. Jones and Frederick Davis, "The 'Air Coach' Experiment and National Air Transport Policy," *Journal of Air Law and Commerce* 17 (Winter 1950): 3.

5. R. E. G. Davies, *Airlines of the United States*, 447–49; Heppenheimer, *Turbulent Skies*, 126; L. S. Willis, "The Non-Skeds," *Flying* 39 (December 1946): 43. Good summaries of the nonscheduled airlines' experience after World War II may be found in Corpening, Forgotten Flights, and in "CAB Regulation of Supplemental Air Carriers," *Harvard Law Review* 76 (1963): 1450-71.

6. Corpening, *Forgotten Flights*, 23.

7. L. S. Willis, "Non-Skeds," 44, 108; Corpening, *Forgotten Flights*, 9; Roger E. Bilstein, "C. R. Smith: An American Original," in Lewis, *Airline Executives and Federal Regulation*, 101.

8. "Coast-to-Coast Flights for $99," *Aviation Week* 48 (March 15, 1948): 45; Esther H. Forbes, "The Battle of the Airlines," *Flying* 44 (February 1949): 25; R. E. G. Davies, *Rebels and Reformers*, 86–87.

9. "Non-Sked's Future Debated," *Western Flying* 29 (March 1949): 12.

10. Andrews, "Coast-to-Coast," 56.

11. Jones and Davis, "'Air Coach' Experiment," 3; Forbes, "Battle of the Airlines," 66.

12. Stubblefield, "Another 99'er Writes," 17.

13. R. E. G. Davies, *Rebels and Reformers*, 87.

14. Stubblefield, "Another 99'er Writes," 17; Solberg, *Conquest of the Skies*, 333–35; U.S. Department of Commerce, Bureau of the Census, *Historical Statistics*, 769.

15. Stubblefield, "Another 99'er Writes," 17.

16. Jacobs, "Coast to Coast for $99," 25.

17. Jones and Davis, "'Air Coach' Experiment," 4.

18. Corpening, *Forgotten Flights*, 11–12.

19. Macris, "Letters," 21.

20. Robert H. Wood, "More Airlines Chop Fare Costs," *Aviation Week* 49 (September 27, 1948): 50. For an outstanding work on the development of low-price airline travel, see Bender, "Flying on the 'Cheap.'"

Chapter 6: Economy and Elegance

1. Miller and Sawers, *Technical Development of Modern Aviation*, 152.

2. Robert H. Wood, "A Break in the Overcast," *Aviation Week* 49 (December 6, 1948): 54.

3. Cherington, *Airline Price Policy*, 90.

4. "NEA Puts New Twist on Family Fare Plan," *Aviation Week* 49 (October 4, 1948): 36; "AA Family Plan Sparks October Gain," *Aviation Week* 49 (December 20, 1948): 41–42; "Family Plan," *Aviation Week* 50 (April 18, 1949): 49–50.

5. "Family Fare," *Aviation Week* 51 (August 29, 1949): 33; Eric Bramley, "Over the Counter," *American Aviation* 13 (October 1, 1949): 59.

6. Solberg, *Conquest of the Skies*, 346; Heppenheimer, *Turbulent Skies*, 125–26.

7. Solberg, *Conquest of the Skies*, 345; "Capital Starts Sky Coach Service," *Aviation Week* 49 (November 15, 1948): 48; "Public Takes to Skycoach Service," *Aviation Week* 49 (December 6, 1948): 42; R. E. G. Davies, *Rebels and Reformers*, 75.

8. Keith Saunders, "Scheduled Air Coach Service Spreads Coast-to-Coast," *American Aviation* 12 (March 1, 1949): 11; Jones and Davis, "'Air Coach' Experiment," 7.

9. R. E. G. Davies, *Airlines of the United States*, 336–37.

10. "Oakland Coach Tops," *Aviation Week* 51 (December 26, 1949): 39.

11. Solberg, *Conquest of the Skies*, 348.

12. U.S. Civil Aeronautics Board, *Handbook of Airline Statistics*, 1973, 34; "So They Tell Us," *Aviation Week* 57 (August 11, 1952): 56.

13. Wood, "Wanted: Millions of First Flighters," 78.

14. Eric Bramley, "Airline Commentary," *American Aviation* 17 (May 1954): 54.

15. Cited in Caves, *Air Transport and Its Regulators*, 37–39.

16. DeVoto, "Transcontinental Flight," 48–49; Mr. Harper, "Flying with a Map," *Harper's Magazine* 205 (November 1952): 101; Serling, *Legend and Legacy*, 41–49.

17. DeVoto, "Transcontinental Flight," 48; Mr. Harper, "Flying with a Map," 101.

18. DeVoto, "Transcontinental Flight," 50.

19. Comstock, "How to Leave Home and Like It," 107; Eric Bramley, "Airline Commentary," *American Aviation* 17 (December 21, 1953): 52.

20. Heppenheimer, *Turbulent Skies*, 128–30; Miller and Sawers, *Technical Development of Modern Aviation*, 146–48; Gunston, *Illustrated Encyclopedia of Propeller Airliners*, 162–63, 188–89; Solberg, *Conquest of the Skies*, 353.

21. Dirk Mathison, "The Saga of the Red-Eye," *Los Angeles Magazine* 44 (February 1999): 58.

22. Comstock, "How to Leave Home and Like It," 40.

23. Eric Bramley, "Airline Commentary," *American Aviation* 17 (December 7, 1953): 82; Eric Bramley, "Airline Commentary," *American Aviation* 18 (August 16, 1954): 52; Serling, Eagle, 268.

24. Serling, *Eagle*, 269.

25. D. F. Magarrell, "To Tickle the Palate," *Air Transportation* 7 (November 1945): 24–25.

26. A. L. Roby, "Caterers to the Airborne," *Air Transportation* 5 (November 1944): 20–21; "Food on the Fly," *Time* 54 (August 15, 1949): 72.

27. Roby, "Caterers to the Airborne," 21–24; "Food on the Fly," 72.

28. Lovegrove, *Airline*, 63.

29. Eric Bramley, "TWA Favors Quick-Freeze Method for Meals Aloft," *American Aviation* 13 (August 1, 1949): 50–51.

30. "WAL Would Do Away with Meals," *Aviation Week* 49 (December 20, 1948): 39.

31. Ibid., 39; "WAL Eliminates Free Meals, Cuts Passenger Fares 5%," *American Aviation* 12 (January 1, 1949): 14; "WAL Cuts Food, Fares," *Aviation Week* 50 (February 7, 1949): 43.

32. Serling, The Only Way to Fly, 253; "WAL Cuts Food, Fares," 43.

33. DeVoto, 'Transcontinental Flight," 49–50; L. Davis, "Inquiring Reporter on Flight 45," 28–29, 72–75.

34. Solberg, *Conquest of the Skies*, 378; Berchtold, "Food," 357; "PAA Innovation," *Aviation Week* 49 (December 6, 1948): 46.

35. Solberg, *Conquest of the Skies*, 104–105.

36. "AM 23-3," 114.

37. Solberg, *Conquest of the Skies*, 223.

38. Sheridan, "A Pilot Looks at the Passenger," 25.

39. "Flying Tastes," 98, 101.

40. Solberg, *Conquest of the Skies*, 378–79; "The Not-Too-High Club," *Aviation Week* 60 (March 29, 1954): 72.

41. "'Champagne' Flights," *Aviation Week* 60 (June 28, 1954): 87; Serling, *The Only Way to Fly*, 282–91; William J. Coughlin, "Customer Is King in West Coast Battle," *Aviation Week* 62 (June 6, 1955): 127; "Dry Blue Yonder," *Time* 66 (September 19, 1955): 102.

42. "Airline Stewardesses Want Dry Planes," *Christian Century* 72 (June 8, 1955): 676; Capt. Dave Kuhn, "The Thrust Lever," *Flying* 68 (April 1961): 58.

43. "Dry Blue Yonder," 102; "Airlines Warned on Serving Liquor," *Christian Century* 72 (September 28, 1955): 1107–1108; "Low Altitude," *Newsweek* 48 (July 16, 1956): 76; "Airlines Turn Down Liquor Service Code," *Aviation Week* 63 (November 14, 1955): 147.

44. "Low Altitude," 76.

45. "Drys v. Wets," *Time* 70 (August 26, 1957): 74; "Air Safety Endangered by Liquor Service," *Christian Century* 75 (April 2, 1958): 398–99; "Prohibition Aloft?" *Newsweek* 53 (June 15, 1959): 33; "Cocktails in the Clouds," *Newsweek* 54 (August 10, 1959): 26.

46. "No Drinks for Drunks," *Time* 75 (January 18, 1960): 19; Rochester, Takeoff at Mid-Century, 185–86.

47. "United Bows to In-Flight Movies," *Business Week* (October 1, 1966): 150.

48. Civil Aeronautics Board, *Reports*, "Passenger Credit Plans Investigation," 37 CAB 404, Docket 10917 (E-19197), 409; "Flying on the Cuff," *Business Week* (June 27, 1964): 115–16; Milton Van Slyck, "Credit Takes Wings," *Flying* 27 (October 1940): 36, 64; "Aviation Travel Credit," *Aviation Week* 60 (April 12, 1954): 86.

49. Leary, "Safety in the Air," in William M. Leary, ed., *From Airships to Airbus*, 1:97–98; U.S. Federal Aviation Agency, *FAA Statistical Handbook*, 1959 ed., 119; Holgar J. Johnson, "Up Goes Safety, Down Go Insurance Rates," *Air Transportation* 8 (June 1946): 12–14; "Better Aviation Insurance," *Western Flying* 25 (June 1945).

50. Robert H. Wood, "Cheaper Airline Trip Insurance," *Aviation Week* 60 (March 29, 1954): 74; "Passenger Insurance for Boeing Arranged," *Aviation* 28 (May 17, 1930): 1010.

51. Robert H. Wood, "Crashes and Perspective," *Aviation Week* 56 (March 17, 1952): 90; R. H. Wood, "Cheaper Airline Trip Insurance," 74.

52. Lydia Strong, "Sky High Odds," *Travel* 105 (February 1956): 48–51.

53. Ibid., 51.

54. "Women Say Yes to Air Travel," *Aviation Week* 47 (September 1, 1947): 37.

55. "Among the Airlines," *American Aviation* 13 (April 1, 1950): 4.

56. "Convention Bound," *Independent Woman* 16 (April 1937): 127; "Selling Airline Travel to Women," *Business Week* (September 25, 1954): 116–20; Glenn Garrison, "More Women Traveling – Airlines Increase Promotions to Ladies," *Aviation Week* 67 (July 15, 1957): 40–41.

57. Karsner, "Leaving on a Jet Plane," 300–303; "Selling Airline Travel to Women," 116–17, 120.

58. Grossman, *Air Passenger Traffic*, 195.

59. Sheridan, "A Pilot Looks at the Passenger," 47.

60. Petzinger, *Hard Landing*, 30.

61. "Flying 'Men Only' Gains," *New York Times* (April 20, 1957): 30; "Discrimination Ended," *Airline Management and Marketing* 2 (February 1970): 16; "Another 'Men-Only' Barrier Falls: United Drops Its Shoes-and-Jackets-Off Flight," *New York Times* (January 16, 1970): 34; Petzinger, *Hard Landing*, 30.

62. "Assault on the Sanctuary," *Fortune* 57 (March 1958): 69.

63. "Another 'Men-Only' Barrier Falls," 34.

64. While there is a wide variety of material pertaining to segregation on trains, buses, and steamships, there is a dearth of sources related to the topic of African Americans and air travel. Relevant sources include Robert G. Dixon, Jr., "Civil Rights in Air Transportation and Government Initiative," *Virginia Law Review* 49 (March 1963): 205–31; Sarah M. Lemmon, "Transportation Segregation in the Federal Courts since 1865," *Journal of Negro History* 38 (April 1953): 174–93; W. Robert Ming, "Disabilities Affecting Negroes as to Carrier Accommodations, Property, and Judicial Proceedings," *Journal of Negro Education* 8 (July 1939): 406–15; Frank E. Quindry, "Airline Passenger Discrimination," *Journal of Air Law* 3 (October 1932): 479–515; and Welke, *Recasting American Liberty*. The quotation is from Woodward, *Strange Career of Jim Crow*, 117.

65. Lewis and Newton, *Delta*, 92.

66. Rampersad, *Jackie Robinson*, 135–39; Robinson, *Jackie Robinson*, 46–48; "Curb on Negroes Eased by Airport," *New York Times* (June 28, 1961).

67. Dixon, "Civil Rights in Air Transportation," 209–12; Gourse, *Ella Fitzgerald Companion*, 87; *Civil Aeronautics Act of 1938*.

68. Dixon, "Civil Rights in Air Transportation," 205–31; Claude Sitton, "Race Bars Easing at Waiting Rooms," *New York Times* (July 26, 1959); "U.S. Sues to Halt Airport Race Ban," *New York Times* (July 27, 1961); "Alabama Airport Target of U.S. Suit," *New York Times* (July 27, 1961).

69. "Job Outlooks," *Aviation Week* 50 (April 18, 1949): 51; U.S. Federal Aviation Agency, *FAA Statistical Handbook*, 1950 ed., 53.

70. G. Johnson, *Abominable Airlines*, 197, 201–202; Kuhn, "Thrust Lever," 54.

71. G. Johnson, *Abominable Airlines*, 202.

72. Solberg, Conquest of the Skies, 364–65; Heppenheimer, *Turbulent Skies*, 178–80.

73. Kurt Rand, "The D Ships," *Popular Aviation* 26 (April 1940): 72; "Plane Talk," *Aviation Week* 50 (February 21, 1949): 33; DeVoto, "Transcontinental Flight," 47.

74. Shelley Berman, *Inside Shelley Berman* (Verve Records, 1958), LP recording.

75. *Saturday Evening Post* 225 (November 8, 1952): 3.

76. Boyne, *Smithsonian Book of Flight*, 116; We Seven, 3–7.

77. U.S. Department of Commerce, Department of the Census, *Historical Statistics*, 769; U.S. Civil Aeronautics Board, *Handbook of Airline Statistics*, 1973, 28, 31, 605; R. E. G. Davies, *Airlines of the United States*, 450–53.

78. "Skeds Bid for Mass Trade," *Business Week* (November 15, 1952): 106.

Chapter 7: Leaving on a Jet Plane

1. Cook, Road to the 707, 98–99; Miller and Sawers, *Technical Development of Modern Aviation*, 153.

2. Heppenheimer, *Turbulent Skies*, 75–79; Constant, *Origins of the Turbojet Revolution*, 1–98.

3. Solberg, *Conquest of the Skies*, 354.

4. Serling, *Jet Age*, 22–23; Constant, *Origins of the Turbojet Revolution*, 254.

5. Miller and Sawers, *Technical Development of Modern Aviation*, 157–85; Eugene Rodgers, *Flying High*, 149–50; Cook, *Road to the 707*, 97–114; John McDonald, "Jet Airliners: Year of Decision; II," *Fortune* 47 (May 1953): 128.

6. Miller and Sawers, *Technical Development of Modern Aviation*, 179–80; Serling, *Jet Age*, 19–37.

7. Serling, *Jet Age*, 33–42; Heppenheimer, *Turbulent Skies*, 158–60.

8. Rodgers, *Flying High*, 151–90.

9. Cook, *Road to the 707*, 211–26; Bowers, *Boeing Aircraft since 1916*, 358.

10. Francillon, *McDonnell Douglas Aircraft*, 513–16.

11. Serling, *Howard Hughes' Airline*, 312.

12. "The Airlines' Golden Age," *Business Week* (March 28, 1964): 52; Solberg, *Conquest of the Skies*, 395, 406.

13. L. Davis, "Inquiring Reporter on Flight 45," 72.

14. Ibid., 29, 72.

15. C. S. Forester, "The Trouble with Travel," *Saturday Evening Post* 232 (November 28, 1959): 67.

16. E. A. Wood, *Science from Your Airplane Window*, 122.

17. Ibid., 123.

18. James, "40 Years Ago," 15, 16.

19. "The Boeing Mail Plane," *Aviation* 23 (July 4, 1927): 18; "The Boeing Model 80-A Transport," *Aero Digest* 15 (October 1929): 134.

20. Snow, "Meeting Women's Aircraft Demands," 1800; Serling, *Howard Hughes' Airline*, 11, 261–63.

21. "Inflight," *New Yorker* 38 (June 2, 1962): 22–23.

22. "United Bows to In-flight Movies," 150.

23. Bilstein, *Flight in America*, 234.

24. "Come Fly with Me," *Time* 85 (June 25, 1965): 92; Horace Sutton, "Getting There Is Half the Difficulty," *Saturday Review* 48 (October 2, 1965): 34; Serling, *Howard Hughes' Airline*, 313.

25. "How to Cut Ground Travel Time," *Aviation Week* 51 (July 4, 1949): 42–43; E. Brown, *Helicopter in Civil Operations*, 99–108; William Burrows, "Airports: When Will the Ground Catch Up with the Sky?" *Holiday* 46 (July 1969): 48.

26. L. Davis, "Inquiring Reporter on Flight 45," 28.

27. Ibid.; Garvey and Fisher, *Age of Flight*, 214.

28. Petzinger, *Hard Landing*, 29–31.

29. Diane Tedeschi, "You've Come a Long Way, Barbie!" *Air and Space Smithsonian* 10 (June–July 1995): 16–17.

30. Serling, *Eagle*, 250–52.

31. *San Francisco Call-Bulletin* (November 30, 1955): 28, quoted in I. Willis Russell, "Among the New Words," *American Speech* 41 (May 1966): 139–40.

32. Dr. Ross A. McFarland, "Smoking Impairs Your Vision," *Aviation Week* 61 (November 1, 1954): 96.

33. "Airline Observer," *Aviation Week and Space Technology* 91 (December 15, 1969): 35; "Smoking in Aircraft under Attack in Congress, by Citizens Groups," *Aviation Week and Space Technology* 92 (January 19, 1970): 29.

34. "Smoking in Aircraft under Attack," 29.

35. "Smokescreen," *AMM/AA* 2 (March 1970): 13–14.

36. "CAB Proposes Rule Requiring Segregated Smoking Areas," *Aviation Week and Space Technology* 97 (September 15, 1972): 29; Sheldon R. Shane, ""Let's Clear the Air," *Travel-Holiday* 169 (June 1988): 4.

37. "The Right to Smoke," *New Republic* 177 (December 10, 1977): 8–9.

38. Gottdiener, *Life in the Air*, 120–21; Cecelia Preble, "Academy Urges Smoking Ban in U.S. Commercial Aircraft," *Aviation Week and Space Technology* 125 (August 18, 1986): 31.

39. Preble, "Academy Urges Smoking Ban," 31; James Ott, "Smoking Ban Sought on Domestic Flights," *Aviation Week and Space Technology* 125 (December 8, 1986): 31–32; J. A. Donoghue, "The Smoking Lamp Is Out," *Air Transport World* 27 (June 1990): 2; "Smoking Lamp Is Out," *Aviation Week and Space Technology* 132 (March 12, 1990): 13.

40. See Field, *Mainliner Denver*.

41. Phillips, *Skyjack*, 42–77; "The Constitutionality of Airport Searches," *Michigan Law Review* 72 (November 1973): 128.

42. Phillips, *Skyjack*, 42–77; Kent, *Safe, Separated, and Soaring*, 333–36.

43. "Constitutionality of Airport Searches," 128–31; "Airport Security Searches and the Fourth Amendment," *Columbia Law Review* 71 (June 1971): 1039–40; Kent, *Safe, Separated, and Soaring*, 337–52; Preston, *Troubled Passage*, 35–56.

44. Horace Sutton, "Flicks in Flight," *Saturday Review* (May 8, 1965): 46.

45. C. R. Smith, quoted in Peterson and Glab, *Rapid Descent*, 30.

46. "For Ladies Only," *Airline Management* 3 (September 1971): 10; "Piano Flight," *Airline Management* 3 (October 1971): 10; Joe Sutter, *747*, 80–103, 163. There are at least two popular explanations for the 747's cockpit location above the single deck. One is that the basic design of the 747 was taken from Boeing's failed bid in the competition with the Lockheed to design a large military cargo aircraft that would become the C-5 Galaxy; and the other is that Pan Am's Juan Trippe insisted that the 747 be designed with cargo carrying in mind, that is, with a hinged nose door for loading containers directly into the aircraft. Joe Sutter, the leader of the 747's design team, refutes both explanations in his book, *747*. He claims that the design team benefited from Boeing's

entry in the C-5 competition solely because the project advanced the development of large turbofan engines, which would be used to power the 747. He also asserts that Juan Trippe fully intended for the 747 to be a double-decked aircraft. But Sutter and his team believed the 747 should feature one wide deck with easy access for loading cargo containers. Only after seeing mock-ups of two possible fuselage cross sections, one with two decks and the other with a single deck below the flight deck, did Trippe agree to the single-deck design, featuring the possible incorporation of a hinged nose door.

47. R. E. G. Davies, *TWA*, 74; John Lake, "Classic Airliner: Aerospatiale/BAC Concorde," *Flightpath* 1 (Summer 2003): 56–119; see also Horwitch, *Clipped Wings.*

48. Federal Aviation Administration, *FAA Statistical Handbook*, 1981 ed., 46.

49. See Peterson and Glab, *Rapid Descent*, and Petzinger, *Hard Landing.*

Chapter 8: The Age of Deregulation and 9/11

1. Meyer and Oster, *Deregulation and the Future of Intercity Passenger Travel*, 56.

2. Larry D. Sall, in Leary, *Encyclopedia of American Business History*, 300.

3. "A New Kind of Flight Plan for Small Freight," *Business Week* (November 3, 1973): 66.

4. Button, *Airline Deregulation*, 21; Meyer and Oster, *Deregulation and the Future*, 60.

5. Button, *Airline Deregulation*, 22.

6. Meyer and Oster, *Deregulation and the Future*, 60.

7. Howard Banks, "A Sixties Industry in a Nineties Economy," *Forbes* 153 (May 9, 1994): 108.

8. R. E. G. Davies, *Airlines of the United States*, 677; Heppenheimer, *Turbulent Skies*, 342.

9. See Freiberg and Freiberg, *Nuts!*

10. Furchgott, "Flying on a Discount," F59.

11. Gary Stoller, "Fliers Wanting Food, Fun; Better Bring Wallets," *USA Today* (April 25, 2006).

12. Heppenheimer, *Turbulent Skies*, 342–43.

13. Petzinger, *Hard Landing*, 138–41.

14. Dan Reed, "Frequent Fliers Turn a Skeptical Eye to the Skies," *USA Today* (May 31, 2006); Jay Clarke, "The Games Airlines – and the Rest of Us – Play," *Miami Herald* (April 2, 2006).

15. Cheryl Rosen, "Internet Shatters Travel Model," *InformationWeek* 816 (December 11, 2000): 56–60.

16. Roger Yu, "Airline Service Evolves into Do-it-Yourself," *USA Today* (February 20, 2006).

17. Kane, Air Transportation, 498; "Why Flying Is Hell," *Newsweek* 137 (April 23, 2001): 34–37.

18. "The Two Worst Headaches in Air Travel," *Changing Times* 21 (February 1967): 33–36; "The Five Worst Hassles in Air Travel," *Changing Times* 31 (August 1977): 41–44; Barbara J. Janesh, "Exercising Your Flight Rights," *Travel-Holiday* 171 (June 1989): 35–39; Julian L. Simon, "A Scheme to Improve Air Travel," *Journal of Policy Analysis and Management* 2 (Spring 1983): 465.

19. Landro, "Finicky Traveler."

20. National Council on Disability, *Enforcing the Rights of Air Travelers*, part 1.1.

21. Solberg, *Conquest of the Skies*, 206–208.

22. "North America Report," *Air Transport World* 27 (May 1990): 7; Christopher P. Fotos, "Transportation Department Issues Handicapped Access Rules for Airlines," *Aviation Week and Space Technology* 132 (March 12, 1990): 69–70.

23. Nancy Eisenhauer, "Implied Causes of Action under Federal Statutes: The Air Carriers Access Act of 1986," *University of Chicago Law Review* 59 (Summer 1992): 1183–84; Samantha Stainburn, "On a Wing and Crutch," *Government Executive* 29 (July 1997): 76; National Council on Disability, *Enforcing the Civil Rights of Air Travelers*, part 6.4.2, table 3; Calmetta Y. Coleman, "Unfriendly Skies for the Handicapped," *Wall Street Journal* (October 11, 1996).

24. "Terrorist Attacks on World Trade Center and Pentagon," *American Journal of International Law* 96 (January 2002): 237–38.

25. "U.S. Airlines Face Financial Armageddon," *Air Transport World* 38 (October 2001): 9.

26. Anna Quindlen, "Armed with Only a Neutral Lipstick," *Newsweek* (March 18, 2002): 72.

27. Jeremy W. Peters and James Kanter, "U.S. Transportation Security Agency Prohibits Liquids and Gels on Flights," *New York Times* (August 11, 2006); Laura Bly, "Veteran Travelers Find it Hard to Carry On," *USA Today* (August 15, 2006).

Bibliography

PRIMARY ACCOUNTS

Andrews, Paul. "Coast-to-Coast by Sky-Coach." *Aviation Week* 49 (October 18, 1948): 56, 58.

Bisgood, Elizabeth M. "Twelve Strangers in the Night." *Forum and Century* 90 (September 1933): 180–83.

Borkland, C. R. "We Take a Little Trip." *Popular Aviation* 2 (May 1928): 14–16, 92.

Bowen, Pansy. "A Postman's Holiday." *Western Flying* 13 (March 1933): 16–18.

Comstock, Louisa M. "How to Leave Home and Like It." *House Beautiful* 96 (August 1954): 40, 107.

Darling, Velva G. "Across the Continent in Forty-Eight Hours." *World's Work* 58 (September 1929): 52–56.ho

Davenport, Marcia. "Covered Wagon – 1932." *Good Housekeeping* 95 (October 1932): 32–33, 140–149.

Davis, Lou. "The Inquiring Reporter on Flight 45." *Flying* 66 (March 1960): 28–29, 72–75.

DeVoto, Bernard. "Transcontinental Flight." *Harper's Magazine* 205 (July 1952): 47–50.

Drake, Francis Vivian. "Pegasus Express." *Atlantic Monthly* 149 (June 1932): 663–74.

Eddy, Don. "Bumped Off." *American Magazine* 139 (February 1945): 32–33, 130–32.

Fisher, Katherine A. "Luncheon a Mile Up." *Good Housekeeping* 91 (July 1930): 84, 223.

Furchgott, Roy. "Flying on a Discount and Some Pretzels." *Business Week* (8 February 1999): 59.

Gray, Jessie. "A Diary of a Coast to Coast Flight." *Journal of the National Education Association* 21 (June 1932): 185.

Jacobs, Larry. "Coast to Coast for $99." *Flying* 44 (June 1949): 24–25, 58.

James, Harry C. "40 Years Ago from 30,000 Feet Up." *Desert* 22 (June 1960): 15–18.

Kerr, Sophie. "Six Thousand Miles by Air." *Woman's Home Companion* 60 (April 1933): 12, 75.

Landro, Laura. "The Finicky Traveler: Class Struggles – As Airlines Tout Deluxe Cabins, We Put Them to the Test; Dirty Floors, Dripping Water." *Wall Street Journal* (July 6, 2001).

Lane, D. R. "Flying with the Western Air Mails." *Sunset* 58 (May 1927): 12–14, 54, 56.

Macris, Georgia. "Letters: She Went Nonsked." *Aviation Week* 53 (October 2, 1950): 21–22.

Mead, George J. "Journeying with the Boeing Air Mail." *Aviation* 23 (October 24, 1927): 990–94.

Parrish, Wayne W. "Spanning the Continent from Dusk-to-Dawn." *Literary Digest* 118 (August 25, 1934): 26–27.

———. "TWA Stratoliner Tops in Passenger Comfort; Cuts Flying Time to Coast." *American Aviation* 4 (July 15, 1940): 28.

Porter, M. de M. "Flying from Ocean to Ocean." Nation 229 (July 10, 1929): 36–37.

Reiss, George R. "From Coast to Coast in a Modern Airliner." *Popular Science* 127 (October 1935): 25–28, 109–10.

Rogers, Will. "Flying and Eating My Way East." *Saturday Evening Post* 200 (January 21, 1928): 3–4, 110–14, 117; continued in "Bucking a Head Wind," *Saturday Evening Post* 200 (January 28, 1928): 6–7, 36–40.

Samuels, F. E. "Coast to Coast in a Fokker F-10." *Aero Digest* 15 (September 1929): 188.

Skinner, Cornelia Oris. "Ground-Minded." *New Yorker* 12 (June 6, 1936): 30–32.

Stearns, Myron M. "All Aboard by Air." *World's Work* 58 (April 1929): 31–41, 144–50.

———. "Flying across America." *Ladies' Home Journal* 46 (January 1929): 17, 79.

Stubblefield, Blaine. "Another 99'er Writes." *Aviation Week* 49 (November 15, 1948): 17.

Wood, Robert H. "Wanted: Millions of First Flighters." *Aviation Week* 60 (March 1, 1954): 78.

GOVERNMENT DOCUMENTS

Air Commerce Act of 1926. U.S. *Statutes at Large* 44 (1926).

Civil Aeronautics Act of 1938. U.S. *Statutes at Large* 52 (1938).

Federal Aviation Act of 1958. U.S. *Statutes at Large* 60 (1958).

Kent, Richard J. *Safe, Separated, and Soaring*. Washington, D.C.: GPO, 1980.

Komons, Nick A. *Bonfires to Beacons: Federal Civil Aviation Policy under the Air Commerce Act, 1926–1938*. Washington, D.C.: U.S. Department of Transportation, Federal Aviation Administration, 1978.

———— *The Cutting Air Crash: A Study in Early Federal Aviation Policy.* Washington, D.C.: U.S. Department of Transportation, Federal Aviation Administration, 1984.

National Council on Disability. *Enforcing the Civil Rights of Air Travelers with Disabilities.* www.ncd.gov/newsroom/publications/1999/ acaa.htm.

Preston, Edmund. *Troubled Passage: The Federal Aviation Administration during the Nixon-Ford Term, 1973–1977.* Washington, D.C.: GPO, 1987.

Rochester, Stuart I. *Takeoff at Mid-Century: Federal Civil Aviation Policy in the Eisenhower Years, 1953–1961.* Washington, D.C.: U.S. Department of Transportation, Federal Aviation Administration, 1976.

U.S. Bureau of Labor Statistics. *Bulletin of the U.S. Bureau of Labor Statistics.* Washington, D.C.: GPO, January 1933.

U. S. Civil Aeronautics Board. *Handbook of Airline Statistics.* Washington, D.C.: GPO, 1961–73.

———— Bureau of Safety Investigation. *Comparative Safety Statistics in United States Airline Operations, Part II: 1946–1952.* Washington, D.C.: GPO, August 15, 1953.

U.S. Department of Commerce. Aeronautics Branch. *Air Commerce Bulletin.* Washington, D.C.: GPO, July 15, 1929, to December 15, 1939.

———— Bureau of the Census. *Historical Statistics of the United States: Colonial Time to 1970, Part 2.* Washington, D.C.: GPO, 1975.

———— Bureau of the Census. *Statistical Abstract of the United States: 1961.* Washington, D.C.: GPO, 1961.

———— Civil Aeronautics Administration. *CAA Statistical Handbook of Civil Aviation.* Washington, D.C.: GPO, 1945.

U.S. Department of Transportation. Bureau of Transportation Statistics. *1995 American Travel Survey.* Washington, D.C.: GPO, October 1997.

U.S. Federal Aviation Agency. *FAA Statistical Handbook of Aviation.* 1950, 1959, and 1981 editions. Washington, D.C.: GPO, 1950, 1959, and 1981.

Wilson, John R. M. *Turbulence Aloft: The Civil Aeronautics Administration amid Wars and Rumors of Wars, 1938–1953.* Washington, D.C.: U.S. Department of Transportation, Federal Aviation Administration, 1979.

BOOKS

Allen, Oliver E. *The Airline Builders.* Alexandria, Va.: Time-Life Books, 1981.

Angelucci, Enzo, ed. *World Encyclopedia of Civil Aircraft.* Edison, N.J.: Chartwell Books, 2001.

Armstrong, Harry G. *Principles and Practice of Aviation Medicine.* Baltimore: Williams and Wilkins Co., 1939.

The Aviation Industry: A Study of Underlying Trends. Philadelphia: Curtis Publishing Co., 1930.

Bain, David Howard. *Empire Express: Building the First Transcontinental Railroad.* New York: Viking Penguin, 1999.

Barlay, Stephen. *Cleared for Take-off: Behind the Scenes of Air Travel.* London: Kyle Cathie, 1994.

Bartlett, Hall. *Social Studies for the Air Age.* New York: Macmillan, 1942.

Bauer, George R. *A Century of Kansas City Aviation History: The Dreamer and the Doers.* Kansas City, Mo.: Historic Preservation Press, 1999.

Bednarek, Janet R. Daly. *America's Airports: Airfield Development, 1918–1947.* College Station: Texas A&M University Press, 2001.

Berg, A. Scott. *Lindbergh.* New York: G. P. Putnam's Sons, 1998.

Biddle, Wayne. *Barons of the Sky.* New York: Simon and Schuster, 1991.

Bilstein, Roger E. *Flight in America 1900–1983: From the Wrights to the Astronauts.* Baltimore: Johns Hopkins University Press, 1984.

Birth of an Industry: A Nostalgic Collection of Airline Schedules for the Years 1929 through 1939 (in Facsimile). New York: Reuben H. Donnelley Corp., 1969.

Bliss, Carey S. *Autos across America: A Bibliography of Transcontinental Automobile Travel; 1903–1940.* Austin, Tex.: Jenkins and Reese Companies, 1982.

Boeing Company. *A Brief History of the Boeing Company.* Seattle: Boeing Historical Services, 1998.

Bor, Robert. *Anxiety at 35,000 Feet: An Introduction to Clinical Aerospace Psychology.* London and New York: Karnac, 2004.

Bor, Robert, and Lucas van Gerwen, eds. *Psychological Perspectives on Fear of Flying.* Hampshire, England: Ashgate, 2003.

Bowers, Peter M. *Boeing Aircraft since 1916.* London: Putnam and Co., 1966.

Boyne, Walter J. *Beyond the Horizons: The Lockheed Story.* New York: St. Martin's Press, 1998.

———— *De Havilland DH-4: From Flaming Coffin to Living Legend.* Washington, D.C.: Smithsonian Institution Press, 1984.

———— *The Smithsonian Book of Flight.* New York: Orion Books, 1987.

Brooks, Peter W. *The Modern Airliner.* Manhattan, Kans.: Sunflower University Press, 1982.

Brown, Eric, Capt. *The Helicopter in Civil Operations.* New York: Van Nostrand Reinhold, 1981.

Brown, Dee. *Hear That Lonesome Whistle Blow: The Epic Story of the Transcontinental Railroads.* New York: Henry Hold and Co., 2001.

Brown, Jim. *Hubbard: The Forgotten Boeing Aviator.* Seattle: Peanut Butter Publishing, 1996.

Bryant, Keith L, Jr. *History of the Atchison, Topeka and Santa Fe Railway.* New York: Macmillan, 1974.

Burkhardt, Robert. *CAB—The Civil Aeronautics Board.* Dulles International Airport, Va.: Green Hills, 1974.

Button, Kenneth, ed. *Airline Deregulation.* London: David Fulton, 1991.

Carter, Susan B. *Historical Statistics of the United States.* New York: Cambridge University Press, 2006.

Caves, Richard E. *Air Transport and Its Regulators: An Industry Study.* Cambridge, Mass.: Harvard University Press, 1962.

Chant, Christopher. *Boeing: The World's Greatest Planemakers.* Secaucus, N.J.: Chartwell, 1982.

Cherington, Paul W. *Airline Price Policy: A Study of Domestic Airline Passenger Fares.* Boston: Harvard University Press, 1958.

Citrine, Sir Walter. *My American Diary.* London: George Routledge and Sons, 1941.

Constant, Edward W., III. *The Origins of the Turbojet Revolution.* Baltimore and London: Johns Hopkins University Press, 1980.

Cook, William H. *The Road to the 707.* Bellevue, Wash.: TYC, 1991.

Corn, Joseph J. *The Winged Gospel: America's Romance with Aviation, 1900–1950.* New York: Oxford University Press, 1985.

Corpening, John T. *Forgotten Flights.* Self-published, 2003.

Cott, Nate, and Stewart Kampel. *Fly without Fear.* Chicago: Henry Regnery, 1973.

Cottenham, Earl of (Mark Pepys). *Mine Host, America.* London: Collins, 1937.

Courtwright, David T. *Sky as Frontier: Adventure, Aviation, and Empire.* College Station: Texas A&M University Press, 2005.

Dahlberg, Angela. *Air Rage: The Underestimated Safety Risk.* Burlington, Vt., 2001.

Damon, Ralph S. *"TWA" Nearly Three Decades in the Air.* New York: Newcomen Society in North America, 1952.

David, Paul T. *The Economics of Air Mail Transportation.* Washington, D.C.: Brookings Institution, 1934.

Davies, Pete. *American Road: The Story of an Epic Transcontinental Journey at the Dawn of the Motor Age.* New York: Henry Holt and Co., 2002.

Davies, R. E. G. *Airlines of the United States since 1914.* Washington, D.C.: Smithsonian Institution Press, 1972.

———— *Delta.* Miami: Paladwr Press, 1990.

———— *Fallacies and Fantasies of Air Transport History.* McLean, Va.: Paladwr Press, 1994.

———— *A History of the World's Airlines.* London: Oxford University Press, 1964.

———— *Rebels and Reformers of the Airways.* Washington, D.C.: Smithsonian Institution Press, 1987.

———— *TWA: An Airline and Its Aircraft.* McLean, Va.: Paladwr Press, 2000.

Davies, R. E. G., and I. E. Quastler. *Commuter Airlines of the United States.* Washington and London: Smithsonian Institution Press, 1995.

Dierikx, Marc. *Fokker: A Transatlantic Biography.* Washington and London: Smithsonian Institution Press, 1997.

Douglas, Deborah G. *Women and Flight since 1940.* Lexington: University Press of Kentucky, 2004.

Douglas, George H. *All Aboard! The Railroad in American Life.* New York: Smithmark, 1996.

Dunn, Ray A. *Aviation and Life Insurance.* New York: Daniel Guggenheim Fund for the Promotion of Aeronautics, 1930.

Edwards, Mary, and Elwyn Edwards. *The Aircraft Cabin: Managing the Human Factors.* Brookfield, Vt.: Gower, 1990.

Evans, David S., and Richard Schmalensee. *Paying with Plastic: The Digital Revolution in Buying and Borrowing.* 2nd ed. Cambridge, Mass.: MIT Press, 2005.

Field, Andrew J. *Mainliner Denver: The Bombing of Flight 629.* Boulder, Colo.: Johnson Books, 2005.

Francillon, Rene J. *McDonnell Douglas Aircraft since 1920.* Vol. 1. Annapolis, Md.: Naval Institute Press, 1988.

Fraser, Chelsea. *Heroes of the Air.* New York: Thomas Y. Crowell Co., 1939.

Frederick, John H. *Commercial Air Transportation*. 5th ed. Homewood, Ill.: Richard D. Irwin and Co., 1961.

Freiberg, Kevin, and Jackie Freiberg. *Nuts!* New York: Broadway Books, 1998.

Freudenthal, Elsbeth E. *The Aviation Business: From Kitty Hawk to Wall Street.* New York: Vanguard Press, 1940.

Garland, Daniel J., et al, eds. *Handbook of Aviation Human Factors.* Mahwah, N.J., and London: Lawrence Erlbaum Associates, 1999.

Garvey, William, and David Fisher. *The Age of Flight: A History of America's Pioneering Airline.* Greensboro, N.C.: Pace Communications, 2002.

Gill, Frederick W., and Gilbert L. Bates. *Airline Competition: A Study of the Effects on the Quality and Price of Airline Service and the Self-Sufficiency of the United States Domestic Airlines.* Boston: Harvard University, 1949.

Glines, Carroll, V. *Airmail—How It All Began.* Blue Ridge Summit, Pa.: TAB Books, 1990.

Gordon, Alastair. *Naked Airport: A Cultural History of the World's Most Revolutionary Structure.* New York: Metropolitan Books, Henry Holt and Co., 2004.

Gorn, Michael H. *Expanding the Envelope: Flight Research at NACA and NASA.* Lexington: University Press of Kentucky, 2001.

Gottdiener, Mark. *Life in the Air: Surviving the New Culture of Air Travel.* Lanham, Md.: Rowman and Littlefield, 2000.

Gourse, Leslie, ed. *The Ella Fitzgerald Companion.* New York: Shirmer Books, 1998.

Greeley, Horace. *An Overland Journey from New York to San Francisco in the Summer of 1859.* Lincoln and London: University of Nebraska Press, 1999. Originally published 1860, C. M. Saxton, Barker, New York.

Greif, Martin. *The Airport Book: From Landing Field to Modern Terminal.* New York: Mayflower Books, 1979.

Gronau, Reuben. *The Value of Time in Passenger Transportation: The Demand for Air Travel.* New York: Columbia University Press, 1970.

Grossman, William L. *Air Passenger Traffic.* New York: Remsen Press Division, Chemical Publishing Co., 1947.

Gunston, Bill, ed. *The Illustrated Encyclopedia of Propeller Airliners.* New York: Exeter Books. 1980.

Hart, Walter. *The Airport Passenger Terminal.* Malabar, Fla.: Krieger, 1991.

Hartman, Cherry, and Julie Sheldon Huffaker. *Fearless Flyer: How to Fly in Comfort and without Trepidation.* Portland, Oreg.: Eighth Mountain Press, 1995.

Heppenheimer, T. A. *A Brief History of Flight: From Balloons to Mach 3 and Beyond.* New York: John Wiley and Sons, 2001.

———. *Turbulent Skies: The History of Commercial Aviation.* New York: John Wiley and Sons, 1995.

Hereford, Jack, and Penny Hereford. *The Flying Years: A History of America's Pioneer Airline.* Western Air Lines, 1946.

Higham, Robin. *100 Years of Air Power and Aviation.* College Station: Texas A&M University Press, 2003.

Holden, Henry M. *The Boeing 247: The First Modern Commercial Airplane.* Blue Ridge Summit, Pa.: Tab Books, 1991.

———. *The Douglas DC-3.* Blue Ridge Summit, Pa.: Tab Books, 1991.

———. *The Fabulous Ford Tri-Motors.* Blue Ridge Summit, Pa.: Tab Books, 1992.

———. *The Legacy of the DC-3.* Niceville, Fla.: Wind Canyon, 1996.

Hollander, Stanley C., ed. *Passenger Transportation: Readings Selected from a Marketing Viewpoint.* East Lansing: Michigan State University, 1968.

Hopkins, George E. *The Airline Pilots: A Study in Elite Unionization.* Cambridge, Mass.: Harvard University Press, 1971.

———. *Flying the Line: The First Half Century of the Air Line Pilots Association.* Washington, D.C.: Air Line Pilots Association, 1982.

———. *Flying the Line.* Vol. 2, The Line Pilot in Crisis: ALPA Battles Airline Deregulation and Other Forces. Washington, D.C.: Air Line Pilots Association, 2000.

Horgan, James J. *City of Flight: The History of Aviation in St. Louis.* St. Louis: Patrice Press, 1984.

Horwitch, Mel. *Clipped Wings: The American SST Conflict.* Cambridge, Mass.: MIT Press, 1982.

Hubbard, Henry V., Miller McClintock, and Frank B. Williams. *Airports: Their Location, Administration and Legal Basis.* Cambridge, Mass.: Harvard University Press, 1930.

Hudson, Kenneth. *Air Travel: A Social History.* Totowa, N.J.: Rowman and Littlefield, 1972.

Hudson, Kenneth, and Julian Pettifer. *Diamonds in the Sky: A Social History of Air Travel.* London: British Broadcasting Corp., 1979.

Ingells, Douglas J. *The Plane That Changed the World: A Biography of the DC-3.* Fallbrook, Calif.: Aero Publishers, 1966.

Initial Study of Air Transportation. Association of American Railroads, 1944.

Jackson, Donald Dale. *Flying the Mail*. Alexandria, Va.: Time-Life Books, 1982.

Jakle, John A. *The Tourist: Travel in Twentieth-Century North America*. Lincoln and London: University of Nebraska Press, 1985.

Jane's All the World's Aircraft. London: Sampson Low, Marston and Co., 1938, 1940.

Jane's All the World's Aircraft. New York: Macmillan, 1941, 1950–51.

Jane's All the World's Aircraft. London: Jane's All the World's Aircraft Publishing Co., 1955–56, 1958–59, 1962–63.

Jensen, Oliver. *The American Heritage History of Railroads in America*. New York: American Heritage, 1975.

Johnson, Daniel A. *Just in Case: A Passenger's Guide to Airplane Safety and Survival*. New York and London: Plenum Press, 1984.

Johnson, George. *The Abominable Airlines*. New York: Macmillan, 1964.

Johnson, Lynn, and Michael O'Leary. *En Route: Label Art from the Golden Age of Air Travel*. San Francisco: Chronicle Books, 1993.

Jordan, William A. *Airline Regulation in America: Effects and Imperfections*. Baltimore and London: Johns Hopkins Press, 1970.

Kane, Robert M. *Air Transportation*, 14th ed. Dubuque, Iowa: Kendall/Hunt, 2003.

Karash, Julius A., and Rick Montgomery. *TWA: Kansas City's Hometown Airline*. Kansas City: Kansas City Star Books, 2001.

Kelly, Charles J., Jr. *The Sky's the Limit: The History of the Airlines*. New York: Coward-McCann, 1963.

Ketchum, Richard M. *Will Rogers: His Life and Times*. New York: American Heritage, 1973.

Lansing, John B. *The Travel Market: 1964–1965*. Ann Arbor: University of Michigan, 1965.

Larkins, William T. *The Ford Tri-Motor*. West Chester, Pa.: Schiffer, 1992.

Launius, Roger D., ed. *Innovation and the Development of Flight*. College Station: Texas A&M University Press, 1999.

Launius, Roger D., and Janet R. Daly Bednarek, eds. *Reconsidering a Century of Flight*. Chapel Hill and London: University of North Carolina Press, 2003.

Leary, William M. *Aerial Pioneers: The U.S. Air Mail Service, 1918–1927*. Washington, D.C.: Smithsonian Institution Press, 1985.

———— ed. *Aviation's Golden Age: Portraits from the 1920s and 1930s*. Iowa City: University of Iowa Press, 1989.

———— ed. *Encyclopedia of American Business History: The Airline Industry*. New York: Facts on File, 1992.

———— ed. *From Airships to Airbus*. Vol. 1. Washington and London: Smithsonian Institution Press, 1995.

———— ed. *Pilots' Directions: The Transcontinental Airway and Its History*. Iowa City: University of Iowa Press, 1990.

LeBow, Eileen F. *Cal Rogers and the Vin Fiz: The First Transcontinental Flight*. Washington and London: Smithsonian Institution Press, 1989.

Lederer, Jerome, M.E. *Safety in the Operation of Air Transportation: A Lecture Delivered by Edward Pearson Warner, Sc.D., under the James Jackson Cabot Professorship of Air Traffic Regulation and Air Transportation at Norwich University, April 20, 1939*. Northfield, Vt.: Norwich University, 1939.

Lewis, W. David, ed. *Airline Executives and Federal Regulation: Case Studies in American Enterprise from the Airmail Era to the Dawn of the Jet Age*. Columbus: Ohio State University Press, 2000.

Lewis, W. David, and Wesley Phillips Newton. *Delta: The History of an Airline*. Athens: University of Georgia Press, 1979.

Lewis, W. David, and William F. Trimble. *The Airway to Everywhere: A History of All American Aviation, 1937–1953*. Pittsburgh: University of Pittsburgh Press, 1988.

Lindbergh, Anne Morrow. *Hour of Gold, Hour of Lead*. New York: Harcourt Brace Jovanovich, 1973.

Lipsyte, Robert, and Peter Levine. *Idols of the Game: A Sporting History of the American Century*. Atlanta: Turner Publishing, 1995.

Lobeck, A. K. *Airways of America: The United Air Lines*. Port Washington, N.Y.: Kennikat Press, 1970. First published in 1933.

Lovegrove, Keith. *Airline: Identity, Design and Culture*. New York: TeNeues, 2000.

Mansfield, Harold. *Vision: The Story of Boeing*. New York: Popular Library, 1966.

Marriott, Leo. *80 Years of Civil Aviation*. Edison, N.J.: Chartwell Books, 1997.

McClement, Fred. *It Doesn't Matter Where You Sit*. Toronto: McClelland and Stewart, 1966.

McConnell, Curt. *Coast to Coast by Automobile: The Pioneering Trips, 1899–1908*. Stanford, Calif.: Stanford University Press, 2000.

———— *"A Reliable Car and a Woman Who Knows It": The First Coast-to-Coast Auto Trips by Women, 1899–1916*. Jefferson, N.C.: McFarland and Co., 2000.

McLaughlin, Helen E. *Footsteps in the Sky: An Informal Review of U.S. Airlines Inflight Service, 1920s to the Present.* Denver, Colo.: State of the Art, 1994.

Meinig, D. W., ed. *The Interpretation of Ordinary Landscapes.* New York: Oxford University Press, 1979.

Meyer, John Robert, and Clinton V. Oster. *Deregulation and the Future of Intercity Passenger Travel.* Cambridge, Mass.: MIT Press, 1987.

Miller, Ronald, and David Sawers. *The Technical Development of Modern Aviation.* New York: Praeger, 1970.

Moffett, Cleveland. *Careers of Danger and Daring.* New York: Century Co., 1911.

Mooney, James E. *Air Travel.* New York: Charles Scribner's Sons, 1930.

Moran, Tom. *Los Angeles International Airport: From Lindbergh's Landing Strip to World Air Center.* Canoga Park, Calif.: CCA Publications, 1993.

Morgan, David P. *Fasten Seat Belts: The Confessions of a Reluctant Airline Passenger.* New York: Arco, 1969.

Morrison, Steven A., and Clifford Winston. *The Evolution of the Airline Industry.* Washington, D.C.: The Brookings Institution, 1995.

Nielson, Dale, ed. *Saga of the U.S. Air Mail Service, 1918–1927.* Air Mail Pioneers, 1962.

Nye, Russel B. A *Baker's Dozen: Thirteen Unusual Americans.* East Lansing: Michigan State University Press, 1956.

O'Callaghan, Timothy J. *The Aviation Legacy of Henry and Edsel Ford.* Ann Arbor, Mich.: Proctor Publications, 2000.

Ormsby, Waterman L. *The Butterfield Overland Mail.* Edited by Lyle H. Wright and Josephine M. Bynum. San Marino, Calif.: Huntington Library, 1942.

Palmer, Henry R., Jr. *This Was Air Travel.* New York: Bonanza Books, 1962.

Pattillo, Donald M. *Pushing the Envelope: The American Aircraft Industry.* Ann Arbor: University of Michigan Press, 1998.

Pearcy, Arthur. *Douglas Propliners: DC-1–DC-7.* Shrewsbury, England: Airlife Publishing, 1995.

Peckham, Betty. *Sky Hostess.* New York: Thomas Nelson and Sons, 1941.

Peterson, Barbara Sturken, and James Glab. *Rapid Descent.* New York: Simon and Schuster, 1994.

Petzinger, Thomas, Jr. *Hard Landing: The Epic Contest for Power and Profits That Plunged the Airlines into Chaos.* New York: Times Books, Random House, 1995.

Phillips, David. *Skyjack: The Story of Air Piracy.* London: George G. Harrap and Co., 1973.

Pisano, Dominick A. *The Airplane in American Culture.* Ann Arbor: University of Michigan Press, 2003.

Plank, Charles E. *Women with Wings.* New York and London: Harper and Brothers, 1942.

Plehinger, Russell. *Marathon Flyers.* Detroit: Harlo, 1989.

Quarantiello, Laura E. *Air Ways: The Insider's Guide to Air Travel.* Lake Geneva, Wisc.: LimeLight Books, 2000.

Rampersad, Arnold. *Jackie Robinson: A Biography.* New York: Alfred A. Knopf, 1997.

Reiss, Bob. *Frequent Flyer: One Plane, One Passenger, and the Spectacular Feat of Commercial Flight.* New York: Simon and Schuster, 1994.

Rickenbacker, Edward V. *Rickenbacker.* Englewood Cliffs, N.J.: Prentice-Hall, 1967.

Robinson, Rachel. *Jackie Robinson: An Intimate Portrait.* New York: Abrams, 1996.

Rogers, Betty Blake. *Will Rogers: His Wife's Story.* Norman: University of Oklahoma Press, 1979.

Rogers, Eugene. *Flying High.* New York: Atlantic Monthly Press, 1996.

Rogers, Will. *Autobiography.* Selected and edited by Donald Day, with a foreword by Bill and Jim Rogers. Boston: Houghton Mifflin, 1949.

Rose, Joseph R. *American Wartime Transportation.* New York: Thomas Y. Crowell, 1953.

Rummel, Robert W. *Howard Hughes and TWA.* Washington and London: Smithsonian Institution Press, 1991.

Salmon, Marguerite A. *"I'll Take the High Road."* Unpublished manuscript. TWA Collection, St. Louis Mercantile Library.

Schivelbusch, Wolfgang. *The Railway Journey: The Industrialization of Time and Space in the 19th Century.* Berkeley: University of California Press, 1986.

Schmeckebier, Laurence F. *The Aeronautics Branch, Department of Commerce: Its History, Activities and Organization.* Washington, D.C.: Brookings Institution, 1930.

Schoneberger, William A., and Paul Sonnenburg. *California Wings: A History of Aviation in the Golden State.* Woodland Hills, Calif.: Windsor Publications, 1984.

Schwantes, Carlos Arnaldo. *Going Places.* Bloomington: Indiana University Press, 2003.

———— *Long Day's Journey: The Steamboat and Stagecoach Era in the Northern West.* Seattle and London: University of Washington Press, 1999.

———— *Railroad Signatures across the Pacific Northwest.* Seattle and London: University of Washington Press, 1993.

Sealy, Kenneth R. *The Geography of Air Transport.* Chicago: Aldine, 1968.

Serling, Robert J. *Eagle: The Story of American Airlines.* New York: St. Martin's Press, 1985.

———— *Howard Hughes' Airline: An Informal History of TWA.* New York: St. Martin's Press, 1983.

———— *The Jet Age.* Alexandria, Va.: Time-Life Books, 1982.

———— *Legend and Legacy: The Story of Boeing and Its People.* New York: St. Martin's Press, 1992.

———— *Maverick: The Story of Robert Six and Continental Airlines.* New York: Doubleday, 1974.

———— *The Only Way to Fly: The Story of Western Airlines, America's Senior Air Carrier.* Garden City, N.Y.: Doubleday, 1976.

———— *When the Airlines Went to War.* New York: Kensington, 1997.

Shamburger, Page. *Tracks across the Sky: The Story of the Pioneers of the U.S. Air Mail.* Philadelphia and New York: J. B. Lippincott, 1964.

Six, Robert. *Continental Airlines: A Story of Growth.* New York: Newcomen Society in North America, 1959.

Smith, C. R. *"A. A." American Airlines—Since 1926.* New York: Newcomen Society in North America, 1954.

Smith, Frank A. *Transportation in America.* Washington, D.C.: Eno Foundation for Transportation, 1989.

Smith, Henry Ladd. *Airways: The History of Commercial Aviation in the United States.* New York: Alfred A. Knopf, 1942.

Smith, Henry Nash. *Virgin Land: The American West as Symbol and Myth.* Cambridge, Mass.: Harvard University Press, 1950.

Smith, Richard K. *Seventy-Five Years of Inflight Refueling.* Washington, D.C.: Air Force History and Museums Program, 1998.

Solberg, Carl. *Conquest of the Skies: A History of Commercial Aviation in America.* Boston: Little, Brown, 1979.

Stein, E. P. *Flight of the Vin Fiz.* New York: Arbor House, 1985.

Stilgoe, John R. *Metropolitan Corridor: Railroads and the American Scene.* New Haven and London: Yale University Press, 1983.

Stover, John F. *The Routledge Historical Atlas of the American Railroads.* New York and London: Routledge, 1999.

Stroud, John. *Jetliners in Service Since 1952.* London: Putnam Aeronautical Books, 1994.

Sutter, Joe. *747: Creating the World's First Jumbo Jet and Other Adventures from a Life in Aviation.* New York: HarperCollins, 2006.

Taylor, Frank J. *High Horizons: Daredevil Flying Postmen to Modern Magic Carpet — The United Air Lines Story.* New York: McGraw-Hill, 1951.

Taylor, John W. R. *Passengers, Parcels and Panthers: The Story of Our Working Aircraft.* New York: Roy Publishers, 1956.

Tebbel, John, and Mary Ellen Zuckerman. *The Magazine in America, 1741–1990.* New York: Oxford University Press, 1991.

Trimble, William F., ed., *From Airships to Airbus.* Vol. 2. Washington and London: Smithsonian Institution Press, 1992.

TWA. Wings of Pride: TWA Cabin Attendants; A Pictorial History, 1935–1985. Marceline, Mo.: Walsworth, 1985.

United Air Lines. *Corporate and Legal History of United Air Lines and Its Predecessors and Subsidiaries: 1925–1945.* Chicago: Twentieth Century Press, 1953.

Vance, James E., Jr. *Capturing the Horizon: The Historical Geography of Transportation.* New York: Harper and Row, 1986.

Van der Linden, Robert F. *Airlines and the Air Mail: The Post Office and the Birth of the Commercial Aviation Industry.* Lexington: University Press of Kentucky, 2002.

Van Riper, A. Bowdoin. *Imagining Flight: Aviation and Popular Culture.* College Station: Texas A&M University Press, 2004.

Wallace, Francis. *Knute Rockne.* Garden City, N.Y.: Doubleday, 1960.

Warner, Edward Pearson. *The Early History of Air Transportation: A Lecture Delivered by Edward Pearson Warner, Sc.D., under the James Jackson Cabot Professorship of Air Traffic Regulation and Air Transportation at Norwich University, November 21, 1937.* Northfield, Vt.: Norwich University, 1938.

———— *Technical Development and Its Effect on Air Transportation: A Lecture Delivered by Edward Pearson Warner, Sc.D., under the James Jackson Cabot Professorship of Air Traffic Regulation and Air Transportation at Norwich University, February 23, 1938.* Northfield, Vt.: Norwich University, 1938.

We Seven. New York: Simon and Schuster, 1962.

Welke, Barbara Young. *Recasting American Liberty: Gender, Race, Law, and the Railroad Revolution, 1865–1920.* Cambridge and New York: Cambridge University Press, 2001.

Whitehouse, Arch. *The Sky's the Limit: A History of the U.S. Airlines.* New York: Macmillan, 1971.

Whitnah, Donald R. *Safer Skyways: Federal Control of Aviation, 1926–1966.* Ames: Iowa State University Press, 1966.

Williamson, Ellen. *When We Went First Class.* Ames: Iowa State University Press, 1990.

Willis, P. P. *Your Future Is in the Air: The Story of How American Airlines Made People Air-Travel Conscious.* New York: Prentice-Hall, 1940.

Wilson, G. Lloyd, and Leslie A. Bryan. *Air Transportation.* New York: Prentice-Hall, 1949.

Wilson, Stewart. *Douglas DC-6 and DC-7.* Australia: Notebook Publications, 2001.

Wohl, Robert, *A Passion for Wings: Aviation and the Western Imagination, 1908–1918.* New Haven, Conn., and London: Yale University Press, 1994.

Wood, Elizabeth A. *Science from Your Airplane Window.* New York: Dover, 1975.

Woodward, C. Vann. *The Strange Career of Jim Crow.* 2nd rev. ed. London: Oxford University Press, 1966.

Yagoda, Ben. *Will Rogers: A Biography.* New York: Knopf, 1993.

Young, David M. *Chicago Aviation: An Illustrated History.* De Kalb: Northern Illinois University Press, 2003.

Zukowsky, John. *Building for Air Travel: Architecture and Design for Commercial Aviation.* Munich and New York: Art Institute of Chicago, 1996.

DISSERTATIONS

Bender, Alan Richard. "Flying on the 'Cheap': The Morphogenesis of Affordable Airline Transportation in America." Ph.D. diss., University of California, Berkeley, 1986.

Johnson, Christopher Derek. "Markets in the Air: The Development of American Aviation Culture, 1918–1934." Ph.D. diss., Northwestern University, 1998.

Karsner, Douglas G. "'Leaving on a Jet Plane': Commercial Aviation, Airports and Post-Industrial American Society, 1933–1970." Ph.D. diss., Temple University, 1993.

Kolm, Suzanne Lee. "Women's Labor Aloft: A Cultural History of Airline Flight Attendants in the United States, 1930–1978." Ph.D. diss., Brown University, 1995.

Michaelis, Patricia Ann. "The Development of Passenger Service on Commercial Airlines, 1926–1930." Ph.D. diss., University of Kansas, 1980.

Index

Oakland, Calif., 41, 105, 221

Oakland Municipal Airport, 143–44, 147–48, 155

O'Hare Airport, 199, 224

Omaha, Neb., 10, 23, 26, 35, 39, 40, 69, 76

Overland Mail Company, 10

Ovington, Earl, 22

Ozark Airlines, 98

Pacific Aero Products Company. *See* Boeing Company

Pacific Air Transport, 115. *See also* United Airlines

Pacific Southwest Airlines (PSA), 144, 201, 212

Panama Railroad, 8

Pan American World Airways, 53, 154, 167, 178, 190, 201, 205, 209, 212, 222

Paralyzed Veterans of America, 226

Parrish, Wayne, 100, 119, 123

Parsons, Charles, 185

Passengers, air: African American, 176–79; bumped, 128, 223, 224; Catholic, 122; celebrity, 105; children, 73, 105–107, 175; disabled, 225, 226; emergency, 105, 108, 128; executive, 105, 114, 134, 159, 167, 169, 175–76; first-time, 76–77, 125, 142, 153, 192; intoxicated, 167–69; leisure, 159; men, 25, 105, 175–76; middle class, 134, 138, 149, 171, 173; no-show, 128; politicians, 105, 225; pregnant women, 108; soldiers, 147; standby, 128; VIPs, 128; women, 26, 51, 59–67, 70, 71, 75–77, 107, 114, 142, 147–49, 173–75, 209. *See also* names of individual passengers

Passenger ridership statistics, 103, 183, 223, 231; air, 158, 183, 190–92; bus, 158; railroad, 158

Paulhan, Louis, 5

Patterson, William Allen (Pat), 73, 115, 189

Pennsylvania Railroad, 44

People Express, 215

Philadelphia, Pa., 22, 23, 84

Philadelphia Public Ledger, 22

Pickford, Mary, 48

Pilots: airmail, 30–32; airline, 55, 88, 116–18, 144, 162, 175, 179–82, 231; copilots, 69, 71, 75, 77, 118–19, 145. *See also* names of individual pilots

Pilots' Directions, 104

Plaskett, Tom, 222

Popular Aviation, 40

Port Columbus, Ohio, 46, 48

Porter, M. de M., 82

Portland, Ore., 63, 206, 208

Post, Wiley, 28, 32

Power, James, 21

Pratt & Whitney Aircraft Company, 18, 28

Pressurization, 122–23, 159, 169, 189, 194, 195

Priority system, 128–31

Public Law 87-197, 206. *See also* Skyjacking

Puerto Rico, 153–54

Pucci, Emilio, 200

Pullman cars, 7, 41, 46, 64

Quesada, Elwood, 170

Railroad travel, 92, 93, 131; fares, 102, 105, 155. *See also* Air travel; Bus travel; Stagecoach travel

Railroads: transcontinental, 10; and mail, 23, 36. *See also* names of individual railroads

Rayburn, Sam, 170

Reagan, Ronald, 225

Red Devil (airplane), 3

Red-eye flights, 162

Redman, Ben, 25

Rein, Edythe, 176

Reiss, George R., 102, 119

Reno, Nev., 34, 39, 41, 161

Rentschler, Frederick, 18

Rickenbacker, Eddie, 97, 130

Robertson Aircraft Corporation, 57, 135

Robinson, Jackie, 178

Robinson, Rachel, 178

Rockne, Bonnie, 87

Rockne, Knute, 87–91, 98

Rockwell International Corporation, 19

Rodgers, Calbraith Perry (Cal), 3–7, 22

Rogers, Betty, 30, 35

Rogers, Will, 28–30, 32, 34–36, 39–40, 231

Rohrbach, Adolf K., 97

Roosevelt, Eleanor, 82, 105, 130

Roosevelt, Franklin, 99–100, 225

Roosevelt, Theodore, 225

Roosevelt Field, 36

SABRE (Semi-Automated Business Research Environment), 135, 199

Safety: airline, 99, 103, 105, 171–72; airline compared with automobile, 30, 92, 231

Salt Lake City, Utah, 17, 24–26, 32, 35, 39, 41, 63, 159, 161, 167

Salt Lake City Airport, 118

San Antonio and San Diego Mail Line, 10

San Francisco, Calif., 8, 10, 15, 17, 21–23, 26, 28, 37, 39, 40, 57, 62, 82, 109, 116, 120, 131, 143, 155, 167, 178, 192, 199, 201, 224, 226

Saturday Evening Post, 28, 182

Schedules, 56, 104; transcontinental air, 46–47, 55, 102, 119, 123, 161, 219, 221

Seat, 34; aluminum, 46; assigned, 163; belts, 46, 73; design, 163; jump, 73; movable armrest, 225; pitch, 134, 136; wicker, 46; window, 195–96; reclining, 64, 224

United States Congress, 22, 99, 170

United States Department of Agriculture, 71

United States Department of Commerce, 37, 88–91

United States Department of Transportation, 204, 225–26

United States Post Office (Post Office Department), 15, 21, 23, 36–37

Universal Airlines, 217

Universal Air Transport, 57

Universal Air Travel Plan (UATP), 171

Universal Aviation Corporation, 56

US Airways, 221, 222

Varney, Walter T., 115

Varney Air Lines, 24, 115. *See also* United Airlines

Viking Air Lines, 140, 145

Vin Fiz (airplane), 5

Vogue, 54

Von Ohain, Hans, 186

Wall Street Journal, 224

Walker, Arthur (Art), 109

Walters, Charles, 201

Ward, Jimmy, 5

Washington, D.C., 23, 24, 143, 145, 159, 226

Wayne, John, 201–202

Waynoka, Okla., 46–48

Weather Bureau, 102

Weiss, Stanley D., 140

Western Air Express (WAE), 17, 24–25, 35, 52, 56, 62, 67, 70, 98. *See also* Stewards; TWA

Western Airlines, 148, 165, 168, 169, 222. *See also* Alcohol

Westervelt, George Conrad, 15

Wheelchairs, 225, 226

Whitman, Marcus, 8

Whitman, Narcissa, 8

Whittle, Frank, 186

Wichita, Kans., 47, 76, 131

Willow Run Airport, 217

Wilson, Woodrow, 23

Windows, aircraft, 64; sliding, 34, 51, 62, 70, 195; sizes compared, 195–96

Winnie Mae (airplane), 28

Winslow, Ariz., 44, 69, 71

World War II. *See* Air travel, Second World War

World Wide Airways, 147

Wood, Robert H., 151, 157

Wright EX Flyers, 5

Wright brothers, 3, 5, 111, 147, 158

Wright, Wilbur, 111

Wright, Orville, 3, 111, 116

Wyman, Jane, 201

Young, Clarence M., 71

Zimbalist, Efrem Jr., 196

Zimbalist, Stephanie, 62

Design: Karen Hayes Thumann and Eric H. Anderson.
Map: Cong Zhang
Printed and bound in Korea by Pac-Com Korea, Inc.